Russian Diplomacy and Eastern Europe

1914-1917

RUSSIAN INSTITUTE
OCCASIONAL PAPERS
COLUMBIA UNIVERSITY

Russian Diplomacy and Eastern Europe 1914-1917

by ALEXANDER DALLIN
MERRITT ABRASH
GIFFORD D. MALONE
MICHAEL BORO PETROVICH
JAMES M. POTTS
ALFRED J. RIEBER
with an Introduction by
HENRY L. ROBERTS

KING'S CROWN PRESS, New York, 1963

The transliteration system used in this series is based on the Library of Congress system with some modifications

The Russian Institute of Columbia University

The Russian Institute was established by Columbia University in 1946 to serve two major objectives: the training of a limited number of well-qualified Americans for scholarly and professional careers in the field of Russian studies, and the development of research in the social sciences and the humanities as they relate to Russia and the Soviet Union. The research program of the Russian Institute is conducted through the efforts of its faculty members, of scholars invited to participate as Senior Fellows, and of candidates for the Certificate of the Institute and for the degree of Doctor of Philosophy.

Of the books that are a direct outgrowth of the research program, some are presented in the Studies of the Russian Institute of Columbia University. Other materials—research monographs, anthologies, bibliographies, memoirs and other archival records, and, in general, materials of scholarly interest—are published as Russian Institute Occasional Papers.

The faculty of the Institute, without necessarily agreeing with the conclusions reached in these works, believe that they merit publication.

The financial assistance given by the Rockefeller Foundation to the research and publication program of the Russian Institute is gratefully acknowledged.

STUDIES OF THE RUSSIAN INSTITUTE

Contents

HENRY L. ROBERTS

Introduction

The studies that follow are revised and abridged versions of
essays prepared in the course of the last decade in the international relations seminars of the Russian Institute at Columbia University. While written in different years—and
with no initial thought of a symposium—they do, in fact,
deal with closely related topics, all of which concern Russian
policy in Central and Eastern Europe in the period between
the outbreak of the First World War and the eruption of
the March Revolution.

In the study of twentieth century diplomacy, the war years
1914-18 have received far less attention than those either
preceding or following.[1] This lack of emphasis is partly a
reflection of the availability of sources; European governments, on the whole, have been slow to publish their wartime
records. It is also a reflection of principal areas of international
interest and debate: the origins and causes of the war, the
creation and eventual destruction of the Versailles system.
Hence, the present studies, based in good part upon relatively
unexploited documentary publications by the Soviet government, serve to fill a gap in the historical record.

---

[1] This is less the case now than when the preparation of this volume
was first contemplated. Later studies include: C. Jay Smith, Jr., *The
Russian Struggle for Power, 1914-1917: A Study of Russian Foreign Policy
during the First World War* (New York, 1956); Victor S. Mamatey, *The
United States and East Central Europe 1914-1918: A Study in Wilsonian
Diplomacy and Propaganda* (Princeton, 1957); Wolfram W. Gottlieb,
Studies in Secret Diplomacy during the First World War (London, 1957);
Titus Komarnicki, *Rebirth of the Polish Republic: A Study in the Diplo-
matic History of Europe, 1914-1920* (London, 1957); and Z. A. B. Zeman,
*The Break-up of the Habsburg Empire, 1914-1918: A Study in National
and Social Revolution* (London and New York, 1961).

But the interest of these studies is more than just that of historical gap-filling—which is likely to be an unrewarding activity unless it is relevant to living concerns—since they deal with two very lively and important issues: (a) the behavior of the tsarist regime in its last days and the bearing of this behavior upon the advent of the Russian Revolution; and (b) the relationship, if any, between "traditional" Russian foreign policy and that of the Soviet Union.

As one reviews tsarist policy regarding the problems and opportunities the First World War brought to Russia's western frontiers, the picture that emerges is of uncertainty, divided counsels and cross-purposes. In dealing with the reemerging Polish question, with the Slavic populations in the Dual Monarchy, with the neutral Balkan states and with the major antagonist, Germany, the imperial government was repeatedly subject to contending and contradictory impulses, no one of which was able to gain clear ascendancy. The consequence in each case was either a failure of policy—as in Bulgaria's joining the Central Powers—or a belated victory which came too late to do much good—as in Rumania's disastrous plunge into war—or a situation in which the terms of the problem repeated themselves without resolution until the regime was overthrown.

At first glance this would seem to provide decisive evidence of a political system blundering toward a catastrophe of its own making, and there is no question but that these failures and tardy gains in foreign policy contributed to both the military disasters and the domestic discontents that destroyed the old order.

Yet there are two other possibilities. Perhaps these topical essays, with the sense of confusion and frustration they convey, fail, in dealing with particular issues, to get at the central purpose of tsarist policy, which might have been less contradictory than would appear in any one sector. Indeed, such a possibility is suggested in several of the essays themselves. It is interesting to note how frequently faltering policies in one area are ascribed to the fact that this was a field of secondary interest to the regime, sacrificed, as it were, to other considerations of higher priority. More specifically, in several instances Constantinople and the Straits are pointed to as the object of chief concern in Russia's wartime foreign policy. These two unquestionably important interests are, however, touched on only tangentially in the present studies.

Still, one may doubt whether a close study of the Straits question during the First World War would, in fact, show Russian policy to have been more coherent and consistent in its purposes. A great deal has been written, by Russians as well as others, about Russia's perennial preoccupation with the control of the Straits, with an outlet to the Mediterranean and with Constantinople. But whenever, throughout the nineteenth and early twentieth centuries, we look closely at this preoccupation—in the Treaty of Unkiar-Skelessi, in the Crimean War, in 1878, or in Izvol'skii's unhappy negotiations with Aehrenthal in 1908—the real interest becomes peculiarly elusive. Certain vague urges to move southward produce an odd combination of ambitious scheming and cautious conservatism. Did the Russians really want the Straits opened or closed? and to whose ships? and under what circumstances? Was Constantinople the key to the Straits, or were the Straits the key to hegemony in the Balkans or were the Balkans the road to Constantinople? The answers are murky.

Even during the First World War—while Turkey's abrupt entry as an enemy was greeted with the Tsar's pronouncement that it was now time for Russia to fulfill its historic mission, and while public demands in the press and in the Duma were aimed at the Straits and Constantinople—it is impossible to discern a coherent policy. Although an official memorandum on the Straits question made an elaborate distinction at the end of 1914 between a "passive" and an "active" solution and recommended the latter, this distinction is far from clear, and the decision for an "active" solution remained without means for its realization. Capturing the Straits would not have been of significant aid in defeating the German army —the question of supplies from the West was not a vital one at this time—and indeed the fighting on the eastern front made it impossible to spare troops for a drive to the Bosporus. So while Foreign Minister Sazonov had to plead for military forces to bolster his diplomatic efforts to achieve a position in the Straits, the military leaders were reduced to demanding that he gain the area by diplomacy alone.

Nor was there agreement at first as to whether Constantinople should be included among the Russian war aims or whether it should be "internationalized." The eventual decision to demand the city came, not from any victory against the enemy, but as a compensation for inability to participate in the unwelcome Dardanelles campaign in company with Russia's allies.

When, in 1915, the British and French agreed to the inclusion of Constantinople within the Russian Empire, this hardly signified the achievement of ancient hopes. Rather, through the compensations accorded the Western allies and through the partitioning of Asiatic Turkey which the agreement foreshadowed, Russia had the prospect not of control over the crossroads and unimpeded access to the Mediterranean but of a direct and awkward confrontation with the Western powers which were moving rapidly to establish positions in the Near East.

Russian policy toward the Straits does not, then, give any more persuasive evidence of coherence or consistency than do the other policies discussed in the following essays. Yet the indication of persistent and long-standing ambiguity with respect to this question suggests a second possible explanation for faltering policy other than fatuity and purblindness on the part of the rulers. May it not be that the difficulty in defining a consistent policy with respect to the Straits lies less in confusion of leadership—though that certainly existed— than in the nature of the problem itself? And if that be so, may not it apply equally to other areas of Russian policy in Eastern Europe: Poland, the Balkans, the Habsburg Monarchy and German-Russian relations?

It is not appropriate here to examine in detail the background of these various problems, but it is worth noting that they are all of relatively long duration and that they comprise some of the most notable sore points in Europe's historical geography. The Balkans have been a perpetual symbol of vexed and infinitely complicated diplomatic intrigue. Poland, with its disputed frontiers, ethnic make-up and role in the European *Staatensystem*, has been a major problem to diplomats of the eighteenth century and to those of today. It has ceased to be such only when stricken from the map by its neighbors, but then with destructive consequences to the rest of Europe. The nationalities problems within the Habsburg Monarchy not only resisted all domestic efforts at a solution that was at once stable and acceptable to Germans, Magyars and Slavs, but were a perennial difficulty in the Monarchy's relations with its neighbors. Most of these problems reemerged, in altered but recognizable form, among the successor states after 1918. As for German-Russian relations, while dynastic connections, conservatism and a common stake in a partitioned Poland had served as mutual bonds in the nineteenth century, the specter, often no more than that, of a great German-Slav clash for hegemony in Eastern Europe always lurked in the background, unexorcised and subtly coloring all diplomatic plans and strategies.

Thus, the issues which came to the fore as explicit challenges with the outbreak of general war in Europe had never been susceptible of easy or self-evident solution, and we can hardly attribute any special folly to Russian officials and diplomats for fumbling them in those hectic and desperate years.

One reason, of course, why they were so difficult, for Russian and other statesmen, was precisely their intimate involvement with Russia's status as a great power. For geographic, ethnic and historical reasons they all touched, directly or by fairly obvious implication, on the question whether Russia was to gain a dominant position in Eastern Europe, with all the consequences that entailed for other nations great and small, or whether Russia was to be outflanked, its sphere of influence pressed back by other expanding continental and maritime powers.

Here we encounter one of the most disputed problems of Russian history: Has Russia's role in Eastern Europe been offensive or defensive, aggressive or protective? The historical record shows that the tide has flowed both ways. Poles were in Moscow in 1610, as was Napoleon in 1812, but then Russian forces were in Turin in 1799, in the Hungarian plain in 1849, and frequently passed the Galatz gap on their way southward along the Black Sea coast. The picture of Russia as the recurrent victim of a Germanic *Drang nach Osten* or of a naval incursion through the Straits is hardly complete.

Admittedly, in a world of strenuous power politics, and such has been the character of much East European history, measures taken by one state as indispensable for the security of its interests and frontiers often constitute a threat to its neighbors. In examining the origins of particular crises and conflicts in Eastern Europe, the diplomatic historian repeatedly finds this interplay of mutual fears and suspicions to have been the immediate source of trouble. For example, Nicholas I's apprehensiveness in 1854 led to acts which the French and British necessarily found alarming; the Crimean War is a classic case of a war erupting from such measures and countermeasures.

Still, there is more to this problem than just mutual fears and suspicions—somehow Russia *had* managed to expand, eastward and westward, from the Duchy of Muscovy to a vast empire spanning the Eastern Hemisphere. Presumably something more than precautionary measures was at work in this expansion. To be sure, in the same centuries we find the United States spreading across another continent, and insular Britain creating its huge overseas empire. Russia was not alone in successful territorial acquisition and settlement. Nevertheless, Russia's expansion, at least to the west, involved not empty spaces, primitive peoples or remote kingdoms, but the immediate interests of other great European powers which, at least until 1914, were the principal players in the great game of world politics. In other words, in the Russian case we find a combination of three elements: the defensive-offensive maneuvering of power politics, the expansion of an empire and intimate concern with areas decisive for the whole European balance of power. It is this combination which rendered, and still renders, the diplomatic and national controversies in Eastern Europe so refractory.

If the uncertainties of Russian wartime policy in Eastern Europe are to be attributed to these enduring and deeply grounded facts of history and geography, can we say, as some have, that there is, therefore, a real continuity between tsarist and Soviet policy? That these facts will largely determine the content of Russian policy regardless of the political system in control? For example, some years ago Walter Lippmann remarked: "The Soviet government has been run by Marxian revolutionists for thirty years; what has to be explained by a planner of American foreign policy is why in 1945 the Soviet government expanded its frontiers and its orbit, and what was the plan and pattern of its expansion. That can be done only by remembering that the Soviet government is a Russian government. . . ."[2]

It is obvious that terrain, resources, and human geography exert an enormous influence on the foreign policy of any nation and create the material framework within which political decisions must be made. There are, moreover, many striking and precise parallels between Russian ambitions in 1914-17 and Soviet claims or achievements during and after the Second World War: the division of the Bukovina along roughly ethnic

[2] Walter Lippmann, *The Cold War: A Study in U.S. Foreign Policy* (New York, 1947), p. 31.

lines, the preoccupation with the approaches to the Straits, the interest in Sub-Carpathian Ruthenia.

Beyond this correspondence in areas of concern, there is undoubtedly a parallel between certain imperialist or messianic strands in Russian political thought and the expansionist drive of the Soviet Union. In the writings of Danilevskii or in the diplomatic efforts of Ignat'ev we find expansionist aims of impressive magnitude combined with active hostility toward Western Europe, its society and culture.

But at this point one must be careful not to press the parallel too far. Differences must not be overlooked, and in the last analysis they are probably more important, for the present and the future, than the similarities. In the first place, the stated motive for the expansion of the Soviet Union and the Communist sphere of control is obviously not that of Pan-Slavism or Russian imperialism but of Marxism-Leninism: the growth and extension of a new revolutionary social order whose limits, in principle at least, are the globe itself. As Mr. Khrushchev observed in 1959 at a meeting with the German comrades: "For the world there are not two ways but only one way—the way of Communism."[3] Whether or not the present Soviet rulers have the revolutionary fervor of their predecessors in the early 1920s, there is no convincing evidence of an abandonment of basic expectations or of a reluctance to act, when practicable, in furthering them.

An equally important, and related, difference is the fact that, while a strong expansionist and even messianic strand runs through Russian history, it is only one of several in the political life of tsarist Russia, and often not the prevailing one. Along with the Pan-Slavists we find diplomatists who understood and wished to work within the Concert of Europe, whether in conservative alliance with Austria and Germany or in an entente with France and Great Britain. While some Russian plans tended to unsettle the European equilibrium, others were aimed at stabilization and pacification. Indeed,

[3] As quoted in *The New York Times*, March 8, 1959.

in the essays that follow we see that a real variety of opinions and pressures made themselves felt, for good or ill, within the framework of the autocracy. For the practicing diplomat of other powers, this play of opinion, in Russia as in other countries, was a significant element in the calculations and maneuvers of diplomacy.

But this sense of a plurality of voices is precisely what is lacking, at most times, in the Soviet system. To be sure, differences of opinion do exist—no form of political organization can overcome the uncertainties of choice and decision—and at times they have broken to the surface, as in the Stalin-Trotsky battle over China policy in the 1920s. But the central tenet of Soviet organization and procedure—so-called democratic centralism—exists precisely to prevent a discordance of voices, a lively diversity of opinions. In consequence, whereas the expansionist impulse in tsarist policy, while important, was only one of several, the expansionist and revolutionary ideology of the Soviet Union is not only a dominating one but, by the nature of the whole political institution, is usually the only one permitted articulation. If the diplomatist of another country attempts to seek out some other strand in Soviet affairs, some other voice to which public or private appeal might be made, he is usually reduced to speculation about possible schisms in the Kremlin but has no effective way to judge or get at them, if indeed they do exist.

Nor is this striking uniformity just a procedural matter having no relation to the aims of Soviet policy. On the contrary, the structure of Soviet institutions and of the Communist Party originated in, and was created to serve, the guiding purposes of Marxism-Leninism.

In 1914, in the rather confused efforts to determine the Russian stake in Constantinople and the Straits, the naval officer A. V. Nemits was instructed to draft a memorandum on the subject. While this memorandum gives a definitely expansionist meaning to Russia's "historic mission," it also, when discussing the status of Constantinople, has this to say:

Enormous interests of "world" significance have long met and
entangled in a subtle and complex fashion in Constantinople
—in this world city which will never be, in any manner or condition, the city of a single nationality. In Constantinople, the
point of contact between western Europe and Asia Minor, global
forces are alive and active. The state which seizes Constantinople by force will immediately come into opposition to all
those powerful factors behind which stand all the great powers
of the world, above all our allies. . . . No serious Russian patriot
can want for his country either a fictitious rule in Constantinople or a conflict with Europe, and consequently he must
reflect on the form to give to Russian sovereignty over this
city. . . . Russia ought to take what is indispensable for it,
but it ought to take it in a fashion that would not weaken, but
would reinforce, the ties which unite it to France, to England,
to a reorganized Germany, to Rumania, to Bulgaria, to Serbia,
Greece and Italy.[4]

The world today would appear brighter if a flicker of this
sense of restraint and international responsibility were evident
in Soviet considerations of policy.

[4] Evgenii A. Adamov, ed., *Konstantinopl' i prolivy: Po sekretnym dokumentam b. Ministerstva inostrannykh del* (Moscow, 1925-26), I, 191-92.

Russian Diplomacy and Eastern Europe

1914-1917

EASTERN EUROPE IN 1914

From *The Triumph of Tyranny*, by Stephen
Borsody (London, Jonathan Cape, 1960)

ALEXANDER DALLIN

The Future of Poland

By 1914, Polish national aspirations—though articulated by only a minority of the population—had survived more than a century of partition among Russia, Austria and Germany. In the Russian-held Kingdom of Poland attempts at Russification had been followed by revolts, which in turn provoked new waves of Russification. The formation of political parties, related to the social and economic development of the country, had finally provided a new basis of alignment and means of expression for Polish patriots. Years before the outbreak of the First World War both the conservative National Democrats (ND's) and the Social Democrats (SD's)—the latter favoring centralized government and opposed to splintering into national groups—had, out of entirely different considerations, come to hope for continued ties with Russia. On the other hand, Pilsudski's right wing of the Polish Socialist Party (PPS) included more extreme elements striving for complete independence.

If the Russian Revolution of 1905 provided a fillip for the crystallization of programs such as Polish autonomy, it also promoted a rapprochement between the Russian and Polish conservatives. In addition to the loyalty of pro-tsarist Polish nobles like the Wielopolski family, Polish-Russian ties developed, for instance, between ND and Russian "Cadet" (Constitutional Democrat) leaders, and the Polish delegation to the all-Russian Duma—known as the *koło*—came to be accepted as a vigorous and vociferous force.

Though the failure of the revolution and the onset of reaction about 1907 meant a setback for the cause of autonomy

by Russian consent, the pro-Russian sentiments, previously
limited in scope, spread among politically conscious Poles as
the possibility of an anti-German coalition, including both
Russia and the Western powers, increased. The man most
responsible for this reorientation of Polish thinking was Roman Dmowski. Appealing to the deep hostility of the Poles
for their Teutonic neighbors—political, religious and cultural
foes of long standing—Dmowski, in his *Germany, Russia and
the Polish Question*, elaborated the imperative of Russo-Polish
collaboration against the common enemy. And it was as the
price of this solidarity with Russia that he demanded a new
deal for Poland: "In order to prevent Europe's being ruled
from Berlin in the future, the Polish people must obtain the
conditions for rapid development and the opportunity for
far-reaching creative labor and in that way set out on a long
and difficult secular struggle"[1] against Germany.

Dmowski's ideas fell on fertile ground, as events were to
show (in 1914 both the Polish peasantry and bourgeoisie in the
Kingdom—whether out of conviction or inertia—behaved,
in the main, like loyal subjects of the Tsar). At the same time
a vigorous Austrian patriotism had developed in Galicia,
where cultural as well as political conditions were far better
than in the other two parts of Poland. To many Galicians,
only continued status within the Habsburg monarchy could
bring an improvement in their fate and Poland's. Various
groups of Polish radicals also pinned their hopes on Austria
and made Galicia their base of operations. Only in German
Poland was there strong disaffection among the Polish inhabitants.

Though successful in arousing some Russian political elements to the need for action,[2] Dmowski and like-minded ND's

---

[1] Roman Dmowski, *Germaniia, Rossiia i pol'skii vopros* (St. Petersburg,
1909), p. 292.

[2] The new effusion of Polish "confidence" in Russia was reciprocated,
in the years preceding the First World War, by growing Russian advocacy
of reforms in Poland, not only by Trubetskoi and Sazonov but by moderates and liberals from Count Kokovtsev to Fëdor Rodichev. See,
for example, *Padenie tsarskogo rezhima: Stenograficheskie otchëty doprosov*

were singularly ineffective in persuading the authorities in
St. Petersburg to initiate reforms in the Kingdom. And while
he himself became increasingly subservient to Russian government demands, other spokesmen of the Polish landowning
and middle classes were distressed by the failure of "reconciliation." Indeed, limitations on the use of the Polish language, the rights of the Catholic Church and the employment
of Poles in Russian service remained unchanged. Russians
continued to occupy key positions in the administration of
Poland. As in the past, the Russian press was forbidden to use
the term "autonomy" in reference to Polish aspirations. Finally, German influence at the Imperial court had traditionally
operated to the detriment of the Poles, and a number of Russian aristocrats maintained a "pan-monarchical," pro-German
outlook, which led them to endorse the sternest Russian opposition to all Polish efforts toward liberalization as attempts
to "undermine autocracy."[3]

Paradoxically, in Russia and Poland alike, both the extreme
reactionary wing and the extreme left produced some adherents to the cause of the Central Powers. As the war approached,
the conservative and moderate elements tended to side with
the Allies. Many Polish anti-tsarists, too, lined up in the
Russian camp, in the expectation that, whatever the disposition of the St. Petersburg autocracy, at least Russia's allies
would not let the Poles down. This expectation was based on
the argument—still very insubstantial in 1914—that the fate
of Poland was a matter not exclusively of Polish and Russian
concern but of international responsibility. True, at various
times in the nineteenth century, pro-Polish elements in France

---

*i pokazanii, dannykh v 1917 g. v Chrezvychainoi sledstvennoi komissii
Vremennego pravitel'stva,* ed. P. E. Shchegolev (Leningrad, 1924-27),
VII, 235 (the title is hereafter abbreviated as PTR); and Boris E. Nol'de,
Dalëkoe i blizkoe: Istoricheskie ocherki (Paris, 1930), pp. 230-31.

[3] Even such loyal Poles as Dmowski complained bitterly about the
great number of Russian officials of German origin who were assigned
to superior positions in the Kingdom. See his *Polityka polska i odbudowanie
państwa* (2d ed.; Warsaw, 1926), pp. 132-33; also Sergei D. Sazonov,
Vospominaniia (Paris, 1927), p. 374; and PTR, VII, 239.

and England had pointed to the international settlement arrived at in Vienna in 1815 as the legitimation of Poland's status and to the corollary responsibility of the signatories for her fate. Russia, of course, had strenuously—and, until this time, successfully—resisted this line of argument. The "internationalization" of the Polish problem was therefore bound to be a focus of contention during the First World War.

The outbreak of the war projected Poland into the center of international attention. "Pacified" during a century of peace among the dividing powers, Poland was the inevitable battleground of the warring powers, and each naturally sought to win Polish sympathy and support.

What was Russian policy to be? One course suggested itself to the realists. In the words of Baron Roman Rosen, a shrewd but exceedingly partisan Russian diplomat:

The partition of Poland had unquestionably been a crime. . . . But in committing this crime Russia had had two accomplices, Prussia and Austria, and she could remain in the tranquil enjoyment of the fruits of the crime only so long as she avoided falling out with her accomplices. Once, however, the rupture with these two powers had taken place, there was only one rational policy to adopt, and that was to make reparations as fully as lay in her power.[4]

Such a policy, however, did not commend itself to all Russian political leaders. The need, the scope, the timing and the form of "reparations" to Poland were precisely at the center of the struggle that ensued in St. Petersburg.

THE GRAND DUCAL PROCLAMATION

Initially the population of Russian Poland proved to be more loyal than might have been expected.[5] Russia's primary interest in the Kingdom, which had of late been strongly economic, was now manifestly strategic—Poland was the door

[4] Roman R. Rosen, *Forty Years of Diplomacy* (New York, 1922), II, 178-79.
[5] See Dmowski, *Polityka polska*, p. 108; Vasilii Gurko, *Memories and Impressions of War and Revolution in Russia* (London, 1918), p. 14; and *Ezhegodnik gazety Rech', 1916* (Petrograd, 1916), p. 65.

that either closed or opened Russia to Germany. Yet, conveniently enough (as Pavel Miliukov was quick to point out), Russia's strategic plans coincided with the task of "uniting" with the Slavic inhabitants of Austrian Galicia.[6] At this moment, the annexation of Galicia was indeed the only avowed territorial war aim of Russia; it was in this direction that Russian operations were most successfully pushed.

Though largely grounded in fear and hatred of Germany (a fear partly offset by friendship for the Dual Monarchy), Polish support for the Russian cause was substantially enhanced by Russian protestations of cordiality and rosy pronouncements regarding the future. It reached its peak in the latter half of August, 1914, after the historic appeal of the Russian commander in chief, Grand Duke Nikolai Nikolaevich.

When Roman Dmowski arrived in Petrograd on August 12, he was pleased to learn not only that his colleagues had responded "loyally" at the outbreak of war[7] but that the Russian government on its part was drafting an appeal to the Polish people. The idea of such a proclamation appears to have been first voiced by Prince Grigorii Trubetskoi, an articulate liberal, who as early as the Balkan wars had submitted a memorandum to the Tsar urging a reorientation of Russian policy toward Poland; there were neo-Slavist overtones in his argument. Foreign Minister Sergei Sazonov, who had gradually embraced the thesis of Russo-Polish reconciliation, was quick to grasp the political benefit to be gained from a revival of faith in Russian intentions, in both Poland and France, if Poland was promised self-government. Finally Trubetskoi, at Sazonov's request, drafted the text of the appeal. The original wording of the manifesto promised the Poles autonomy, but opposition to the term arose, and on August 13 it was re-

---

[6] See Miliukov, "Territorial'nyia priobreteniia Rossii," in *Chego zhdët Rossiia ot voiny* (Petrograd, 1915), pp. 49-50.

[7] The conservative Polish *koło* members pledged their fullest support during the early days of the war, apparently accepting the notion of *Burgfrieden* without raising any Polish demands. See, for instance, Kazimierz Kumaniecki, *Odbudowa panstwowości polskiej* (Kraków, 1924), pp. 29-30; and Dmowski, *Polityka polska*, pp. 154-55.

placed by the weaker and more ambiguous expression "self-government." (Self-government had indeed been the semilegitimate garb under which it had been possible to present Polish national aspirations in Russia since 1905.) Dmowski, to whom Sazonov showed the text, willingly accepted the formula and professed understanding for the inevitable delay in the implementation of the promises.

The few Poles who had access to Russian government leaders urged them not to delay the manifesto; notably, Count Zygmunt Wielopolski—a man of many connections—prodded the old Premier,[8] Goremykin, to publish it promptly. And on August 11 Sazonov called on Wielopolski to translate the draft into Polish.

Who was to sign the proclamation? Sazonov favored the Tsar himself; but the reactionary members of the cabinet, to whom the entire notion of promises to Poland was repugnant, objected that the appeal, addressed as it was to Poles under German and Austrian rule as well, could not very well come from a foreign monarch. It was therefore decided that the commander in chief, Grand Duke Nikolai Nikolaevich, should be the signer. By this maneuver the right wing sought to divest the Tsar and the government of any responsibility for implementing the promises contained in the manifesto. Nicholas II approved, and bearing the date of August 14, the proclamation was made public.[9] It made eloquent reading:

Poles! The hour has come when the dream of your fathers and forefathers can at length be realized. A century and a half ago the living body of Poland was torn to pieces, but her soul

[8] For convenience the Council of Ministers will be referred to also as the cabinet, and its Chairman as the Premier.

[9] It was not actually published until August 16, and the actual signatures —one in Russian (Nikolai) and the other in Polish (Mikołaj)—were not affixed until August 17. The foregoing account is based on Wielopolski's testimony, in PTR, VI, 28; Dmowski, *Polityka polska*, pp. 155-56; Szymon Askenasy, *Uwagi* (Warsaw, 1924), pp. 397, 424; *Russko-pol'skie otnosheniia v period mirovoi voiny*, ed. M. N. Lapinskii (Moscow, 1926), pp. 140-41 (hereafter cited as RPO); "Perepiska V. A. Sukhomlinova s N. N. Ianushkevichem," *Krasnyi Arkhiv* (Moscow), I (1922), 215; Nol'de, *Dalëkoe i blizkoe, passim*; and Nol'de, "Les desseins politiques de la Russie pendant la Grande Guerre," *Le Monde Slave* (Paris), No. 2 (1931), pp. 165-66.

has not perished. She lived in the hope that the time would
come for the resurrection of the Polish nation and its fraternal
reconciliation with Great Russia. The Russian armies bring
you the glad tidings of this reconciliation. May the boundaries
vanish which have cut asunder the Polish people! May it once
more be united under the scepter of the Russian Emperor!
Under this scepter Poland will arise again free in faith, language and self-government.

After an exhortation to provide equal consideration for non-
Polish nationalities in Poland, the appeal continued:

With open heart, with hand fraternally outstretched, Great
Russia comes to you. She believes that the sword has not rusted
which slew the foe at Grunwald. From the shores of the Pacific
Ocean to the Arctic seas the Russian war hosts are in motion.
The dawn of a new life is rising for you. May there shine re-
splendent in the dawn the Sign of the Cross, the symbol of the
Passion and Resurrection of nations![10]

Essentially, the promise consisted in the unification of Poland
and the establishment of self-government—both under the
"scepter of the Russian Emperor."

The authors of the proclamation were proud of it as a statement of ideals as well as an apt instrument of *Realpolitik*.
Maurice Paléologue, the French ambassador, recounted a discussion with Sazonov at the time, during which they

philosophized about the accession of strength Russia would
gain from the reconciliation of the two nations under the scepter
of the Romanovs. German expansion eastward would thus
be definitely arrested; all the problems of Eastern Europe
would wear a new aspect, to the great advantage of Slavism. . . .[11]
I quoted to him what Father [Grétry had] said in 1863: "Since
the partition of Poland, Europe has been in a state of mortal sin."
"Then I've done good work for the salvation of Europe,"[12]
[Sazonov retorted].

The Polish ND's and their associates were no less enthusiastic. The manifesto marked, after all, the triumph of Dmow-

[10] RPO, p. 155.
[11] Maurice Paléologue, *An Ambassador's Memoirs* (5th ed., London,
1925), I, 81-82.
[12] *Ibid.*, p. 84.

ski's political orientation. In a variety of messages the pro-Russian Poles now hailed the proclamation and offered their services.[13] Russians and Poles alike, it is true, were aware of the somewhat hypocritical nature of the proclamation. There were a good many mental reservations and doubts, typified by the remark Count Józef Potocki was reported to have made in private: "Not for a moment did I believe in [the sincerity of Russian intentions], but in reading the manifesto I wept copiously just the same."[14] An astute literary critic, Mikhail Lemke, summarized the prevalent comment in informed Russian quarters: "A costly promissory note has been issued. Though it has no seal on it, eventually it will have to be paid. . . . The sincerity of the issuer of the note and the support of the tsar-endorser as well as of the ruling circles arouse general doubt."[15]

In the opinion of Roman Rosen, who hoped for a peace with Germany, if only because of Russia's apparent inability to withstand the strains and stresses of war and the absence of compelling war aims, "hardly anything more illogical [than the proclamation], more senseless and unsatisfactory, to Poles as well as to Russians, could have been devised." It made peace overtures more difficult, aroused vain hopes among the Poles and "impudently" told the Russian people "they were going to die for Poland."[16] Witte expressed himself in similar terms,

[13] Four Polish parties—the ND's, the Progressives (*Postępowcy*), the Realists and the Polish Progressive Union—jointly "welcomed" the Grand Duke's proclamation as "an act of the greatest historical weight." They declared that "the blood of [Polish] sons shed in the common struggle against Germany will represent a sacrifice on the altar of the resurrected fatherland." English text in *The Times* (London), September 25, 1914.
    A group of sixty-nine leading Polish politicians and spokesmen of various organizations, including Roman Dmowski, Władysław Grabski and Maurycy Zamoyski, enthusiastically applauded the proclamation in a wire to the Emperor. Kumaniecki, p. 28. From Paris the grandson of a Polish émigré, Jan Chodźko, wrote the Russian envoy to France: "Yesterday perhaps many of us would have hesitated to give our lives for the Emperor of Russia; tomorrow none will hesitate to spill his blood for the King of Poland." *Ezhegoanik gazety Rech'*, *1916* (Petrograd, 1916), p. 60.
[14] Anatolii V. Nekludoff (Nekliudov), *Diplomatic Reminiscences before and during the Worla War, 1911-1917* (2d ed.; London, 1920), p. 324.
[15] Mikhail K. Lemke, *250 dnei v tsarskoi stavke* (Petrograd, 1920), p. 15.
[16] Rosen, II, 179-80.

adding, "The moment we annex Austria's and Prussia's Polish territories, we shall lose the whole of Russian Poland. Don't you make any mistake: when Poland has recovered her territorial integrity, she won't be content with the autonomy she's been so stupidly promised. She'll claim—and get—her absolute independence."[17]

Open expression of such views, however, was rather rare. The principal opposition in Russia came from chauvinists and reactionaries—including rightist cabinet members, deputies, editors, and churchmen, as well as courtiers, bureaucrats and Empress Alexandra Fëdorovna and her "Friend," Grigorii Rasputin. These groups, who were to assume such importance at a later stage of the war, had been stunned by the first wave of national unity and élan that the outbreak of the conflict had produced. Furthermore, the official sanction given to the proclamation precluded a frontal attack. The right-wing cabinet members therefore confined themselves to efforts to obstruct its realization.

The right wing had several articulate representatives in the government, notably Nikolai Maklakov, the Minister of the Interior, who had turned down Prince Trubetskoi's Polish project in 1912, Ivan Shcheglovitov, the Minister of Justice, and Procurator Sabler of the Holy Synod. They promptly rallied to oppose what seemed to be Sazonov's efforts on behalf of Poland. Shcheglovitov and Maklakov declared at a cabinet session that the Poles had been promised "too much."[18]

Contrary opinion notwithstanding, there is evidence that Nicholas II favored the modest plan for a self-governing and united Poland and trusted, perhaps naïvely, in the prospect of brotherly reconciliation. While his underlings deterred him from signing the proclamation of August 14, the Tsar himself

---

[17] Quoted in Paléologue, I, 123.
[18] V. A. Sukhomlinov, "Dnevnik," Dela i dni, I (Petrograd, 1920), 222. Premier Goremykin, though distinctly a rightist, was sufficiently subservient to the wishes of the Tsar not to oppose him openly. Moreover, he had at least a modicum of understanding of Polish affairs from the days of his own service in Poland.

repeatedly indicated his endorsement. To Count Wielopolski, his "favorite Pole," he said of the manifesto: "It is my appeal as well—we composed it together";[19] and, according to Dmowski, he told the Poles that he wished to consult them about its implementation.[20]

Yet in all likelihood the appeal would never have been formulated and sanctioned had it not been for Sazonov, the leading advocate of the new orientation in the cabinet. Moderate by comparison with his colleagues, strongly committed to a pro-British and pro-French policy, a man of far greater competence than the majority of the courtiers and officials, he had become a "realist" with regard to Poland—not out of moral or emotional considerations but in recognition of the imperatives of practical policy. "Without counting on support from any quarter," he later recalled, "I decided to take the cause of Russo-Polish reconciliation into my own hands and try, so far as it was in my power, to end the deadlock in this matter."[21] Before the war he had opposed Polish independence on the ground that its grant would provoke war between Russia and Germany; yet by February, 1914, he was prepared to argue for a reversal of the traditional monarchical concord in favor of a pro-Polish course as a matter of competition with Austria-Hungary: "We must create a real interest binding the Poles to the Russian state."[22]

While granting that the partition of Poland had been an injustice, Sazonov's arguments centered around the harm which its annexation had caused the Russian state; it had played

[19] PTR, VI, 33. In an audience on November 21, 1914, the Tsar told the French ambassador that for herself Russia wanted but a rectification of frontiers in the west—an elastic term, to be sure—and for Poland, "Poznań and possibly a portion of Silesia will be indispensable [for her reconstitution]." Paléologue, I, 192-94. The present paper concerns itself largely with the problems of Poland's status, not with alternative boundary proposals. The question of Poland's western borders as a part of the Allied war aims vis-à-vis the Central Powers is discussed in the articles by Merritt Abrash and Gifford Malone in this volume.
[20] Dmowski, *Polityka polska*, p. 156.
[21] Sazonov, p. 383.
[22] A. J. P. Taylor, *The Struggle for Mastery in Europe 1848-1918* (Oxford, 1954), p. 509.

"the part of a tumor or hernia in the then normal body politic
of the Russian state."[23] And it was in terms of Russian interests
—interpreted from the point of view of a faithful monarchist—
that he advocated a new course. However pliant under the
influence of liberal or internationalist advisers, Sazonov earnestly remarked to Paléologue in 1915 that "to me, there is no
Russia without tsarism."[24] It was therefore incumbent upon
the Tsar (and his ministers) to take the initiative in effecting
the needed "reconciliation."[25]

There were distinct limits to what Sazonov was prepared
to "offer" the Poles. He consistently opposed a grant of full
independence. Even in his postwar apologia he justified this
stand on the ground that "it would have provided a dangerous
precedent for Finland, which was of first-rate importance for
the defense of the capital and all of Northern Russia."[26] In
short, Sazonov was no Polonophile; he was above all a faithful
servant of the Russian emperor, but also a realist with a sense
of urgency about the Polish problem, which virtually all of
his cabinet colleagues lacked.

RUSSIAN POLICY IN POLAND

Within a few weeks it became evident that Russian policy
in Poland was not going to be changed as a consequence of
the proclamation. Maklakov's Ministry of the Interior promptly
issued a secret directive to the Russian press, instructing it to
keep comment on the manifesto to a minimum. Moreover,
the ban on the term "autonomy" continued in effect, so that
the Russian press was substantially "deprived of the possibility

---

[23] Sazonov, p. 369; see also pp. 372-75.
[24] Paléologue, I, 268-69.
[25] Sazonov, p. 384.
[26] *Ibid.*, pp. 373-74. When on August 23, 1914, Ambassador Bakh-
met'ev inquired from Washington about the details of Russian policy
toward Poland, Sazonov replied that the proclamation contained merely
"general principles, which can obviously be made specific only at the end
of the war, with the resumption of legislative activity." *Mezhdunarodnye
otnosheniia v epokhu imperializma*, Series III (Moscow, 1931-38), VI,
Part 1, 125; the abbreviation MOEI used hereafter refers to this title,
Series III.

of discussing the Polish question."[27] In Russian Poland restrictions on the appointment of Poles and on the official use of the Polish language and other discriminatory practices continued in effect.[28]

The offhand comment of the acting Governor General that the manifesto was but a piece of paper found more formal and sophisticated reflection in a confidential memorandum by Maklakov in which he sought to reduce it to an appeal to Poles outside the Kingdom: "It has in view only the Polish territories not belonging to the Russian Empire, which the Grand Duke will be able to conquer in the course of military operations. . . . Until this has taken place, one is merely to apply the mandatory regulations to the Polish population with the greatest good will."[29]

It is true that, at the Stavka (Field Headquarters) and in some "higher" circles in Petrograd, apparently sincere expressions of friendship for Poland were voiced.[30] Yet on the lower levels practice was in sharp contrast with the spirit of reconciliation. As Alexander Lednicki put it, there was "on the one hand, a seemingly benevolent attitude on the part of Headquarters, going a long way in meeting [what he con-

[27] PTR, VII, 238; see also Askenasy, p. 424; Sazonov, p. 373; and *Ezhegodnik gazety Rech', 1915* (Petrograd, 1915), p. 249.

[28] "Perepiska V. A. Sukhomlinova s N. N. Ianushkevichem," p. 261; V. Korostovetz, *The Rebirth of Poland* (London, 1928), p. 14; and PTR, VII, 238-39.

[29] No original of this memorandum is available. It has been widely cited and reprinted, and no question of its authenticity seems to have been raised. It appears in the otherwise wholly authentic collection compiled by Stanisław Fiłasiewicz, *La question polonaise pendant la guerre mondiale* (Paris, 1920), p. 14. When Engalychev took over as Governor General of Warsaw he publicly stated that he had come to "disillusion" the Poles about their future, and that only after the war would the Tsar "reward" those who had shown their good will by actively helping the Russian cause. Marcel Handelsman, *La Pologne: Sa vie économique et sociale pendant la guerre* (Paris, 1932), I, 54; and *Revue de Pologne* (Paris), No. 1-2 (1915), p. 38.

[30] The Tsar, the Grand Duke Nikolai Nikolaevich and General Samsonov addressed various expressions of thanks to the Polish population. Some "excessively" anti-Polish officials, such as Generals Utgof (Uthof) and von Essen, were removed. See Fiłasiewicz, p. ix; RPO, pp. 138, 141-43; PTR, VI, 29; Józef Błociszewski, *La restauration de la Pologne et la diplomatie européenne* (Paris, 1927), p. 10.

sidered Polish] demands; and, on the other hand, practical measures carried out with all the ruthlessness of force, making a great and unfavorable impression on public opinion."[31] The honeymoon in Russo-Polish relations was already over.

In October, 1914, the Polish question was submitted to the Russian Council of Ministers when General Ianushkevich, on behalf of Grand Duke Nikolai Nikolaevich, asked for instructions concerning the policy he was to pursue toward the Poles in newly occupied territory.[32] Ianushkevich himself suggested that "the time would seem to have come to give the Poles certain positive assurances regarding the contemplated concessions in their favor."[33] The cabinet devoted five sessions to this issue in November, discussing various courses on the basis of two projects, one introduced by Sazonov and the other by Ministers Maklakov, Shcheglovitov and Kasso (during the discussions Kasso, Minister of Education, was temporarily replaced by Acting Minister Baron Taube).

Both projects agreed that a future Poland must be reestablished in her "ethnic" borders, that is, not in her pre-Partition

---

[31] PTR, VII, 239.

[32] A further deterioration in Russo-Polish feelings resulted from Russian policy and behavior in occupied Galicia, a subject outside the framework of the present paper. On this question see Fiłasiewicz, p. 13; Handelsman, p. 53; Edmond Privat, *La Pologne sous la rafale* (Paris, 1915), pp. 57-64; *Odezwy i rozporzadzenia z czasów okupacji rosyjskiej Lwowa 1914-1915 rr.* (Lwów, 1916); Iurii Danilov, *Russland im Weltkrieg* (Jena, 1925), pp. 246-47; and Bernard Pares, *The Fall of the Russian Monarchy* (New York, 1939), p. 234. The split among the members of Piłsudski's Supreme National Committee (NKN) in Galicia, the cooperation of some Galician ND's with the Russians and the establishment of a Polish legion by Austria-Hungary are likewise outside the scope of this paper. For a general survey see *The Cambridge History of Poland*, Vol. II: *1697-1935* (Cambridge, England, 1951), Chap. 20. For Russian concern about a Polish legion see Błociszewski, p. 11; RPO, pp. 138-39; Bazili to Stepanov, in "Stavka i Ministerstvo inostrannykh del," *Krasnyi Arkhiv*, XXVI, 1-2; and MOEI, VI, Part 1, 269-72, 318-19. The leader of the Galician ND's, Stanisław Grabski, appealed to Petrograd for permission to convene a conference of Poles from all three parts to discuss the future of the country. Though Grabski was deemed conservative—not to say reactionary—enough to be trusted, both military and civil authorities repeatedly postponed decision; finally (February, 1915) the entire issue was turned over to the cabinet in Petrograd, which apparently took no action. RPO, pp. 27-39.

[33] RPO, p. 16.

expanse, and that a viceroy (*namestnik*) should be established to represent the emperor in Poland; both sides were likewise prepared to make some concessions in regard to local self-government as well as linguistic and religious policy. The Maklakov wing, however, wished to circumscribe the concessions so strictly and postpone their realization so indefinitely as to reduce the project to little more than lip service to the proclamation. Even Sazonov's proposals of a more extensive transfer of church, school, local economic and judicial matters to the Poles still constituted a rather modest program.

After a fairly frank debate—punctuated by comments of Maklakov that "our aim is not to satisfy the Poles but to keep them from separating"[34]—Sazonov's project was carried in a somewhat watered-down version. It called for a Polish kingdom within ethnic borders, under the scepter of the Russian emperor, and including (after the war) the Polish areas of Germany and Austria. It provided for the wider employment of Poles, and the Polish language, in education and administration. The viceroy was to be advised by a council consisting of government appointees as well as men elected by Polish local and regional assemblies. Implicitly, foreign and military affairs and other matters of state were to remain under the jurisdiction of the Russian government.

Even so weak a proposal was too much for the reactionaries. Shcheglovitov, Maklakov and Taube formally dissented and outlined their own position in a separate memorandum forwarded to Nicholas II. Stressing the necessity of "serving the interests of Russia exclusively," they insisted that if the war "were to lead merely to the unification of Poland . . . such an outcome might result in exceedingly deep discontent and disillusionment among the masses of the Russian people."[35] In relation to the broad gamut of Russian war aims—including, principally, the Straits, eastern Galicia, northern Bukovina and Sub-Carpathian Ruthenia—Poland was but a "very sec-

[34] *Ibid.*, p. 15.
[35] *Ibid.*, pp. 20, 22.

ondary" problem. Poland was, moreover, a purely Russian
concern (French and British interest in it must be ignored),
and the policy of Russia there must be decided on the basis
of her own interests, which demanded the postponement of
any action until the end of the war.[36]

While the majority and minority views were being transmitted to the Tsar, the "Russian Poles" learned about the
cabinet drafts (probably through Count Wielopolski, a member
of the State Council) and unhesitatingly came out against
both schemes. Even Dmowski agreed that neither the Maklakov scheme nor the Sazonov project was adequate in any
respect. Under the circumstances, he felt, it was more advantageous to leave the Polish question open, for at a future
date the Poles might be in a more favorable position to wring
concessions from Petrograd.[37]

Yet this was precisely what Sazonov sought to avoid. In
the fall and winter of 1914, the Russian armies were advancing
in Galicia. Events were to show that Russia's willingness to
yield to Polish demands varied in rough proportion to the
reverses she suffered on the field of battle and to the weakening of her system at home.

INCH BY INCH

Months were passing, and the Russian bill for the future
Poland was only slowly taking shape. In the face of increasing
Polish disappointment in Petrograd's policy, pro-Russian Polish leaders like Roman Dmowski and Zygmunt Wielopolski
continued to profess their steadfast alignment on the side of
Russia.[38] (Their seemingly blind endorsement of the Russian
autocracy at this time provoked a furious and prolonged

---

[36] *Ibid.*, pp. 19-23. For a fuller discussion of the minority memorandum
see Malone, in this volume, pages 138-40.

[37] Dmowski, *Polityka polska*, pp. 160-61. See also William Martin,
"La question polonaise et l'Europe au cours de la guerre," *Quarterly
Review* (London), CCXXX (1918), 479.

[38] On behalf of Russo-Polish friendship, Leo Kozłowski compiled a
volume of speeches and articles by Russian officials and pro-Russian
Poles and Westerners, *Voina i Pol'sha* (Moscow, 1914).

debate in postwar Poland during which Dmowski was accused of folly and insincerity.)

Yet grumbling and disaffection continued to grow unmistakably as the war dragged on, not only among the rank and file but also on the part of some of the Polish leaders in Petrograd.[39] Indeed, some of the skeptical Poles abroad, notably the "passivists" working out of Lausanne, openly demanded that the Polish issue cease to be treated as an internal Russian affair and become an inter-Allied concern.[40] Similarly a correspondent of Le Temps, after returning from Poland, declared that "son sort n'est pas une question russe. . . . C'est un devoir européen."[41] This was precisely what Sazonov had dreaded and sought to forestall. When the Russian embassies in the Western capitals reported on the favorable response to the appeal of Nikolai Nikolaevich—Benckendorff reported from London that it had helped neutralize anti-Russian feeling over the Polish, Jewish and Finnish questions—Sazonov, characteristically enough, urged them to play down the whole matter; as for precise "juridical formulas" for Poland, their crystallization, he added, was "premature."[42]

Sazonov's stand did not prevent Poles and non-Poles from embarking on active propaganda in favor of wider autonomy for the Kingdom—as was true of groups of Polish extraction in the United States[43]—nor from asking Russia to prove the

[39] When Count Józef Potocki returned to Petrograd in October, he told the French ambassador: "We are already feeling that the Russians are trying to get out of their promises. They are giving us to understand —and later this will be their excuse—that the manifesto was signed by the Grand Duke [Nikolai] and not by the Emperor. . . . They will resort to other subterfuges, no doubt. And in any case these magnificent promises are conditional on the conquest of Prussian Poland." Paléologue was forced to admit that reactionaries were working hard to "secure that the manifesto of August 16 [sic] shall remain a dead letter." Paléologue, I, 164-65.

[40] See, for instance, Michał Lempicki, Le grand problème international (Lausanne, 1915), pp. 88-89.

[41] Privat, p. 9.

[42] MOEI, VI, Part 1, 120-21, 124-25. See also Kozłowski, comp., Voina i Pol'sha, pp. 101ff.; and Le Temps, September 24, 1914.

[43] See Harold H. Fisher, America and the New Poland (New York, 1928), and the interesting but more controversial Louis L. Gerson, Woodrow Wilson and the Rebirth of Poland, 1914-1920 (New Haven, 1953).

sincerity of her apparent *volte-face*.[44] And for the first time
one of the Western governments was constrained to declare
its formal interest in the fate of Poland. In reply to an interpellation in the House of Commons, Sir Edward Grey stated
on March 2, 1915, that, "if the Honourable Member's question
is to be assured that His Majesty's Government are not out
of sympathy with the [Grand Ducal Proclamation], I can
assure him that this is so."[45]

The future of Poland inevitably came into question in the
discreet negotiations which Paris was conducting with Petrograd on the future map of Europe. At an early date Sazonov
informed Paléologue that Russia's war aims included the annexation of East Prussian and East Galician territory to Russia,
and of Poznań, Silesia and Western Galicia to Poland.[46] And
French Foreign Minister Delcassé, after some bickering, renounced French interest in at least the Austrian part of Poland,
a move to which even Paléologue objected as unnecessarily
magnanimous; he himself followed a careful path of encouraging
the Poles to back the Russians and of prodding Sazonov to
promote the pro-Polish reforms, but he avoided all appearance
of open interference.[47]

Despite Paléologue's protests, Delcassé's policy prevailed,
and for nearly a year the Polish question all but disappeared
from international diplomatic correspondence. As yet neither
public opinion nor government circles in the West were sufficiently aroused to intervene in what was officially termed
an internal matter of the Russian Empire, and therefore outside pressure was as yet insufficient to force a speeding up or

[44] See, for example, the "open letter" to Nikolai Nikolaevich in *Stockholm Dagbladet*, October 27, 1914, translated in Lempicki, pp. 97-107.
In Paris a French society lady took upon herself the mission of intervening
on behalf of the Poles with Ambassador Izvol'skii, who was forced to
admit that "the assurances of the Grand Duke had unfortunately not
been actually confirmed by the Emperor's signature and might therefore
be set aside, if convenient, as if of no account." Francis Bertie, *The
Diary of Lord Bertie of Thame* (London, 1924), I, 154-55.
[45] *Hansard*, LVII, 654.
[46] MOEI, VI, Part 1, 247-48.
[47] Paléologue, I, 246; see also *ibid.*, pp. 164-65.

a widening of the scope of Russian deliberation on the future
of Poland.[48]

At the end of November, 1914, the Tsar received the two
cabinet reports on Poland. During his stay at field headquarters
he turned over the file to the Grand Duke, who on December 5
informed Goremykin of his agreement to the principles (though
not all details) expressed in the majority report.[49] After a
further delay, in January, 1915, Nicholas II ordered the cabinet to take up the majority plan for detailed consideration,
and the Council of Ministers promptly resumed its discussions
of the Polish problem.[50]

The decision adopted (and forwarded to the Tsar as the
minutes of the March 3 session) was a conservative modifica-
tion of the earlier Sazonov draft. Army, navy, foreign affairs,
finances, communications, law courts and transportation were
to remain under Russian control. The cabinet voted for the
proclamation of the new Polish status by Imperial *Reskript*,
to be followed by detailed legislative implementation. On
various issues such as the status of the Catholic Church, the
official use of the Polish language and local self-government,
the new draft was distinctly vaguer or provided for slower
action, but otherwise followed the sense of the 1914 proposal.[51]
In March, 1915, when Russia's military position still appeared
rather favorable, the modestly "reformist" tendencies of the cabinet majority stopped at the high-water mark set by this project.

The Council of Ministers pointed to two issues for possible
action before adoption of an overall decree. One was liber-

---

[48] On this point see Titus Komarnicki, *Rebirth of the Polish Republic*
(London, 1957), pp. 41-63.

[49] RPO, pp. 23-24; *Krasnyi Arkhiv*, II, 150.

[50] RPO, p. 41; Sukhomlinov, "Dnevnik," *Dela i Dni*, I, 227. A few
days earlier the Cadets had taken the lead in urging a substantial number
of reforms, which included self-government to the Poles. The speeches
before the Duma on August 2, 1915, in which Miliukov and Shingarev
gave a detailed account of the Cadet demands and their reception by
Goremykin were censored and omitted from the official record of the Duma
sessions. PTR, VI, 310-11.

[51] RPO, pp. 40-47; and Nol'de, *Dalëkoe i blizkoe*, p. 172.

alization of policy toward the Catholic Church, but the Stavka raised objections to it in time of war.[52] Thus only the issue of municipal self-government received immediate attention. On March 30, 1915, with the approval of the Emperor, the Russian Urban Statute, adopted under Stolypin, was extended to the towns of the Kingdom of Poland.[53] This step was the only significant concession which the tsarist government made to the Poles during the entire period of the First World War. It was of course meant to appease the Poles; yet after the build-up of previous months and the expectations aroused by the proclamation of August 14, it was bound to produce little besides disappointment. Indeed, some predicted such a response and sought to dissuade the government from issuing the act.[54]

The "Russian Poles" decided to let no more time pass without speaking up. Nicholas II clearly intended to proceed with the reform project; in late April he asked the cabinet to edit the final text of the contemplated edict on the future status of Poland, and from Engalychev's letter to Goremykin it is apparent that he planned to promulgate it when and if he visited Warsaw.[55] On May 10 Zygmunt Wielopolski sent a memorandum to the Tsar, Goremykin and Engalychev, urging the final reconciliation of Russians and Poles as "fraternal nations within the borders of a single state." He was quick to point out that the Act of March 30 had been approved in principle before the war and that it fell short of the various promises since made by Russia. He singled out the German influence in Russia as responsible for delays in Russo-Polish understanding. Now, with the war exacting a heavy toll

---

[52] RPO, pp. 47-49; and "Stavka i MID," *Krasnyi Arkhiv*, XXVI, *passim*. Apparently Ianushkevich was the major restraining element.

[53] The act also permitted the use of the Polish language in municipal administration. On the other hand, it formalized the separation of the government of Chełm from the Polish Kingdom—a measure which had been approved by the Duma in 1912 but to which (since it meant a diminution of Poland) Polish circles had emphatically objected. For the text of the act of March 30, see Fiłasiewicz, pp. 19-20.

[54] RPO, p. 54; Dmowski, *Polityka polska*, p. 160; and PTR, VII, 242.

[55] RPO, p. 49; and *Perepiska Nikolaia i Aleksandry Romanovykh* (Moscow, 1923-27), III, 154.

among Russians and Poles alike, "the hour has struck to speak up clearly and unequivocally. " Fundamentally, the six points suggested by the memorandum as the basis of a Russo-Polish understanding coincided with the government project; it merely emphasized the urgency of action.[56]

The memorandum helped crystallize the decision, taken after the Tsar conferred with Goremykin, to call on Polish representatives to participate in future conferences on the status of Poland.[57] Yet in all likelihood this decision, taken in May, 1915, was more significantly influenced by the sudden turn of fortune on the battlefield. On May 2 a fierce German-Austrian offensive was launched on the eastern front. A fortnight later the German Army was advancing at a rapid pace —and making enticing appeals to the Polish population. As usual, Petrograd was more apt to listen to the Poles when the going was rough.[58]

Polish spokesmen were invited to attend a long conference on June 3, 1915, which amounted to a series of addresses by the Poles. The record reveals nothing novel in their arguments. Dmowski reiterated his idée fixe of the community of Russian and Polish interests in stopping Germany; Zygmunt Wielopolski merely expanded on his memorandum to the Emperor; Ignacy Szebeko, also a member of the State Council, acknowledged, a bit more bluntly than heretofore, widespread Polish suspicion of Russian motives, but assured the gathering that the limited reform bill would satisfy them and—equally important—cut the ground from under more radical elements; Jan Harusewicz, a member of the Duma, demanded that the "Russian Poles" be kept properly informed and consulted in

[56] The text is in RPO, pp. 50-ᴜ3; see also PTR, VI, 30, 34. It is likely that Wielopolski did not draft the memorandum himself. The six points were: the granting of legislative autonomy in local affairs in Poland; a separate regional government under an appointive viceroy; official recognition of the Polish language in government; use of Polish in all schools of the Kingdom, which were to come under local supervision; use of Poles in Russian government service; and the lifting of limitations on the Catholic Church in Poland.

[57] Dmowski, *Polityka polska*, p. 161.

[58] For other notes from this period, see RPO, pp. 53-60, 78-85.

future deliberations; and Władysław Grabski asked for "tangible proof" of Russian good will toward the Polish "masses," of whom he spoke with obvious condescension. Self-government was distinctly the maximum aspired to ("autonomy" being referred to occasionally with regard to education, religion and local government); the demand of Polish "radicals" for a greater degree of "separateness" (*gosudarstvennaia obosoblennost'*) was violently rejected by Szebeko and others. The Poles who met with the Russian leaders represented the highest, most conservative social strata of Poland—the elements most unconditionally loyal to Russia.[59]

Eight days later the Council of Ministers voted to suggest the establishment of a joint Russo-Polish Commission, and on June 19, Nicholas II confirmed this decision. To the accompaniment of German artillery fire as the Russians retreated from Poland, Petrograd—almost a year after the outbreak of war—seemed finally prepared to give the Poles a voice in their own destiny.

RUSSIAN SOCIETY AND POLAND

How the inarticulate mass of the Russian people felt about Poland in the early months of the war remains unknown. In terms of Russian policy-making it did not matter, for policy was formulated by a select and unrepresentative group, and only a few intellectuals, politicians, officials and journalists (stifled as even they were by the prevalent taboos and censor-

---

[59] For the protocol of this meeting, see RPO, pp. 60-77. The Russian participants included the arch-conservative Goremykin and Maklakov. At this session Wielopolski submitted an additional memorandum intended to clarify his earlier draft. The text, referred to in RPO, p. 61, is Appendix II to Sovet Ministrov, *Osobye zhurnaly 1914-1916*, "Protokol soveshchaniia," May 21, 1915, O.S. (Library of Congress microfilm). This microfilm comprises a larger collection of the A. N. Iakhontov papers than those published in Berlin in 1926 (see note 82, below). These additional materials now available at the Library of Congress have served as basis for an article by Kazimierz Grzybowski, "The Jakhontov Papers: Russo-Polish Relations (1914-1916)," *Journal of Central European Affairs*, XVIII, No. 1 (April 1958), 3-24; but they shed little new light on the present subject.

ship regulations) had an opportunity to express themselves publicly on the issue.

At the extreme right, several newspapers were vociferous in their denunciation of the "pro-Polish" orientation. Professor Migulin bluntly declared in *Russkii Ekonomist* [Russian Economist] that Russian soldiers would not die for Poland; he emphasized the necessity of an eventual understanding with Germany, which would be frustrated if Poland were permitted to expand westward.[60] Such periodicals as *Kolokol* [The Bell], *Russkoe Znamia* [Russian Banner], *Zemshchina* and *Tserkovnyi Vestnik* [Church Herald], largely subsidized by the government from clandestine funds, were strenuously opposed to any scheme for Polish autonomy. The Church organs, for instance, vociferously objected to any moves in favor of the Roman Catholic Church.[61] The notorious Markov, editor of *Zemshchina*, repeatedly objected to the Polish statute as "premature." He added that the Poles wanted independence and would not be appeased by such generous gestures as the grant of autonomy; in fact, their desire for independence might well push them into the arms of the Central Powers, and Russia would merely be helping its enemies by yielding to the Poles.[62] Similar views were voiced by the Duma rightists after a conference led by Neidhardt, Sazonov's (and Stolypin's) brother-in-law.[63] Others argued that Poland was being promised something concrete while Russia herself was still uncertain of the gains she would derive from the war.[64]

With the passage of time, however, important men and organs came to adopt a more favorable view toward concessions.

---

[60] Jerzy Jan Sosnowski, *Prawda dziejowa, 1914-1917* (Warsaw, 1925), pp. 330-32; quoted in Walther Recke, *Die polnische Frage als Problem der europaeischen Politik* (Berlin, 1927), p. 237.

[61] Marjan Seyda, *Polska na przełomie dziejów* (Poznań), I (1927), 161-62; and Askenasy, p. 136.

[62] Askenasy believed that Markov expressed Goremykin's views in this matter; see Askenasy, p. 141.

[63] *Ibid.*; and Nekludoff, p. 398.

[64] See, for instance, Paléologue, I, 166-67; and Dmowski, *Polityka polska*, p. 120.

Even such an advocate of negociated peace with Germany as Roman Rosen—writing, it is true, after the war—stated: How clearly indicated was the obvious course that should have been adopted: the restoration, under the Constitution of 1815, of the autonomous Kingdom of Poland, united to Russia solely in the person of the Sovereign—a solution of the Polish problem which was entirely within the power of Russia—could have been effected immediately, would have dealt a most serious blow to both Prussia and Austria, and would have given the Polish nation a real satisfaction instead of shadowy promises whose realization was entirely dependent on the fortune of arms.[65]

Gradually the influential *Novoe Vremia* [New Times] and *Kievlianin* [The Kievan] shifted to a more pro-Polish attitude.[66] Peter Struve appealed to the Russians to help the Poles, who were "bearing the brunt" of the war.[67] Nikolai Berdiaev echoed Dmowski's theme of a Slav brotherhood opposing the Teuton onslaught: "A Poland united in herself and united with Russia by fraternal bonds will be a bastion against the German danger, that eternal enemy of the Slavs."[68]

Another bourgeois publication, *Russkie Vedomosti* [Russian News], commented editorially: "The war is not being waged to replace one hegemony by another, one form of national hatred by another, but in order to create stable conditions for peaceful cooperation of different nationalities on the basis of mutual respect for their rights."[69] This is about as far as censorship would permit Russian moderates to express themselves until the summer of 1915.

Such prominent men of the liberal center as Nikolai L'vov, the Princes Trubetskoi and Peter Struve all agreed on the desirability of Polish autonomy and the maintenance of personal union between Poland and Russia. Most of the liberals were determined opponents of complete Polish independence.[70]

[65] Rosen, II, 180.
[66] Quoted in *Revue de Pologne*, No. 1-2 (1915), pp. 41-42.
[67] *Ibid.*, pp. 45, 47.
[68] *Ibid.*, pp. 48-49.
[69] Quoted in R. Vydrun, in *Sovremennyi Mir* (Petrograd), No. 9 (1915), p. 105.
[70] See Seyda, I, 163.

The Neo-Slavs in various forms and degrees talked of a rebirth of Poland as a prerequisite for Slavic, and Russian, re-
naissance.[71] The most outspoken advocacy of Polish independence came, somewhat surprisingly, in a memorandum
submitted to the Tsar in May, 1915, by a group of Moscow
Neo-Slavs, including Fëdor Samarin, A. A. Kornilov and the
two Golitsyns. Quoting Aksakov and Khomiakov, they insisted that Poland could not be satisfied with autonomy, while
the "Russian Orthodox Tsar cannot simultaneously be Polish
Catholic King." Hence Russia must "step across the line
set by the proclamation [of Nikolai Nikolaevich] and make
out of Poland, in her ethnographic boundaries, an entirely
independent state."[72] The proposal was apparently not pub-
licized. Other than this group, few if any Russian spokesmen
declared in favor of a complete severance of ties with Poland.[73]

The views that carried most weight in moderate quarters
were those of the Miliukov group. Early in the war the Cadets
began elaborating the details of the future status of Poland
in numerous articles and monographs. In one thoroughly
documented study Miliukov proposed a basis for drawing the
future boundaries of Poland which would take into consideration both ethnographic factors and economic utility. In contrast to other Russian writers, Miliukov was willing to give
Poland access to the Baltic Sea, including Danzig and a part
of East Prussia.[74]

After voicing their demand for a Polish statute at the Duma-
Government conference in February, the Central Committee
of the Cadet Party in May, 1915, adopted a detailed project
of autonomy known as the Kokoshkin Plan. It aroused considerable comment but had little effect on government policy.
Under this proposal Poland would have received autonomy
in all matters except foreign, military and customs affairs,

---

[71] See *Revue de Pologne*, No. 1-2 (1915), pp. 40-41.
[72] Quoted in Askenasy, p. 451, note.
[73] See Recke, p. 211.
[74] Miliukov, "Territorial'nyia priobreteniia Rossii," pp. 51-62. See
also Pares, p. 247.

much as in Sazonov's plan. In addition, the Kokoshkin Plan
would have provided for constitutional guarantees of civil
rights, universal suffrage and cabinet responsibility to the
Sejm—stipulations that were distinctly less than welcome to
the pro-Russian Polish magnates.[75]

Though not spokesmen of any party, a number of scholars
and intellectuals also took a liberal stand on the Polish question.
The well-known historian N. I. Kareev, in an article on the
historical aspects of the problem, concluded: "On both sides
a good deal of the past must be forgotten, but a good deal
must also be remembered so as to serve as a lesson on the
mistakes which it would be unpardonable to repeat at a moment
when the Polish question is being raised so extensively."[76]

The socialist parties took no vigorous stand on the issue
of the future Poland. Both Socialist Revolutionaries and
Social Democrats were on record as favoring far-reaching autonomy and did not alter their views on this question during
the war. The national question, however, underwent a serious
revision in Bolshevik circles during the war. While Piatakov
and Bukharin continued to argue that "the slogan of 'self-
determination' is above all utopian and harmful" and advocated propagandizing "indifferentism with regard to 'fatherland' and 'nation,'"[77] Lenin in 1914-1916 adopted a stand
in favor of Polish self-determination in the widest sense, even
over the opposition of the Polish Zimmerwaldists themselves.[78]

[75] See, for instance, Alexander Lednicki, "Voina i Pol'sha," *Russkaia
Mysl'* (Moscow), No. 6 (1915), p. 121; Miliukov, "Tseli voiny," in *Ezhegodnik gazety Rech'*, 1916, p. 66; "Kadety v dni galitsiiskogo razgroma,"
Krasnyi Arkhiv, LIX (1933), 110-44; and *ibid.*, LIV-LV (1932), 19-20,
note. See also pp. 65-66, this volume.

[76] Kareev, "Pol'skii vopros v istoricheskom osveshchenii," in M. I.
Tugan-Baranovskii, ed., *Voprosy mirovoi voiny* (Petrograd, 1915), p. 85.

[77] Piatakov, Bosh and Bukharin, November 19, 1915, quoted in M.
N. Pokrovskii, ed., *Ocherki po istorii oktiabr'skoi revoliutsii* (Moscow,
1927), I, 516-18.

[78] V. I. Lenin, *Sochineniia* (4th ed.; Moscow), XXI (1948), 371-76,
and XXII, 132-45. A convenient and well-documented summary of
Lenin's and Radek's views is contained in Olga Genkin and H. H. Fisher,
The Bolsheviks and the World War (Stanford, 1940), pp. 500-21. See also
Richard Pipes, *The Formation of the Soviet Union* (Cambridge, Massa-

Virtually all Russians, whatever their differences on the future of Poland, did see eye to eye on one point—Poland was a matter to be decided by Russia and not by the Allies jointly. "Internationalization" of the Polish question, vaguely hinted at by Poles and Frenchmen from time to time, was out of the question. A. A. Stolypin, editor of *Novoe Vremia*, insisted that it was up to Russia, shedding blood for Poland, to decide her future within the "great Slav family."[79] Berdiaev argued that "the Polish question is an *internal*, deep wound of the Russian nation."[80] Even Miliukov, in an interview with a correspondent of the Italian *Messagero* (April 18, 1915), declared that Poland would get her autonomy after the war, but that it was Russia's business to decide how much.[81] With this, all the parties from Cadets to extreme rightists agreed.

THE SUMMER CRISIS OF 1915

While the Russian government was considering changes in the status of Poland, the Russian forces were in headlong retreat, and Russian policy was alienating increasingly large segments of the Polish people. In an inept semblance of "scorched-earth" tactics, the tsarist authorities arrested thousands of Poles and Jews once it became evident that Warsaw would have to be abandoned. At the request of the army, Russian gendarmes raided homes and jailed thousands—including children from the age of twelve. Many more thousands of Polish families were forced to flee into the interior of Russia. Though the *razzias* provoked angry cries of protest—an interpellation by Alexander Kerensky in the Duma resulted in the release of some 1,300 Poles—several thousand were nonetheless deported to Siberia on the flimsiest of pretexts. Even the cabinet agreed that the action was as stupid as it was unjustified, and voted to release all minors and those against whom no

chusetts, 1954), Chap. 1; and Bertram D. Wolfe, *Three Who Made a Revolution* (New York, 1948), Chap. 33.

[79] Quoted in *Revue de Pologne*, No. 1-2 (1915), pp. 42-43.
[80] Quoted *ibid.*, p. 48.
[81] Quoted in *Polen* (Vienna), I, No. 18 (1915), 10.

charges were preferred, but the damage was done.[82] Benckendorff had reason to write Sazonov that Russian policy in
Poland was provoking hostility, which "may reverse the sympathies" of England.[83] It was easy for the cabinet to blame the military. The
Russian government itself was floundering in an atmosphere of
crisis. The reverses on the battlefield produced unrest and a
marked decline in morale; economic difficulties led to a wave
of strikes; official inefficiency prompted a resumption of political
warfare at home, and the Duma was becoming frankly more
hostile to the government. One by one, the most reactionary
cabinet ministers (including Maklakov and Shcheglovitov) were
eased out, but without appreciable increase in the government's popularity. Nor did the Tsar give the cabinet his
confidence. By the end of the summer—to quote Sazonov—"the
government hung in mid-air, without support from either
above or below."[84]

On June 19 the government announced, with the Emperor's
approval, the creation of the joint Russo-Polish commission.
Within a fortnight the commission was convened, consisting
of six Russians and six Poles. State Secretary Kryzhanovskii,
a man of Polish origin who had become a stalwart Russified
reactionary, soon replaced the ailing Goremykin as acting
chairman. All twelve members of the commission were past
or present members of the Duma or State Council and, except
for two (Bagaliev and Sviatopolk-Mirskii), represented the most
conservative elements of society.[85]

[82] See PTR, VII, 245; RPO, pp. 144-48; Askenasy, p. 444; Handelsman, pp. 57-58; and minutes of cabinet session of August 29, 1915, in
A. N. Iakhontov, ed., "Tiazhëlye dni," in *Arkhiv russkoi revoliutsii* (Berlin),
XVIII (1926), 74-75.
[83] MOEI, VIII, 11.
[84] Sazonov, pp. 376-78. Just before their dismissal Shcheglovitov and
Sabler had petitioned the Tsar to give up the idea of a joint commission,
"representing that the autonomy of any part of the Empire [was] incom-
patible with the sacrosanct principles of autocratic absolutism." Paléologue, II, 23.
[85] See Fiłasiewicz, p. 23; and PTR, V, 442-43. For the cabinet protocol of June 11 establishing the commission, and the Tsar's approval
dated June 19, see Sovet Ministrov, *Osobye zhurnaly*, May 21, 1915 (O.S.).

In the course of the commission's nine sessions in early July, it quickly became apparent that the Russian and Polish views could not be reconciled at this stage. Moreover, the Russians did not see eye to eye among themselves. Goremykin opened the conference on a discouraging note: "The manifesto of the Grand Duke contains two promises: unification of the Polish lands and self-government. When God gives unification, there shall be self-government; and if there is no unification, there will be no self-government."[86] The Poles were apparently eager to reach an agreement, insisting that they did not seek full independence. Dmowski suggested shrewdly that by letting the Poles run their own affairs Russia could profitably concentrate on her major foreign policy aim, the acquisition of the Straits. Other Polish spokesmen even agreed that the controversial borderlands known as the *kresy*—historically Polish but inhabited predominantly by Eastern Slavs —were not to be a part of postwar Poland.[87]

As the commission's work proceeded, two distinct projects took shape, one supported by the Russian members, the other by the Poles. Kryzhanovskii made a futile attempt to reconcile them and had a "compromise proposal" drafted. Yet in the end the commission agreed to disagree.[88] While Sazonov blamed the failure on the split within the Russian government and the low caliber of the commission's membership, Dmowski declared that the breakdown was a blessing in disguise, for it saved the Poles from an entirely "undesirable" manifesto![89]

In view of the failure by agreement and the unfavorable developments at the front, Sazonov now suggested the im-

---

The Russian members were Bagaliev (Bahalii), Balashov, A. G. Khvostov Nikol'skii, Shubinskii and Prince Sviatopolk-Mirskii. The Poles were Szebeko, Dmowski, Grabski, Harusewicz, Dobecki and Zygmunt Wielopolski.

[86] Recke, p. 213.

[87] No stenographic record of the commission's sessions is available. Askenasy (pp. 437-43) provides an entirely credible account of its work, based apparently on a contemporary publication in Petrograd. See also Błociszewski, p. 21; and Recke, pp. 213-17.

[88] RPO, p. 89; PTR, V, 442-43, and VI, 38, 46; Nekludoff, p. 441; and *Ezhegodnik gazety Rech', 1916*, pp. 67-68.

[89] Sazonov, p. 381; and Dmowski, *Polityka polska*, p. 162.

mediate proclamation of Polish self-government by imperial
decree. "Such an act," he told his colleagues, "will produce
an excellent impression among our allies, who are distressed
by the uncertainty and vacillations of our Polish policy. The
Poles, in turn, will see that Russia, forced by adverse military
fortune to evacuate the Polish lands temporarily, does not
cease to concern herself with her sister nation and is preparing
for the future the conditions for just coexistence." The manifesto would have to be "posted on the walls of Warsaw before our forces leave." But all the other ministers objected.
Krivoshein protested against such an "act of impermissible
cowardice." Kharitonov asserted that "the Germans will
counter by proclaiming a Polish kingdom," while Polivanov
insisted that it was too late: "The days of Warsaw are numbered." Concluding the vigorous debate, Goremykin declared:

I do not deem myself empowered to submit to the Emperor's
signature and to countersign an act regarding the unity and
the future structure of Russia. This is not a measure of military
necessity and must be resolved in the course of normal legislative action. If the Poles are willing to trust in the sincerity
of the government, my statement to be made before the Duma
on behalf of the Emperor will suffice.[90]

Goremykin had in mind the speech he was to deliver at the
opening of the legislative session on August 1. The spirit had
changed radically since the solemn dedication to the war effort
a year earlier. Cabinet members were under outspoken attack, and some speeches were deemed so compromising that
the censor did not permit their publication. Goremykin in
his address for the first time acknowledged that the Grand
Ducal proclamation represented Russian government policy.
For the first time he used the long-censored term "autonomy"
in referring to Poland:

    [90] Session of July 29, 1915, in Iakhontov, ed., pp. 22-23. See also
Günther Frantz, *Russland auf aem Wege zur Katastrophe* (Berlin, 1926),
pp. 274-75.

The Polish question can of course be solved fully only after the end of the war. . . . But at this time it is important for the Polish people to know and trust that its future is definitely and irrevocably laid down by the appeal of the Commander in Chief, made with the Emperor's sanction in the first days of war. . . . The Emperor has deigned to authorize me, gentlemen of the State Duma, to inform you that His Majesty has ordered the Council of Ministers to work out a bill granting Poland, after the war, the right freely to build its national, cultural and economic life on the basis of autonomy, under the scepter of the Russian Emperor and with the maintenance of the unity of the state.[91]

While the Polish *koło* professed to be "satisfied,"[92] the legal opposition, liberal and socialist alike, spoke up bluntly in accusing the government of "bankruptcy."[93] But to the stand-patters Goremykin's "promise" was a welcome device. General Ianushkevich told Kudashev, the acting Foreign Office representative at the Stavka: "The declaration of I. L. Goremykin on the autonomy of Poland was very opportune. Now let the Poles choose between us and the Germans. If it should become clear that they prefer the latter, it will free us of all promises past and present." Informing Sazonov of this conversation, Kudashev commented: "This statement, I think, shows the genuinely hostile attitude of the General toward the Poles and his lack of sympathy for any concessions whatever to their political aspirations."[94]

The time for talk had passed. The political problem was assuming an increasingly academic character for tsarist Russia, which had lost the opportunity to rally the people of Poland to its side by sincere and meaningful reform—just as it failed to rally its own people. On August 5, 1915, the Germans entered Warsaw and rapidly rolled on eastward. Kovno, Wilno and Grodno fell. Riots broke out in several Russian cities.

[91] The text is given in Fiłasiewicz, pp. 27-28.
[92] PTR, VI, 31; and Handelsman, p. 58.
[93] *Gosudarstvennaia Duma, IV sozyv, IV sessiia, zasedanie I: Steno-graficheskie otchëty* (Petrograd, 1915), pp. 86-87, 95-96; and Vydrun, pp. 108-9.
[94] "Stavka i MID," *Krasnyi Arkhiv*, XXVII, 44.

Ammunition, food and arms were dangerously short. Nicholas II was persuaded to make Grand Duke Nikolai Nikolaevich the scapegoat for the defeats.[95] This was an early achievement of the Rasputin clique, which henceforth played a major part, thanks in large measure to the Empress herself.

When the Tsar decided to assume the supreme command himself, the majority of the cabinet, led by Sazonov, promptly voiced their opposition to so dangerous a step, fearing that further setbacks at the front might jeopardize the shaky monarchical system itself. All in vain. Nicholas II took the Grand Duke's place, leaving operational supervision to his chief of staff, General Alekseev. Ianushkevich departed with the Grand Duke to the Caucasian front. But the ministers' protest was not forgotten. Empress Alexandra singled out Sazonov for special stricture and enmity. Not only had he formulated a foreign policy that ran counter to her views (or those of the reactionary camarilla), but Sazonov—in reality motivated by a fervent desire to strengthen the monarchy— had even dared protest against the will of the Emperor!

After the Tsar departed to the Stavka, Alexandra Fëdorovna began to take a more active part in government affairs. In her frequent letters, with news and gossip about events in the capital, she would report time and again on Sazonov's doings in the most disparaging terms. "Sazonov is the worst, cries, excites all," she complained in her somewhat awkward English on September 19, 1915. "Fred[ericks, Minister of the Court] ought to tell him from you that you have heard of it and are very displeased, I find. I call it a strike of the ministers." The next day she urged her husband to think of a "successor to Sazonov, who . . . has lost his head, cries and agitates against Goremykin." And again: "Clean out all, give Goremykin new ministers to work with, and God will bless you and their work. Please, lovebird, and quickly. I wrote to [Goremykin] to give

[95] When in March, 1915 War Minister Sukhomlinov suggested Nikolai Nikolaevich for the post of viceroy of Poland, the latter had made it known that he cherished the "dream of not returning to any official duty after the war." Krasnyi Arkhiv, III, 38-41.

a list, as you asked, but he begged you to think of Sazonov's successor."[96]

The naïvely insistent arguments of his wife were bound to carry weight with Nicholas. Moreover Goremykin, himself angry at Sazonov, sought to have him and others in the cabinet replaced. Kryzhanovskii was virtually told that he would become Minister of the Interior.[97] Rumors of Sazonov's impending dismissal were so widespread that the press took note of them. Yet when Sazonov inquired, Nicholas assured him that he knew nothing of them and had nothing of the sort in mind.[98] Indeed, for another four months, the cabinet remained intact.

The increasing tension between the Duma and the government pushed the Polish question into the background. Nonetheless, the demands of the Progressive bloc, published on September 7, 1915, included "the solution of the Russo-Polish question: abolition of the restrictions on the rights of Poles in the entire territory of Russia, completion and introduction without delay of a bill for the establishment of autonomy in the Kingdom of Poland, and the simultaneous revision of the legislation concerning Polish landholding."[99]

The government "solved" one part of the crisis by proroguing the Duma. Now, however, the "Russian Poles" were restless. They openly complained of delays and trickery. The least Russia could do, Harusewicz argued, was to prove its good will by revoking limitations on the use of the Polish language and on the civil rights of Poles on the territory of Russia proper. He too now threatened to play what was the

---

[96] *Pis'ma imperatritsy Aleksandry Fëdorovny k imperatoru Nikolaiu II* (Berlin, 1922), I, 519-21, 528; see also pp. 535-36. The Empress thought neither Izvol'skii, Neratov, Girs (Giers) nor Benckendorff would do as successor to Sazonov.

[97] According to Kryzhanovskii's account in his *Memoirs*, he would not have accepted the offer unless there was "an agreement with the Poles . . . by means of concessions on the future of Poland." Sergei Efimovich Kryzhanovskii, *Vospominaniia* (Berlin, 1938 [?]), pp. 160-61.

[98] MOEI, IX, 134-35; see also pp. 158-59.

[99] *Ezhegodnik gazety Rech'*, *1915*, p. 277; see also A. A. Polivanov, *Memuary*, I (Moscow, 1924), 220; and "Progressivnyi blok v 1915-1917 gg.," *Krasnyi Arkhiv*, L (1932), 130-32.

highest trump in the deck of the pro-Allied Poles—he warned
Petrograd that Poland was potentially a matter of international
interest, not merely a Russian issue.[100]
Ambassador Paléologue aptly summed up the status of the
Polish question in the winter of 1915-1916:

The Russian government persists in remaining silent about the
restoration of Poland. Paris, where the Polish committees of
Switzerland are carrying on a very energetic and skillful propaganda, is getting anxious about it. At this end, I neglect no
opportunity of pointing out that the Imperial Government is
making a grievous mistake in delaying the establishment of
the autonomy of Poland on a broad basis; it risks being fore-
stalled by the Teutonic powers. Of course, I am obliged to be
very diplomatic, as Russian nationalism has not yet forgotten
the events of 1863.[101]

The tsarist government had had ample time to take advantage of the initial good will of many Poles, to make tangible
concessions and win them over. It had missed this chance.
As 1916 approached, Poland was in enemy hands, and the
Poles active in politics in Russia and abroad had all but lost
faith in Russia. There were signs that the Western Allies were
beginning to take a more active interest in the future of Poland,
at the very moment when Polish spokesmen sought to place
the destiny of their country on an international basis. In
Russia the Polish statute had become a facet of the fierce
conflict between the extreme right and the liberals, between
the Rasputin clique and the Sazonov wing, between elements
committed to the alliance with France and Britain and those
toying with separate peace.

LOOKING WEST

On February 15, 1916, Boris Stürmer replaced Goremykin
as Chairman of the Council of Ministers. Sir George Buchanan,

---

[100] See *Revue de Pologne* No. 1-2 (1916), p. 15; also PTR, VI, 59-60.
[101] Paléologue, II, 198-99. Paléologue believed that "the Emperor
himself has been won over to the principle of a generous autonomy.
Provided that Poland remains under the scepter of the Romanovs, he
would concede most of the Polish claims. Sazonov shares his views and
bravely exhorts him to adhere to them." *Ibid.*

the British envoy, aptly described Stürmer as a man of "second-rate intelligence, without any experience, [and] extremely ambitious, [who] owed his new appointment to the fact that he was a friend of Rasputin and that he was backed by the empress' camarilla."[102] As for Poland, Stürmer insisted (as he put it a year later) that "the Russian people get what was coming to them and know what they could expect first."[103] As the Western powers at this time objected to the publication of inter-Allied agreements concerning the Straits, Stürmer maintained, Russian public opinion would tolerate no promises to Poland.[104]

In his opening speech on government policy, on February 22, Stürmer spoke of "our obligation to realize all the principles of national reunion which were proclaimed as early as the first days of war and were thereafter, by Imperial order, confirmed from this tribune [in the Duma] by my predecessor. In accordance with the wish of the Emperor, a new life is opening for Poland, assuring the Polish people of the free development of its essential genius and of its cultural and economic aspirations."[105] Sazonov's speech, the same day, did little to balance these vague platitudes. While reaffirming the Russian pledge for a united and autonomous Poland and alerting the Poles to the intentions behind the German plans for a Polish army and a Polish university, Sazonov added nothing new, except for a symptomatic reference to the "sympathetic" attitude of France and Britain.[106]

Until early in 1916 Poland had scarcely figured in the diplomatic negotiations among the Allies. There had been informal references to her future, especially in the frank per-

---

[102] George Buchanan, *My Mission to Russia and Other Diplomatic Memories* (London, 1923), II, 3.

[103] PTR, I, 227. A cabinet colleague of Stürmer asserted that the new Premier held the Grand Ducal proclamation to be merely an *obiter dictum* without binding force. M. S. Balabanov, *Tsarskaia Rossiia XX veka* (Moscow, 1927), p. 95.

[104] PTR, VI, 48

[105] Fiłasiewicz, p. 39.

[106] *Ibid.*, pp. 40-42.

sonal talks between Paléologue and Sazonov, and the question
was indirectly considered in the official but secret conversations
regarding Russia's postwar boundary in the west.[107] Yet the
internal organization of the future Poland had been conceded
by France and Britain to be the exclusive concern of the Russian government.

In the winter of 1915-16 the diplomatic situation began
to change. While consenting to Russian gains, Britain and
France were still striving for a better quid pro quo.[108] The
deterioration of Russia's military position placed the West
in a more advantageous bargaining situation. Briand, moreover, had replaced Delcassé in the new Viviani cabinet, and
leftist elements in France—more vociferous and independent
than before—provided a fertile ground for pro-Polish sentiments. There was also a growing realization in the West that
a German-sponsored Polish army might seriously handicap
the Allied position on the battlefield. Finally, it may be sur-
mised that hopes for a liberalization in Russia had been dashed
by Stürmer's appointment and that the delays in Petrograd
made Paris more impatient about the entire Polish issue. On
November 3, 1915, Briand mentioned the future Polish state
in the Chamber of Deputies, and on December 7 an Italian
deputy, Montresor, introduced a bill that would have made a
"free and independent Poland" one of the Allied war aims.[109]

A decisive role in raising the Polish question to the level of
international consideration was played by the émigré Poles
themselves. The continued setbacks, increasing difficulties and
seeming hypocrisy of the Russian government had produced
a noticeable cooling in Polish feeling toward Russia, even in
the most loyal quarters. While among many Poles the Central
Powers were still viewed with suspicion, the logical locus for
the propagation of the idea of an independent Poland was
now found in Western Europe. In the course of the war,

[107] See the articles by Abrash and Malone in this volume.
[108] See MOEI, X, 398-401.
[109] Fiłasiewicz, p. 33; and Handelsman, p. 66.

as Nol'de wrote afterwards, Russian soil gradually proved to be no longer necessary for the advancement of Polish ideals. Even Wielopolski and Harusewicz, finding Stürmer's speech narrower in interpretation than Goremykin's address of the previous year, manifested their growing disaffection. In the words of Wielopolski, "If [after the Goremykin speech] we could say, 'We will of course support the government,' this could no longer be asserted in reply to Stürmer."[110]

In November, 1915, Roman Dmowski left Russia for Western Europe. Though he still professed adherence to his Slav-versus-Teuton conception, his departure was indicative of the shift in primary reliance from the eastern ally to the western Entente. If earlier the fear of a German move had prompted Russian action—paper action—with regard to Poland, now the fear that the West might take or claim a hand in the solution of the Polish question united the various legal parties in Russia; in February, 1916, they were agreed to oppose all French efforts to interfere in the matter. On the other hand, the prospect of "internationalization" eased the way to advocacy of full independence for Poland—both out of sincere conviction and as a means of anticipating the intervention of the West.[111]

Early in 1916 Russian diplomats abroad began to urge their government to act on the Polish question without delay. On January 29 Izvol'skii sent Sazonov a report suggesting, in view of the menace of German-Austrian plans for Poland, that at least a statement formally confirming the Grand Ducal proclamation and specifying the future status of Poland be issued—a statement with which the Allies might declare their solidarity. Izvol'skii felt that continued Russian indecision would be "exceedingly harmful" both in settling the Straits

---

[110] PTR, VI, 35.

[111] Dmowski, *Polityka polska*, pp. 179ff.; Askenasy, p. 141; Handelsman, p. 62; *Russkoe slovo* (Moscow), January 9, 1916, quoted in *Revue de Pologne*, No. 3 (1916), pp. 78-82. Moderate socialists, such as Kerensky, Chkheidze and Nekrasov, joined a "Circle of Friends of Polish Independence." Even Prince Evgenii Trubetskoi, the neo-Slav publicist, urged an independent Poland with an outlet to the Baltic Sea, with Russia "as guardian of her integrity."

issue and in influencing public opinion in the West. (It is significant that on January 28 Louis Barthou had listed among the war aims "la liberté de la Pologne.")[112] On March 3 Benckendorff likewise insisted from London that Russian policy toward Poland "be made amply clear and precise so as to neutralize all hostile efforts."[113]

Now the Polish émigrés started their offensive. Erasmus Piltz, one of the senior pro-Russian Polish leaders of the Lausanne committee, informed Bakherakht, the Russian minister to Switzerland, of details in the German-Austrian project for Polish autonomy and military service. After disappointing efforts to drum up support for the Polish cause in Rome and at the Vatican, Roman Dmowski and Count Plater explained to Bakherakht that, if the Central Powers were to proclaim Polish autonomy or even independence, the "Russian Poles" would be hard pressed to hold their ground, that the only solution was to forestall them.[114]

Dmowski, still not satisfied with the results of his mission, proceeded to Paris, where he asked to see Izvol'skii. At the end of a two-hour talk, he urged, for the first time, the inclusion of no less than Polish independence among the Allied war aims. A few days later, at Izvol'skii's suggestion, Dmowski handed him a paper, incorporating the substance of the earlier remarks—a bit milder than his verbal demands had been, but still opposing the idea of personal union of the king of Poland and the emperor of Russia.

The memorandum expanded at length on the question of German war guilt, evidently in an attempt by Dmowski to prove his unalterable opposition to the Central Powers, and stressed the hardships the Poles were suffering for the Allied cause. Dmowski argued that the Poles were as much a nation ("*naród w pełnem znaczeniu słowa*") as were the South Slavs

[112] MOEI, X, 113-14.
[113] *Ibid.*, p. 344.
[114] *Ibid.*, pp. 23, 198-99. While the Poles were unquestionably using the German bogey to wring concessions from Russia, Berlin and Vienna were indeed preparing a new Polish statute.

or the Czechs. Germany's efforts, skulduggery though they were, promised to win the sympathies of the Poles unless Russia carried out the "national idea" in an act that would recognize Poland's "just place among the peoples of Europe" and thereby restore the faith of the Polish people and the world in the Russian Empire before it was "too late."[115]

Interest in the Polish question did not ebb in France. Petrograd was not greatly concerned, as French censorship, despite considerable opposition to the ruling, still barred discussion of Polish independence. The Swiss press, readily available in France, frankly debated all aspects of the Polish question, much to the annoyance of Izvol'skii, who was in favor of exerting influence on the French press—with the expenditure of considerable sums—to demonstrate that an independent Poland would become a tool of Germany.

When he transmitted the Dmowski memorandum, Izvol'skii at the same time informed Sazonov that he had

learned that government circles here are seriously disturbed by the reports concerning Germany's intention to declare Poland's independence with the aim of recruiting troops in the occupied Polish areas. It must not be forgotten that the French government leans with one wing on the extreme parliamentary factions which are especially apt to wax enthusiastic about the thought of reestablishing Poland.[116]

Sazonov was well aware of this segment of opinion, and looked upon it with strong repugnance. The journal of the Ministry of Foreign Affairs for March 8 reiterated Sazonov's motif in his instructions for the impending inter-Allied conference in Paris: "It is essential to insist on the exclusion of

---

[115] The French original of the memorandum is not available. MOEI refers to it but does not print it. A Polish translation appears as appendix to Dmowski, *Polityka polska* (pp. 433-40), under the heading "Memorjał w sprawie uznania niepodległości Polski" (Memorial on Recognition of the Independence of Poland). Izvol'skii commented that in fact Dmowski would have been satisfied with a Polish state in personal union with Russia and without a separate foreign policy, but with a separate army. MOEI, X, 398-401. Sazonov acknowledged receipt of the memorandum from Paris but failed to tell the Poles in Petrograd of its existence. Dmowski, *Polityka polska*, pp. 183, 233.

[116] MOEI, X, 401.

the Polish question from the subjects of international deliberation."[117] Sazonov maintained the same attitude in his conversations with Paléologue; on March 2 the latter noted that
Sazonov had told him: "Be careful! Poland is a dangerous
quarter for an ambassador of France."[118] He repeatedly
pointed to the failure of earlier French attempts to intervene
in Russian affairs, to Stanisław Leszczyński's plight,[119] to
Napoleon's attempt to use the Duchy of Warsaw against Russia, to French incitement of the Poles in the nineteenth century
and to Russian neutrality in the Franco-Prussian war of 1870,
which, he maintained, had been the result of this French
policy. Said Sazonov: "If I were a Frenchman or a Pole,
I would have a superstitious fear either of granting my protection to Poland or accepting if from France."[120]

At this moment France was anxious not to alienate the
Russians, not to conduct a policy which—with the Stürmer
group already in power—might tend to increase the influence
of what were assumed to be the elements favoring separate
peace. And yet the Polish question did come up, as Sazonov
had feared. Evidently under pressure from the left and with
the approval of Briand himself, Jules Cambon, Secretary-
General at the Quai d'Orsay, asked Izvol'skii how the Russian
government would react to an offer of a collective demonstra-
tion of the Allies in favor of Polish unification and autonomy.
Izvol'skii "most decisively" replied that such a suggestion
was absolutely unacceptable, that Russian public opinion would
never acquiesce in making Poland the subject of international
negotiations. Russia had agreed to give France a free hand
in the solution of the question of Alsace-Lorraine, he pointed
out; a suitable quid pro quo would be a similar recognition

---

[117] "Dnevnik Ministerstva Inostrannykh Del za 1915-1916 gg.," *Krasnyi
Arkhiv*, XXXII, 23.
[118] Paléologue, II, 199.
[119] With French support, Stanisław Leszczyński (1677-1766) was twice
elected King of Poland, in opposition to the Russian-backed candidate.
As a result of the Treaty of Vienna (1735), however, he finally lost the
Polish throne, but became Duke of Lorraine and father-in-law of Louis XV.
[120] Sazonov, pp. 384-85.

of the Russian position in regard to Poland. Cambon offered a formula that would encompass both Poland and Alsace-Lorraine, but Izvol'skii again refused. Still, Briand decided to take another step. In exceedingly careful wording, perhaps suspecting that the Russians were deciphering foreign diplomatic correspondence, Briand wired Paléologue a statement that officially raised the question of Poland's future:

En présence de la propagande habile des allemands et des mesures récentes . . . nous ne doutons pas que le gouvernement russe saura de son côté prendre les mesures et faire des déclarations de nature à rassurer le peuple polonais et à conserver sa fidelité à la Russie. Nous ne pouvons que nous en remettre à notre allié du soin d'agir avec la sagesse et le libéralisme qu'impose la situation.[121]

While ostensibly "not doubting" Russia's good will and efficiency, the note in effect did question them and urged Petrograd to act.

It appears that Paléologue somewhat backhandedly mentioned this note to Sazonov but at the very same time assured him that Poland would not become an international issue. Sazonov, on his part, assured the French diplomat that the Russian government and public had the best intentions toward Poland. Paléologue thereupon wired Briand that France could rest assured of Petrograd's good intentions. The affair was embarrassing to both parties and rested there, without any effect except increasing suspicion at both ends.[122]

At the inter-Allied conference on March 27-28, 1916, Léon Bourgeois suggested the formal reaffirmation of the "liberty and dignity of peoples." The proposal was evidently a surprise to Briand himself. On the basis of Bourgeois' known sympathies Izvol'skii had no doubt that he had Poland in mind and feared such a statement might provide a lever for the internationalization of the problem. During an inter-

---

[121] Confidential dispatch from Izvol'skii to Sazonov, March 16, 1916, in MOEI, X, 411-12.

[122] Izvol'skii to Sazonov, March 19, 1916, and Sazonov to Izvol'skii, March 20, in MOEI, X, 428-29, 431; excerpt from the Journal of the Ministry of Foreign Affairs, ibid., pp. 414-15.

mission Izvol'skii therefore hurriedly conferred with Briand, who tactfully managed to get Bourgeois to withdraw the proposal.[123] The cloud had passed, but the Polish weather was no longer made in Petrograd alone.

From France, Dmowski traveled on to London, where the future of Poland still aroused less interest than in Paris. Under-Secretary Arthur Nicolson, who received him, described him to Benckendorff as a superior and trustworthy man, "très polonais, mais très slave."[124] Dmowski once again urged extensive and immediate action on the Russian envoy, who in reply insisted on the adequacy of earlier Russian promises. The Dmowski in London was a different man from the studiedly militant separatist of Paris a fortnight earlier. Intent on erasing any impression of disloyalty, he eagerly acknowledged the primacy of Russia's interests in Polish matters and declared that he would be satisfied if the Western Allies were merely to accede to Russia's Polish statute without taking an active hand in it.[125]

On the whole Dmowski's efforts in England were less successful than in France. While individuals such as Viscount Bryce championed the Polish cause from the same platform as Dmowski,[126] the British newspapers by and large paid little attention to Polish aspirations.

With the general shift in reliance, among pro-Allied Poles, from Petrograd to Paris, those who remained in Russia increasingly sought out the French envoy there. Paléologue himself mentioned this fact to Sazonov since, as he said, the police "report all my movements to him" anyway. Among those who frequented the embassy were the Wielopolski broth-

---

[123] Izvol'skii to Sazonov, March 30, 1916, *ibid.*, pp. 540-51.
[124] Benckendorff to Sazonov, March 23, 1916, *ibid.*, p. 439.
[125] *Ibid.*, pp. 440-41. Dmowski himself stated (*Polityka polska*, p. 184) that when Benckendorff insisted that he return to Russia, he backed out, even though offered a diplomatic passport. Instead he promised to send Count Konstantin Plater to Petrograd. There is no record of this conversation in MOEI.
[126] *The New York Times*, March 9, 1916.

ers, Counts Zamoyski and Plater, Stanisław Radziwiłł and
Józef Potocki. When a group, including Count Plater just
back in Russia from Britain, lunched with him, a frank exchange developed, which is best described in Paléologue's
own words:

Plater argued that the Allies should take up the Polish question
so as to make it international. I protested vigorously against
this notion. The claim to internationalize the Polish question
would provoke an outburst of indignation in nationalist circles
in the empire and paralyze all the sympathies we have won in
other quarters. Sazonov himself would violently object. And
the whole Stürmer gang would have a fine game denouncing
the democratic Western powers for taking advantage of the
Alliance to interfere in the domestic affairs of Russia. I added:
" You know what the French Government feels about your
cause, and I can promise you its interest is not academic. But
its action will be all the more efficacious if it is discreet and
deprived of any officia character. So far as I personally am
concerned, I never lose an opportunity of inducing the Emperor's ministers to talk to me about Poland and tell me their
views, doubts and difficulties about the grave and complex
problems which the proclamation of Polish autonomy raises.
Although given solely as private opinions, their repeated declarations (for not one of them, not even Stürmer himself, has
ventured to protest against the Emperor's intentions) have at
length constituted a kind of moral obligation which unquestionably would enable the French government to speak with
exceptional authority when the hour of final decision arrives."
Plater has promised me to make this point clear to his compatriots; but he does not hide from me that he will have difficulty in convincing them.[127]

In line with Paléologue's attitude, the diplomatic facet of
the Polish question appears hereafter to have been subordinate.[128] When a French government mission, headed by
Viviani and Albert Thomas, visited Petrograd in May, 1916,

[127] Paléologue, II, 230. See also *ibid.*, pp. 198, 217, 228-29; and MOEI,
X, 543.

[128] This tentative conclusion is based on the fact that only occasional
reference to the question is made in published memoirs of the subsequent
period. The diplomatic record itself is not available. Not only are the
relevant British and French documents inaccessible, but even the MOEI
series was suspended with the volume ending in April, 1916.

one of the purposes of their visit was to "persuade the Imperial government to give a firm and definite undertaking in favor of Poland." Yet after their arrival Paléologue advised Viviani "to postpone any discussion until just before you leave; you can then judge for yourselves whether that topic can be broached. I have my doubts."[129] Indeed, when in their farewell visit on May 18 the French statesmen mentioned Poland to Sazonov, the latter "insisted in the strongest possible terms on the danger to the Alliance of any intervention, even a discreet intervention, by the French government in the Polish question."[130]

On the surface, the none-too-insistent French effort to transfer the Polish question to the international level had failed. Yet it had produced a strong effect in Petrograd, for it had given food for thought both to those favoring concessions to Poland and to those who opposed them. Each faction found itself reinforced in its position, the advocates of the Polish statute seeking to forestall internationalization, and the recalcitrants fearing the identification of Polish and anti-Russian orientations in the West.

SAZONOV AND THE POLISH PROJECTS

Sergei Sazonov held the initiative in Polish matters in Petrograd. Three reasons, he felt, compelled Russia to act without delay. Germany and Austria were readying their own independence projects for the Poles, and it was essential to forestall them. Secondly, prompt action was vital to avoid the interference of the Western Allies. Thirdly, the Poles had to be given enough—though not necessarily more than the minimum—to satisfy them and attach them to the Russian cause. Since a pledge of local self-government would merely insult their dignity (especially at a time when Poland was under German occupation), the Poles "should be given everything compatible with the interests of Russia, without looking

---

[129] Paléologue, II, 250.
[130] *Ibid.*, p. 261.

back into the past."[131] Despite the urgency, the opposition
of influential Russian circles to any meaningful reforms made
it essential to steer a wary course that would be acceptable
to them too. Sazonov saw the best solution in "granting,
from the eminence of the Russian throne, a constitutional
charter to the Polish people."[132] Above all else, Sazonov urged
haste.

It bears repeating that he was neither a Polonophile nor a
sentimentalist. At the end of May, 1916, in an interview with
a London *Times* correspondent, Sazonov still hedged on the
basic issues of the Polish statute and was content to declare
vaguely that "Poland will receive a just and equitable autonomy
in the greatest degree, adjusted to its future life and its economic and industrial development."[133] The stalemate in the cabinet prevented him, until May, 1916, from pushing his ideas
on the Polish statute. An opportunity for action appeared
on May 8, when Izvol'skii forwarded a detailed report on the
Polish situation.

Surveying the increasing pressure from the Poles and from
the French left, Izvol'skii pointed to the Briand-Paléologue
exchange as well as to the Bourgeois proposal as harbingers of
things to come. While the French authorities were helpful
in "hirdering the Polonophile campaign" (Izvol'skii proudly
reported that an issue of the socialist *Victoire* had been con-
fiscated because it contained an article by Gustave Hervé
entitled "Gare à la Pologne"), the problem was becoming increasingly difficult to control.

In his report the envoy transmitted a new proposal of Dmowski to Petrograd:

---

[131] Sazonov, *Vospominaniia*, p. 385.
[132] *Ibid.*, p. 386.
[133] *The New York Times*, May 29, 1916. See also PTR, VI, 207; Sazonov, *Vospominaniia*, p. 387; and Askenasy, pp. 447-48. The early Soviet
interpretation of Sazonov stressed his implicit reliance on Polish landlord
and bureaucratic elements in the future kingdom. Recent Soviet studies
(including the comprehensive *Istoriia Pol'shi*, published by the USSR
Academy of Sciences [3 vols.; Moscow, 1954-55]) completely ignore his
plans.

Russia must immediately work out a project for the solution of the Polish question so as to unite all three parts of Poland and form out of them a national Polish state, united with Russia by such bonds as would guarantee the community of state defense and economic interests. This project might become the subject of an agreement between Russia and her allies; at the same time, there would be no need to announce the existence of such an agreement; it would be entirely sufficient if the Poles were to learn by some means about its existence and contents, for instance, through newspaper dispatches.[134]

Dmowski was thus offering Russia a face-saving device for avoiding the humiliation of Western interference, while in effect sponsoring precisely such an intervention.

Izvol'skii himself, after reviewing the shift in Polish attitudes since the beginning of the war, concluded with a dual appeal. On the one hand, it was "necessary to restore the hope [of the Poles] that an Allied victory will bring them a better future, and for this purpose it is above all essential to restore their faith in the promises of Russia." On the other hand, "the transfer of the Polish question to the international arena . . . is entirely unacceptable to Russia."[135] To be sure, the two concluding points had long since been found to be the common denominator of the views held by most of the contesting factions in Russian political life.

Sazonov now made a detailed report to the Tsar and received his permission to submit a draft constitution for Poland. Early in June Sazonov submitted his report to Nicholas II, in essence incorporating all the major arguments earlier adduced. On the one hand, "it would be tantamount to closing one's eyes to reality to deny the international significance of the Polish question"; on the other, or just for this reason, Russia had to act alone. The Foreign Minister envisaged three possible "solutions": independence, broad autonomy or regional self-government for Poland. At this time (and in contrast to the assertions he made in his memoirs), he most

134 RPO, p. 96.
135 *Ibid.*, p. 97.

firmly opposed the idea of an independent Polish state, which
would lead to German control of the country and would be
interpreted as a sign of Russian weakness. Just as firmly
he rejected self-government as inadequate to gain Polish support and politically impossible after the more substantial earlier
promises. The way out was that of far-reaching autonomy.[136]

The actual draft constitution submitted by the Foreign
Minister consisted of nineteen articles.[137] It embodied no radical departures, no startling innovations from the prevailing
doctrine of the "autonomists." It was bound to please them
and to antagonize the standpatters. It could cause no shifts
in position.

---

[136] The text is given in RPO, pp. 85-90; also in V. P. Semennikov, ed.,
Monarkhiia pered krusheniem, 1914-1917 (Moscow, 1927), pp. 183-87.
The report was dated April 17 (Old Style; April 30, New Style); actually
it was not submitted until several weeks later. This discrepancy in dates
has been interpreted as an effort on Sazonov's part to protect himself against
a possible charge that he had been influenced in his thinking by Thomas
and Viviani, who visited Russia in the first half of May.

Nol'de summarized the proposal subsequently as follows: "Only a
Russo-Polish reconciliation on the basis of recognizing genuine state
autonomy for the Polish people, but with the retention by Russia of the
responsibility for the destiny of Poland, can provide a real line for the
future defense of Russia against Germany—i.e., political, military and
economic defense—and establish a real line of Russo-German demarcation." *Dalëkoe i blizkoe*, p. 85.

[137] The text is given in RPO, pp. 90-94; also in Semennikov, ed., pp.
187-91. The document was apparently drafted by Baron Boris Nol'de;
see his *Dalëkoe i blizkoe*, p. 85. The draft reaffirmed the indivisibility of
the Kingdom of Poland and the Russian state, their community of dynasty
and state affairs. The central government retained control of monarchical
succession, foreign affairs, military affairs, the Orthodox Church, cur-
rency, the national budget, tariffs, banks, some taxes, communications,
aviation, railroad trunk lines and monopolies (Art. III) While thus specifying in considerable detail the areas of Russian jurisdiction, it gave the
Poles complete freedom in internal organization, education, language and
the Catholic religion. The Sazonov plan was narrower than the Cadet
proposal (the Kokoshkin plan of May, 1915; see pp. 24-25) in that the
Polish deputies to the Duma and State Council would have acted as a
delegation participating only in matters concerning their kingdom. The
Nol'de draft provided for a viceroy (Art. VII), a bicameral legislature
(Art. XI) and a council of ministers (Art. XIV). A vaguely defined body
for the settlement of disputes between Poland and Russia was provided
for (Art. XVIII), much as Miliukov had suggested. Finally, the statute
could be abrogated only by consent of the tsar and the Russian legislature,
as well as the Polish Sejm (Art. XIX).

While the finishing touches were being put to the Sazonov plan, another project for Polish autonomy was being drafted by the "Russian Poles" themselves. Count Stanisław Lubomirski, an aristocrat and friend of the Wielopolski brothers, in May, 1916, composed a letter to the Tsar, which Grand Duke Boris Vladimirovich personally took to the Stavka.[138] It rather bluntly declared that Polish attitudes toward Russia had evolved into a widespread suspicion because of the violation of solemn promises, with the result that the Central Powers were successfully winning the support of the Poles. Polish autonomy, Lubomirski insisted, must be granted regardless of the fulfillment of the other major promise, unification of all Polish lands.[139]

The Tsar examined both the Sazonov draft and the Lubomirski letter in early June; on June 8 Stürmer gave him two statements of his own views on these new developments. In his comments Stürmer revealed himself as an uncompromising opponent of wartime concessions to Poland, true to his "Russia first" outlook and his extreme conservative connections. He professed to see neither need nor urgency for changes, considering Lubomirski's appeal to be proof of the increasingly pro-German outlook of the Poles, which he attributed in part to the anti-Russian propaganda of Jews (a charge ludicrous both in fact and in terms of the personalities involved, since many of the leading "Russian Poles" were outspoken anti-Semites). Stürmer stated in effect: " You have done enough for the Poles; let them do something for you."[140]

Thus the lines were drawn. Sazonov and Stürmer had taken opposite positions, and it was up to the Emperor to decide. Over the strenuous opposition of Stürmer and Khvostov, by late June Nicholas II tentatively approved the draft statute

---

[138] RPO, pp. 126-27.

[139] *Ibid.*, pp. 101-3. Wielopolski and his friends criticized various details of the Sazonov project, such as the appointment, not election, of the future governor general of Poland, and the absence of equal rights for the Poles living outside the borders of the Kingdom. Nekludoff, p. 440.

[140] RPO, pp. 98-101, 104-7; and Semennikov, ed., pp. 191-97.

submitted by Sazonov by ordering the cabinet to proceed with its elaboration.[141] Meanwhile Stürmer had become involved in an incident which, perhaps better than anything else, illustrated his attitude toward the Poles.

In their realignment and search for new formulas the "Russian Poles" traveling abroad had established, or reestablished, ties with neutral and even pro-Austrian Poles in the West. Dmowski had felt compelled to go to see Under-Secretary Arthur Nicolson to obtain a denial of a Foreign Office report that had labeled him an Austrian agent. Characteristically, he attributed the reports to Lewis B. Namier, then working at the Foreign Office—"that little Galician Jew," as Dmowski called him.[142] Such reports did not fail to reach Stürmer.

The Russian premier promptly took advantage of these dispatches. In a memorandum to the Tsar, detailing the increasing pro-Austrian sentiment among the Poles, Stürmer indiscriminately lumped together followers of Piłsudski, Prince Czartoryski (leader of the Polish "Centrum" in Galicia) and Roman Dmowski. He charged, without factual basis, that secret meetings held at the Polish House in Moscow had given support to the Austro-German proposals for Poland. "The majority of Poles in Russia," he continued, "are already inclined to accept the Austro-German proposals, and only the National Democrats still delay joining the rest, waiting for the decision of the forthcoming Polish congress in [Kraków]. In this way the Austro-German agitation has achieved its end."[143]

[141] After the Tsar returned the Sazonov draft, the cabinet asked the military leaders for comment. Both Chief of Staff Alekseev and General Brusilov, commander of the southwestern front, proved to be emphatically in favor of the plan. It was no surprise to those who knew him that Alekseev informed Stürmer that "on my part, I associate myself fully with the opinion of General-Adjutant Brusilov and consider that the proposal for the solution of the Polish question is at present the only expedient one and that it would therefore be desirable to carry it out without any delay." RPO, pp. 113-14. See also "Stavka i MID," Krasnyi Arkhiv, XXVIII, 42-43; Sazonov, Vospominaniia, p. 388; and A. A. Brusilov, A Sodier's Notebook (London, 1930), pp. 107-8.

[142] Dmowski, Polityka polska, pp. 194-95.

[143] English translation in British War Office, Daily Review of the Foreign Press (hereafter cited as DRFP), August 11, 1916, pp. 10-11. Factual

The most striking aspect of this incident was the subsequent release of the memorandum to the press. Alexander Lednicki, a Polish historian and politician who was chairman of the Polish House in Moscow and close to the Miliukov group, decided to inquire into the matter. When Kryzhanovskii failed to be helpful, Lednicki succeeded in securing a copy of the memorandum through his friend Stepanov, Deputy Minister of the Interior, and proceeded to write a determined protest to several members of the government (as well as to General Alekseev, for the memorandum had been distributed to all corps headquarters, implying that the Poles fighting on the Russian side were disloyal).[144] The *koło* and Wielopolski protested against the Stürmer memorandum on their own.[145] But the damage was done.

The July Crisis and the Empress

In May, 1916, a delegation of representatives of the major Russian parties went on a tour of western Europe. It included the Cadet leader, Miliukov; the neurotic Vice-chairman of the Duma, Protopopov; and Count Zygmunt Wielopolski, who traveled as a member of the State Council. Inevitably the subject of Poland cropped up in their conversations in the West. Protopopov, who was also Minister of the Interior, declared in Paris, "I can guarantee that the promises given by the Grand Duke will be fulfilled." After the war, he pledged, the Russian government would see to the establishment of a united Poland, with its own parliament, government and

inaccuracies were also to be found in other Stürmer memoranda; see Lemke, pp. 814-17. In his statement concerning the Lubomirski letter Stürmer reiterated the charge against the Polish House in Moscow and labeled the Polish newspaper *Dziennik Pietrogrıdski* [Petrograd Journal] as pro-German.

[144] See PTR, VII, 248-49. The memorandum, distributed within the government in May, 1916, appeared in *Russkoe Slovo* on July 25, 1916 (DRFP, August 11, 1916).

[145] DRFP, August 9, 1916, p. 10, and August 12, 1916, pp. 6-7; PTR, VI, 36-37. Separate replies were sent apparently because the Polish rightists could not abide Lednicki, whom they accused of radicalism and "Judeo-German" sympathies; see Kazimierz Smogorzewski, *La Pologne et la guerre à travers les livres polonais* (Paris, 1929), pp. 75-76.

language—in brief, "the mistress of her own fate."[146] These
and similar statements were due in part to the disturbing
findings of the parliamentary mission. When the delegation
returned, Miliukov gave a full report to the Military and Naval
Committees of the Duma, in the presence of the cabinet and
Duma members. He spoke of the public concern over Poland
in the West, and of the forthcoming German-Austrian proclamation of an independent Poland.[147] Miliukov added his
voice to those demanding prompt proclamation of broad autonomy.[148] Upon his return, Wielopolski, having requested
an audience to submit a new list of Polish desiderata to the
Emperor, first conferred with Paléologue, to whom he predicted that the moderate elements of the Foreign Office and
General Staff were sure to defeat Stürmer. To improve Sazonov's chances, he asked Paléologue to permit a recommendation from him to be added in the Polish memorandum.
And now at last the French ambassador broke his silence and
authorized the Pole to say in his name that "the proclamation
of Polish autonomy would be received in France not merely
as the first act of historical reparation to result from the war
but as an eminently wise step which would have a considerable

---

[146] *Novoe Vremia*, October 6, 1916.

[147] The text of his report on July 2, 1916, was suppressed at the time;
it appears in *Krasnyi Arkhiv*, LVIII (1933), 3-25. Miliukov stressed the
"dangerous" straits into which the Russian government had unnecessarily
maneuvered itself. He warned that "the enemy is not asleep" and that
Polish opinion was already shifting against Russia. To the applause of
the left, he asserted that "the last hour" for Russian action had come and,
to the applause of the right, that under no circumstances must Russia
permit the Polish question to become a subject of international negotiations. *Ibid.*, pp. 10-12.

On the parliamentary mission to Europe, Miliukov had expressed the
same views to Count Zygmunt Wielopolski, who was apparently a little
franker than usual in admitting the intrigues the Poles were weaving,
and to Sir Edward Grey, with whom Miliukov conferred in London. In
talking with the latter, he suggested the establishment of "home rule"
in Poland, but maintained that international action must be limited,
at the maximum, to defining the future borders of Poland by inter-Allied
agreement. Grey agreed to this suggestion, as he did to Miliukov's refusal
to grant Dmowski's demands for Polish independence. *Krasnyi Arkhiv*,
LIV-LV (1932), 16-20, 45. See also Miliukov, *Vospominaniia* (New York,
1955), II, 262.

[148] *Ezhegodnik gazety Rech', 1916*, p. 69.

effect on the future and might facilitate in the most remarkable way the advance of the Russian armies in Poland."[149] In the outcome the Polish memorandum (differing from the Sazonov draft only in relatively minor points, such as the provision that a Pole be named chief of the civil administration in the Kingdom)[150] carried no weight, for a decision had been made before it reached the Tsar.

On July 4 Stürmer wrote the Emperor for permission to hold a cabinet session at the Stavka "in view of the urgency of several matters." Two days later Nicholas II replied that he would receive Stürmer on July 11 and the full cabinet the following day.[151] On July 11 Sazonov obtained the consent of the Tsar to consult General Alekseev, who volunteered to speak to the Tsar in favor of the Sazonov project. On July 12 Sazonov and Alekseev reported to the Emperor, verbally reiterating their arguments for the adoption of the Polish project. After some reflection the Tsar told them that he approved the plan and found the moment opportune for its publication. When Sazonov cautioned that Stürmer and others would surely oppose it, the Tsar—in Sazonov's words—"told me that by law, when the Tsar ranges himself on the side of the minority, its views prevail over those of the majority. This aspect of Russian law was known to me."[152] To Sazonov, then, the prospect was one of using undemocratic procedure on behalf of what appeared to be a democratic move. Sazonov emerged beaming from the audience. At lunch (the head chaplain recalled) the Tsar turned to Wielopolski and told him: "The question has been resolved, and I am very glad. You may give your compatriots my congratulations."[153] And in further conversations, General Hanbury-Williams reported, Nicholas "prophesied that we should make [the Boers] good partners

---

[149] Paléologue, II, 292. See also Nekludoff, p. 425; and PTR, VI, 36-37.

[150] Text in DRFP, August 10, 1916, pp. 7-8.

[151] Semennikov, ed., p. 126.

[152] Sazonov, *Vospominaniia*, p. 388.

[153] Georgii Shavel'skii, *Vospominaniia* (New York, 1954), II, 60.

in the British Empire. Then he added: 'We are going to do the same with Poland.'"[154]

Poland was on the cabinet agenda that afternoon, and the gathering came off better than Sazonov had dared hope. (Fearing he would be outvoted, Stürmer apparently absented himself before the end of the session, on the ground that he had to return to Petrograd.)[155] With the Emperor committed to the autonomy scheme, Sazonov was authorized to introduce the Polish bill formally the following week, and the Tsar asked to be given the text of a proclamation to the Polish people which he would release. Elated and excited, the tired Sazonov hurried back to the capital. The next day, when Neratov, his deputy, was conferring with Paléologue and Buchanan, Sazonov stormed into the Foreign Office: "The Emperor has entirely adopted my views—all my views— though I can assure you we had a pretty warm debate. It's all over now. . . . His Majesty has given orders that a draft manifesto proclaiming the autonomy of Poland be submitted to him without delay."[156]

Sazonov was exhausted by his efforts on the Polish issue. Now, with victory seemingly secure, he decided to go to Finland for a rest. After instructing Kryzhanovskii to write the draft of an imperial proclamation and to forward it to the Stavka for approval, he left the stage on July 15.[157]

It seems certain that the Emperor expected to go through with the Polish proclamation. Nicholas II, who had experienced neither 1830 nor 1863, had not been reared in the same rabid anti-Polish tradition as his predecessors. "The Emperor listened attentively and sympathetically to my reports on the Polish question," Sazonov (admittedly a biased reporter) recalled.[158]

---

[154] John Hanbury-Williams, *The Emperor Nicholas II As I Knew Him* (London, 1922), p. 110.

[155] Buchanan, II, 11-15, Accounts differ on details of this cabinet session.

[156] Paléologue, II, 296-97. Sazonov then informed Stürmer of the decision, who still protested that Russia was "too sensitive to Polish nervousness" and was inviting foreign meddling in her internal affairs. Askenasy, p. 453; see also PTR, I, 286.

[157] PTR, V, 464-65.

[158] Sazonov, *Vospominaniia*, pp. 377-78.

And the chief of the British military mission at the Stavka recorded a conversation he had with the Tsar:

He said that he liked the Poles and appreciated all they had done and how much their country had suffered during the war. He said that he would grant them a measure of self-government with which he thinks they will be content, but it is going to be a difficult and delicate matter to carry through, a policy somewhat similar to our Irish one. He added what a curious thing it was that people living so near one another as the Russians and Poles, or the British, Scotch, and Irish and Welsh, should be so different in many of their characteristics.[159]

The press was already allowed to predict that in his forthcoming speech Sazonov would make an important statement regarding Poland,[160] and the Emperor's faithful factotum, Fredericks, told the British attaché on July 14 that Russia was doing her best to strengthen the alliance with Britain and France. "Poland," he added, would "be a commencement."[161]

Now the lightning struck. On July 20 Nicholas II signed an order dismissing Sazonov as Minister of Foreign Affairs. Deputy Minister Neratov as well as Paléologue and Buchanan feared that he would be succeeded by a man of Stürmer's class. Their efforts to intervene on Sazonov's behalf of necessity failed.[162] Sazonov sent the Tsar a loyal letter, full of expressions of gratitude and no indication of surprise, remorse or bitterness.[163] Yet in fact his dismissal amounted to a minor diplomatic revolution in Russia.

For two weeks the wheels of bureaucracy continued to turn without appreciable change. Kryzhanovskii had speedily drawn up a manifesto for Poland on the basis of the amended Sazonov plan. "By the grace of God, We, Nicholas the Second, Emperor and Autocrat of all the Russias, Tsar of Poland and

[159] Hanbury-Williams, pp. 79-80.
[160] *Ezhegodnik gazety Rech', 1916*, p. 69.
[161] Hanbury-Williams, pp. 111-12.
[162] Paléologue, II, 301-4; Hanbury-Williams, pp. 113-14; and *Sbornik sekretnykh dokumentov iz Arkhiva byvshego Ministerstva inostrannykh del* (Petrograd, 1917-18), pp. 114-15 (a publication of the People's Commissariat of Foreign Affairs).
[163] Semennikov, ed., p. 105.

Grand Duke of Finland," reaffirmed the proclamation of August 14, 1914, and proceeded to list fourteen points which incorporated the provisions of the Sazonov plan. The proclamation gave solemn assurances to the Poles and announced the specific institutional forms of future Russo-Polish relations. On July 19 Acting Foreign Minister Neratov forwarded the draft to the Emperor, and three days later Nicholas II returned the text with the notation "To be examined immediately by the Council of Ministers." Neratov accordingly asked Stürmer to introduce it in the cabinet.[164]

The Council of Ministers discussed the Kryzhanovskii plan at three sessions, and on August 1 Stürmer went to headquarters, where he handed the Emperor a personal letter and the record of the cabinet sessions. In his letter Stürmer favored a change of procedure, by which the Emperor would grant the Poles formal autonomy by decree, while detailed provisions of the statute would be postponed until later. More important, Stürmer now interpreted autonomy to apply not to the Kingdom as an entity but to each of its provinces; the result would have been regional (oblast) self-government, not Polish autonomy.[165]

The record of the cabinet sessions, held in the absence of Sazonov, is revealing. Only four ministers went on record as favoring something in the nature of the Kryzhanovskii plan: War Minister Shuvaev, Navy Minister Grigorovich, Minister of Agriculture Rittikh and to some extent Minister of Education Count P. N. Ignat'ev. They advanced largely the same arguments Sazonov had used, warned that, failing a Russian decision, the question was bound to come up at the peace conference after the war, where Russia would be in a disadvantageous position. The other cabinet members, led by Stürmer and Khvostov, came out against the draft proposal. With the Foreign Minister ousted, the majority swung back to the extreme right. Their arguments can be summarized

---

[164] RPO, pp. 108-12.
[165] The text of the letter is given in Semennikov, ed., p. 180.

af follows: The question of Polish autonomy could not be determined in detail before the future boundaries of Poland were fixed. As for Russian Poland, the Goremykin speech of August 1, 1915, contained adequate assurances. Poland was under German occupation, and Russia did not know what the Polish population wanted. A Russian proclamation might provoke German countermeasures such as the proclamation of an independent Poland. The Polish legions fighting with Austria were proof that the Poles were not loyal to Russia. A proclamation at that time would create, inside and outside Russia, the impression of weakness and invite further demands. The discussion of Poland at the postwar peace conference could not be averted under any circumstances.[166]

The majority therefore submitted a brief draft manifesto to the Tsar limiting themselves to a general statement which promised vaguely "the resurrection of Poland" (consisting of the provinces of Warsaw, Kalisz, Kielce, Łomża, Lublin, Pietrków, Płock, Radom and part of Suwałki), "free in faith, language and self-government." While expressing hope for a "united Poland" and speaking of regional organs of self-government but not autonomy, the majority manifesto was unquestionably far more narrow and anti-Polish than the Sazonov plan.[167]

Count Zygmunt Wielopolski had asked for an audience with the Tsar before the Sazonov dismissal. Only now, a week after the ouster of the Foreign Minister, was Wielopolski granted the imperial audience, during which the Tsar assured him that a manifesto on Poland was about to be published.

---

[166] The record of the cabinet sessions is given in RPO, pp. 114-22. There is a peculiar discrepancy between two versions of the cabinet protocols for July 26, 29 and 31, regarding Minister of Education Ignat'ev. The earlier text (Sovet Ministrov, *Osobye zhurnaly*, for these dates, and Appendix IV) listed Ignat'ev along with the other three dissenters as opposing the majority draft; it included his (as well as Grigorovich's) own draft; and it summarized his separate line of argument. The apparently later, "edited" version (RPO, pp. 114, 116, 120) of the same protocol refers briefly to Ignat'ev's opinion but lists him as voting with the majority and entirely omits his substantive presentation.

[167] RPO, pp. 123-25.

Nicholas advised him to see the Empress Alexandra Fëdorovna upon his return to Petrograd and to inform her of the situation.[168] And on July 31 the Tsar wrote his wife: "Our Wielopolski arrived, and I had a long talk with him. He would very much like to see you and explain this whole stupid business to you in a few words. You know everything and therefore it won't take long."[169]

Alexandra Fëdorovna here emerged in a semi-official capacity in the Polish question. On July 21, the day after Sazonov's unexpected ouster, the newspapers published an official announcement:

Her Imperial Majesty, Empress Alexandra Fëdorovna, with Her most august daughters, deigned to arrive at the Tsar's Stavka on July 7 [Old Style; July 20, New Style]. Fredericks.[170]

In other words, the Empress had secretly been at the Tsar's headquarters when the decision was made to dismiss the Foreign Minister, and all the evidence points to the fact that her role was decisive in bringing about this change.

Since the fall of 1915, when the Tsar had assumed the supreme command in the field, she had actually replaced him at Tsarskoe Selo, and in daily letters gave him advice and information. The sickly, secluded and suspicious Empress was herself under the influence of Grigorii Rasputin, the monk whom she believed to possess mystical powers. Rasputin, in turn, was strongly influenced by various obscurantist and perhaps pro-German elements in the capital. Between Empress and monk, the weak and naïve Nicholas II found himself paralyzed.

In her letters to "Nicky," Alexandra Fëdorovna ("Alix," the Tsar called her) served as Rasputin's messenger. She once wrote frankly: "Listen to me, which means to our Friend."[171] Another time—in the spring of 1915, on the occasion of the

---

[168] PTR, VI, 39-40. Lednicki's account of the audience (PTR, VII, 250-51) appears to be somewhat erroneous.
[169] *Perepiska Nikolaia i Aleksandry Romanovykh*, IV, 377.
[170] *Novoe Vremia*, July 21, 1916.
[171] Letter dated December 13, 1916, in *Pis'ma imperatritsy*, II, 462; see also *ibid.*, I, 463.

Tsar's visit to Lwów—she reported, "Our Friend is delighted and blesses you." She was always ready with political counsel, couched in her unsure English (Alexandra wrote all her letters to Nicholas in English): "God bless and unite—in the fully deep, historical and religious sense of the word—these Slavonic countries to their old Mother Russia. . . . Nevertheless, we must in the 'interior' become yet stronger and more united in every way, so as to govern stronger and with more authority."[172]

Again and again Alexandra Fëdorovna insisted on the autocratic prerogatives of the Emperor and displayed her disdain for parliamentary and democratic institutions. " You are too kind, my sunny angel," she wrote her husband. "Be firmer and when you punish don't forgive at once and give good places—one does not fear you enough—show your power."[173] As time went on, she became even more determined. "Be more self-sure," she wrote. "God has placed you there, it's not pride and you are an anointed one and they dare not forget this. One must feel your power, it's time for the saving of your country and your child's throne."[174] And "Be Peter the Great, Ivan the Terrible, Emperor Paul—crush them all under you !"[175]

Her personal likes and dislikes were in part determined by the attitude of Rasputin. When Grand Duke Nikolai Nikolaevich refused to let Rasputin tour the front, the Empress began a vicious campaign against him. She depicted him as a potential "Nicholas III" and the candidate of the hostile elements, and left off urging his dismissal only when it actually took place.[176]

One of her pet enemies was Sazonov. For one reason, she feared and detested everything that smacked of liberalism. (In her letters she dropped such remarks as "Could one not

[172] *Ibid.*, I, 446.
[173] *Ibid.*, II, 275.
[174] *Ibid.*, p. 443.
[175] *Ibid.*, p. 463.
[176] *Ibid.*, I, 486; and Danilov, p. 154.

hang Guchkov?")[177] Second, Sazonov was the major champion of the alliance with republican France. Third, he was a frank enemy of Rasputin. Finally, the German-born Alexandra was anti-Polish in outlook.

She had been particularly infuriated by Sazonov's leadership of the cabinet faction that opposed the Tsar's assumption of supreme command. In one of her frequent recommendations to her husband on reorganizing the government,[178] she wrote in the spring of 1916: "Wish you could think of a good successor to Sazonov—need not be a diplomat . . . Old Gorem[ykin] and St[ürmer] always disapproved of him as he is such a coward towards Europe and a parliamentarist."[179] Two months later a friend of the well-informed Madame Vyrubova, Alexandra Fëdorovna's confidante, told Paléologue, "I believe Sazonov is going to be dismissed."[180] The wish to see Sazonov ousted had evidently remained in the Tsaritsa's mind.

As for the Poles, even Wielopolski, the most "acceptable" of the Polish magnates, was for her "not a very sympathetic man and such a 'salon' fellow."[181] In general, "one cannot trust these Poles," she wrote the Tsar. "After all we are their enemies and the Catholics must hate us."[182]

In the light of Alexandra Fëdorovna's known prejudices and past maneuvers, it is clear that her action on July 20 was not a sudden whim, but rather a step which had long been contemplated and for which the ground had been carefully prepared. She did not stop with her successful intervention on July 20. When Stürmer told her of the new manifesto draft of August 1, she wrote her husband: "One must indeed be very prudent. . . . One must well weigh over this serious question."[183]

[177] Pis'ma imperatritsy, I, 511.
[178] See, for instance, ibid., pp. 486, 632, 637.
[179] Ibid., II, 313.
[180] Paléologue, II, 266.
[181] Pis'ma imperatritsy, I, 497.
[182] Ibid., p. 382.
[183] Ibid., II, 391.

After the crisis at headquarters, not Zygmunt Wielopolski but his brother Władysław asked for an audience with Alexandra. He had in the past been the host of Nicholas and Alexandra at Spała and Skierniewice; now he ostensibly wished to discuss the affairs of the domain in Łowicz of which he was Imperial Lieutenant.[184]

He was received by the Empress on August 4 and casually told her what he knew about the state of the Polish question. Evidently he was not aware of the critical situation that had developed after his brother's audience with the Tsar. In any case, Alexandra's mind was already made up before the conference (or had been made up for her by others). Shortly before receiving Wielopolski, she had written her husband: "Now I have Velep [Wielopolski]—I rather dread it because I feel sure I shan't agree with him and think wiser one should wait a bit, but in any case not give *too* great liberties, otherwise when Baby's turn comes he will have very hard times to go through."[185]

Her preoccupation with the question of her son's heritage is confirmed by Count Lubomirski's account of the interview, evidently based on information from Władysław Wielopolski: "The Empress asked the Count whether the successor would be happy if Poland were to receive the rights [in question], and remarked that it would be necessary to do likewise with regard to Courland and other regions. According to the Count, he was certain when leaving her that the project for the organization of Poland would not be carried out."[186]

That very afternoon Alix summoned Stürmer and asked him when he intended to go the Stavka: he replied that he foresaw no early visit. The Empress then asked him to dispatch a wire to the Tsar concerning Poland. Stürmer agreed. The telegram, as received at the Stavka, read as follows:

On order from Her Majesty. Today had the honor to see the Empress. [Earlier in the day] she had received Count Wielopolski,

[184] PTR, VI, 39-41.
[185] *Pis'ma imperatritsy*, II, 383-84.
[186] RPO, pp. 128-29.

asked me to inform Your Majesty of her request to hold up
[*zaderzhat'*] solution of the Polish question until the arrival
of Her Majesty at Stavka.

Stürmer
Chairman of Council of Ministers[187]

What business did Stürmer have sending this coded wire?
Its very dispatch is indicative of the extent of the Empress'
extra-official influence. Under interrogation by the Extraordinary Commission of the Provisional Government the following year, Stürmer was asked; "How was it that you permitted
the interference of the Empress in the solution of the Polish
question?"

Stürmer: How could I prevent it? She wanted to talk to the
  Tsar. How could I stop her?
Question: How was it that you, as Chairman of the Council
  of Ministers, did not protest against the interference of the
  Empress in the solution of affairs of state?
Stürmer: But I hadn't asked her to. ... I was merely a tele-
  grapher who sent a wire at her request.
Question: Did it not seem to you that, as Chairman of the
  Council of Ministers you were not suited for the part of a
  telegrapher? ... Could you not say, "Your Majesty, this
  does not fall within your competence"?
Stürmer: No, I could not say that.
Question: You should have said that this was a matter of
  state the solution of which would take place when it was
  deemed necessary.
Stürmer: I did mention that the question also depended on
  our Allies, and then our conversation soon ended.[188]

The effect of the Stürmer telegram was to suspend all action
on the Polish question until August 9, when Alexandra Fëdorovna again arrived at headquarters. The sequel was bound
to be anticlimactic. On August 18 the newspaper *Russkoe
Slovo* [Russian Word], which was frequently used as an official
mouthpiece, informed its readers that the proclamation of the
Polish statute had been postponed until Russian troops re-
entered Poland.[189]

---

[187] RPO, p. 126; and PTR, VII, 249-50. See also Bertie, II, 81-82.
[188] PTR, V, 183-84.
[189] DRFP, September 1, 1916, p. 9. See also PTR, V, 465.

Discussion of the Polish bill did, it is true, continue in the cabinet, and newspapers commented widely on the Polish question. Few details of the cabinet debates at this period and of the further modifications in the draft bill are available.[190] It is known, however, that Stürmer made two more reports to the Tsar on the subject of Poland. On September 3 he saw Nicholas at the Stavka and told him that issuance at that time of a manifesto granting autonomy to Poland—only one of the nationalities of the empire—"would meet with popular perplexity." Other peoples, too, for instance, the Russian, Estonian and Latvian, had suffered greatly from the war. Stürmer therefore urged either the postponement of the Polish bill or its subordination to some proclamation concerning all of Russia. He improved the occasion by pressing again for announcement of the Allied agreement giving Russia the Straits—an idea that had long been close to his heart. The day after this announcement, he suggested, the *Pravitel'stvennyi Vestnik* [Government Messenger] could carry a decree granting Poland autonomy.[191]

Three weeks later, on September 23, Stürmer handed the Tsar a revised cabinet draft of the Polish bill. Now the grant of autonomy was further restricted by limiting it to "all matters of local significance." The Emperor, Stürmer stated in his minutes of the audience, had approved this addendum. Stürmer added that the Tsar had kept the text of the manifesto with him, intending to publish it only when the Russian troops resumed their advance into the Kingdom of Poland.[192]

[190] Stürmer and Khvostov were, as before, the leading brakes on the Polish bill. According to Khvostov (who was transferred from the Ministry of Justice to the Ministry of the Interior in July), Trepov and Makarov, two cabinet members, were instructed to work out an alternative plan, which was then reworked, utilizing parts of the Kryzhanovskii project. PTR, V, 464-65.

[191] Text of Stürmer's report is in Semennikov, ed., pp. 147-48. The draft manifesto appearing in Sovet Ministrov, *Osobye zhurnaly*, "Proekt bol'shinstva Chlenov Soveta Ministrov," contains a notation, certified by Stürmer on September 15, that Nicholas II had personally deleted from the text two paragraphs referring to the changes in the fortunes of war and the victorious return of the Russian troops to Polish soil. This deletion is not indicated in the text given in RPO, p. 126.

[192] Semennikov, ed., pp. 153-54.

Thus the sudden intervention of the reactionary camarilla stifled and indefinitely postponed the proclamation of Polish autonomy, which had seemed already at hand. Such a proclamation would have had only limited effect in rallying the Poles to the Russian side and, moreover, would in no way have arrested the internal process of disintegration in Russia, which was soon to lead to revolution. Yet in the minds of the political figures of the time, the Polish statute and the proclamation connected with it were the crucial test of Russian intentions. The failure of the Sazonov policy was both a symptom and a product of the increasing influence of the Rasputin-Alexandra wing, and of the breakdown of responsible foreign policy under the Tsar.

ANTICLIMAX

The dismissal of Sazonov and the postponement of the Polish proclamation were bound to have a most serious effect on Russian relations with both the Entente Poles and the Western powers. For the Poles they served as further confirmation of the unreliability of tsarist Russia and reinforced pro-Western as well as Austrophile sentiments in their midst. In France and Britain alike, they added to suspicion of Russia's plans and motives, raising considerable doubt regarding her faithful adherence to the Alliance. A fog of gloom settled over Russian foreign relations.

The hitherto loyal Poles Władysław Wielopolski and Maurycy Zamoyski confidentially voiced their feelings of "acute apprehension" to Paléologue, who reported in his diary:

The Poles are convinced that Russia will not emerge from the war victorious, and that tsarism at bay is even now preparing to negotiate a reconciliation with the Teuton empires at the expense of Poland. Under the spur of that notion they feel all their old hatreds reviving, and the sentiment is reinforced by a sarcastic contempt for the Russian colossus, whose weakness, impotence and moral and physical infirmities are now being ruthlessly revealed. But the very fact that they have lost all confidence in Russia absolves them, they think, from all obedience or obligation to her. Henceforth they are fixing all their hopes on France and England, and putting forward national claims which are altogether excessive. Autonomy under the scepter of the Romanovs is not enough: they must have complete and absolute independence, and the wholesale resurrection of the Polish State; they will not stop until they have secured the triumph of their cause at the peace congress. More emphatically than ever they deny the empire of the tsars the right to domination over the Slav peoples, or to speak in their name or control their historical evolution.[193]

In mid-August, 1916, the Polish National Committee for Cooperation with Russia, formed in August, 1914, moved to Lausanne to "concentrate all its hopes on France and England"; and in September, after a bitter exchange, Wielopolski told Stürmer that he declined all responsibility for the future of Russo-Polish relations.[194] Alexander Lednicki now resigned from the Cadet Party and in the Moscow *Echo Polskie* [Polish Echo] published a blistering article contrasting the "sentimental effervescence" of the Poles in 1914 with their "will to act" in 1916; more and more Poles were taking independence, no longer autonomy, as their slogan, and Russian inaction had contributed to this change of outlook.[195]

September also saw the last Polish memorandum on autonomy, written by Count Lubomirski. The latter had returned to Petrograd from Bucharest in August. "When soon thereafter I went to see Count Wielopolski," he later stated, "I was struck by the considerable change, bordering on despair, which his outlook on the future of Poland had undergone. . . . He had lost all of the optimism which, along with his adoration of the former Emperor, had always distinguished him."[196]

---

[193] Paléologue, II, 317-18.
[194] In late August, Wielopolski had given Stürmer further details of the impending German proclamation of Polish independence. After a visit to headquarters Stürmer then assured the Pole that everything would be carried out as agreed, evidently concocting some spurious promises. Wielopolski, eager to pin him down, immediately drafted a telegram to France (probably to Erasmus Piltz) stating that a Russian proclamation would soon be issued. Before dispatching the wire, he submitted it for verification to Stürmer, who "edited" it drastically and asserted that Wielopolski had misunderstood him. The wire (which consisted of fairly meaningless phrases in the first place) was not dispatched at all. PTR, VI, 39-43; Semennikov, ed., pp. 147-48; and DRFP, September 6, 1916, p. 8.
[195] DRFP, October 12, 1916, pp. 7-8; and October 26, 1916, p. 9.
[196] RPO, pp. 127-28.

The most reactionary and faithful of the "Tsar's Poles" were now ranged against him.

The Russian press, despite censorship, commented widely on the Sazonov affair. Miliukov deplored the dismissal and urged haste in publishing the Polish manifesto, both to forestall the Germans and to cut the ground from under Polish radicals. Right-wing publications like *Kolokol* pointed to separatist and "imperialist" pronouncements[197] as evidence of the Poles' hostility to Russia. Count Andronnikov's *Golos Rossii* [Voice of Russia], often reflecting the views of the pro-German aristocracy, asserted that the Grand Ducal proclamation had contained no promises to Poland—a charge to which *Birzhevye Vedomosti* [News of the Bourse] replied bitterly, accusing Andronnikov of seeking peace with Germany at the expense of the Poles. The extreme rightist *Golos Rusi* [Voice of Rus'] promised the Poles a "reward" for good behavior after the war, provided they ignored the Cadets, who wanted to give the Jews equal rights in the future Poland.[198]

The conservative press ran suggestions for a Russian protectorate over Poland and Bulgaria after the war, with cultural autonomy for both. *Novoe Vremia* exhorted the Poles to trust their protector, pointing to the British Empire as a working example of such an unequal combination. In *Kievlianin* the Nationalist-Progressive Shul'gin bluntly stated that "Sazonov retired for no other reason than a disagreement on the Polish question. . . . More than ever it is time to put an end to these misunderstandings."[199]

[197] They apparently had in mind the claims of the more chauvinist Polish circles abroad, who had begun to demand a future Polish state whose borders would exceed ethnic Polish territory and encompass parts of Lithuania, Belorussia and the Ukraine on the basis of Polish "historical" rights. None of the prominent "Russian Poles" appear to have made such claims.

[198] DRFP, August 4, 1916, p. 7; August 9, 1916, p. 10; August 11, 1916, p. 10; August 18, 1916, p. 11; and August 30, 1916, p. 9. *Allied Press Supplement* (an occasional supplement to DRFP), November 8, 1916, p. 8; and November 22, 1916, p. 7.

[199] DRFP, August 18, 1916, p. 11; August 26, 1916, pp. 10-11; August

Various new projects regarding Poland were now advanced. Significantly enough, Grand Duke Nikolai Mikhailovich listed Poland as one of the questions of Russian *foreign* policy and suggested the Tsar appoint a commission of generals, admirals, princes and financiers to study it.[200] The nationalist Chikhachëv outlined a compromise scheme in the conservative *Kievskaia Mysl'* [Kievan Thought]. Honest autonomy was all Russia could offer, he maintained; however, Russia must not become economically and strategically dependent on Poland, and Polish Jews and Galicians must be kept out of Russia. To some quarters in Petrograd this scheme was appealing enough to justify calling Chikhachëv to the capital for discussions.[201]

Thus, while strong divisons remained in the press, Russian spokesmen continued to agree that Poland was and must remain a purely Russian problem, as even the liberal and pro-Western Burtsev insisted in mid-August 1916.[202]

The Cadets occupied a peculiar position in this matter. Their earlier attempts to contribute a solution of their own were distinguished by insistence on representative government and universal suffrage.[203] In the summer of 1916 Miliukov had occasion to discuss this plan with various Polish leaders abroad. The pro-Russians—overwhelmingly rightists—raised numerous objections. Erasmus Piltz, for instance, protested the universal franchise clause, demanding property qualifications for voting and rejecting equal rights for the Jewish population of the Kingdom. Piltz's letter was made public at a Cadet meeting and caused a considerable stir. Professor Dymsza, a Polish deputy in the Duma, wrote Miliukov

28, 1916, p. 8; September 16, 1916, pp. 8-9; and September 27, 1916, p. 8.

[200] *Lettres des Grand-Ducs à Nicolas II* (Paris, 1926), p. 151.

[201] DRFP, October 17, 1916, pp. 5-6. A few months later Chikhachev apparently changed his mind and came to advocate Polish independence as being in Russia's interest. *Allied Press Supplement,* November 29, 1916, p. 6.

[202] In *Rech'* (Petrograd), August 15, 1916; quoted in *Allied Press Supplement,* September 1, 1916.

[203] See pp. 24-25, this volume.

advising him to keep out of Polish affairs and limit himself to
the interests of Russia proper.[204] Yet in terms of practical
politics the Cadets more and more clearly accepted Sazonov's
"middle-of-the-road" solution: autonomy, no more and no
less.[205]

For several months after Sazonov's dismissal it was rumored
that a separate German-Russian peace was about to be concluded. The possibility of reaching such an understanding
is a question beyond the scope of this paper. One reason
why in fact none came about was the long-rumored proclamation of an "independent" Polish state by the Central Powers
on November 5, 1916.[206] Where the Western powers had
failed since 1914, the German-Austrian proclamation succeeded
at once—tsarist Russia was now, willy-nilly, wedded to the
anti-German coalition for good. The German and Austrian
military governors of Poland announced that their two em-
perors had decided to establish a hereditary Polish monarchy
with a constitutional government. Without specifying the
borders of the new state, the proclamation made it clear that
Poland would be closely allied to the Central Powers; neither
Galicia nor Poznań was to be part of the new Poland.

[204] *Novoe Vremia*, August 25, 1916.
[205] Recke, pp. 269-70.
[206] The consideration given Poland in the peace feelers (a subject still
awaiting thorough study) is suggested by a message from the German
Foreign Minister, conveyed to Petrograd indirectly in May, 1915, that
the Central Powers had no plans for a new Polish state, since a Poland
cut off from the Baltic ("Neither Russia nor Germany would think of
sacrificing one of their ports to Poland") would soon be strangled; see Semennikov, ed., p. 222. When the Germans occupied Poland, their peace
feelers began to mention, as partial price of an armistice, Russian cession
of "the part of Poland belonging to her, which [would] form an autonomous
state economically associated with Germany"; Nekludoff, p. 351. Another proposal, late in 1915, apparently suggested the creation of a "Great
Poland, which would serve as a buffer state between Russia and Germany";
MOEI, IX, 433. In mid-1916, the quixotic attempt of Protopopov to
discuss possible peace terms with Warburg, the influential German banker,
while in Stockholm, provoked a German plan to form a Polish state out
of the Russian and Austrian (but not the Prussian) parts of Poland as
part of the settlement; PTR, I, 139; Semennikov, ed., pp. 38-40; and
Nekludoff, pp. 425ff. Though there was apparently some inclination in
Russia to consider a separate peace, all such prospects were shattered
by the proclamation of a Polish kingdom by the Central Powers.

Petrograd was outraged, though the announcement should have come as no surprise. In court circles, Paléologue reveals,

There was a flood of charges and imprecations against the "Polish betrayal," no one doubting that, if Poland had become subject to German allegiance, it is a result of a conspiracy of all the Poles. So it is being said that Russia owes them nothing more, that they have torn up the manifesto of August 14, 1914, with their own hands and they are being threatened with terrible reprisals.

In utter disregard of facts, Petrograd was equally quick to blame the Poles and the West. Count Viazemskii told the French envoy: "You may take it from me, Ambassador, that all this would not have happened if people in France and England had not taken up the cause of Polish independence so warmly."[207]

On November 10 Paléologue urged Stürmer to put some teeth in what appeared to him a "colorless and insipid" Russian government protest.[208] Buchanan, after conferring with Paléologue and Stürmer, issued a statement of his own:

The act which the Germans have just proclaimed proves that, on their side, they ask the Poles to be content with a Polish state consisting of the territories of Russian Poland, without Poznań, without Galicia. On the other hand, we know that the Allies consider it their task to reconstitute the Polish state entirely, including Poznań and Galicia.[209]

This was the first definite British commitment in regard to Poland and could not but arouse some hostility in Petrograd.

Finally, on November 15, the Russian government's note was released, a copy being sent to all allied and neutral powers.

[207] Paléologue, III, 83. See also DRFP, November 29, 1916; *Allied Press Supplement*, November 29, 1916, pp. 5-9; Recke, p. 265; Bertie, II, 53-54; Otto Hoetzsch, *Der Krieg und die grosse Politik* (Leipzig, 1918), III, 113.

[208] Paléologue, III, 84-85.

[209] From *Russkoe Slovo*, November 8, 1916, quoted in Fiłasiewicz, p. 64. Buchanan later claimed that he had kept out of Polish affairs until then out of deference to Sazonov; see Pares, p. 340. As late as August 23 Lord Cecil, when asked whether it was the intention of the British Government to recommend a constitution for Poland, replied, "No, Sir, it is not the intention of His Majesty's Government to make any recommendation on a matter of internal policy of another State"; Komarnicki, p. 58.

At the same time a communiqué to the press confirmed the Russian promise of national, cultural and educational autonomy for the kingdom. The note pledged the formation of a united (*tselokuknaia*) Poland after the termination of the war.[210] Clearly the Russian government continued to consider Poland an "integral" part of its state.

Now at long last Britain and France decided to act. Poincaré was "indignant at the wording of the Russian protest," Lord Bertie noted in Paris. The French President "concurred that the Russians should be told that if the Emperor will confirm the promises made by the Grand Duke [Nikolai] at the beginning of the war, promise a really autonomous Poland to Russian Poland, the Entente will do their best in the peace negotiations to add thereto German and Austrian Polands."[211] The West, it appeared, still had a strong trump to play. The French and British leaders who were just then conferring in Paris decided to send a public note to the Russian government. It concluded:

Nous nous réjouissons sincèrement des généreuses initiatives prises par le gouvernement de Sa Majésté l'Empereur en faveur d'un peuple auquel nous attachent d'antiques sympathies et dont l'union restaurée constituera un élément primordial du futur équilibre européen. Nous sommes heureux de nous solidariser entièrement avec les vues dont le gouvernement impérial entend assurer la réalisation au bénéfice du noble peuple polonais.

Aristide Briand,
Président du Conseil des Ministres
H. H. Asquith,
Premier-Ministre de la Grande Bretagne[212]

While on the surface the statement did little more than associate its signatories with the declarations of the Russian government, it nonetheless amounted to the "internationalization" of the issue which Polish leaders had long urged.[213]

---

[210] Fiłasiewicz, pp. 79-81; and Błociszewski, p. 32.
[211] Bertie, II, 56-57.
[212] *Le Temps*, November 17, 1916.
[213] Fiłasiewicz, pp. 83-84.

Etiquette demanded a Russian reply, and Stürmer wired Briand a few words of gratitude for the "sympathy [of] the French government . . . respecting the future of the noble Polish people."[214] In reality Petrograd was perturbed by the Allied move. Insult was added to injury when the Italian premier, Boselli, associated himself with the Briand-Asquith note and "applauded" the Russian promise of Polish autonomy.[215] Sazonov was reported to have said of the Briand-Asquith note: "They did it in a courteous and very prudent form. But M. Boselli too has deemed it necessary to manifest his feelings. . . . Italy mixing in the Polish question—that is really too much! It would have been so easy to avoid this humiliation, and I greatly regret that the question of Polish autonomy has become an international one."[216]

While the Empress reassured the Tsar that he had done the right thing ("How many reasonable Russians, *entre autres* Shakhovskoi, bless you for not having listened to those who begged you to give Poland freedom, when she no longer belonged to us, as it would have been absolutely ridiculous—and they are perfectly right"),[217] the government was driven to having Protopopov read, to a hostile legislature, a declaration reaffirming the pledges made in the proclamation of August 14, 1914, and Goremykin's speech of August 1, 1915. His statement was received in icy silence.[218]

The "Russian Poles," while responding to the German-Austrian declaration with unequivocal skepticism, failed to hasten back to the Russian banners. Some of them urged the French ambassador to do "anything" to show that France would not abandon them; Paléologue diplomatically replied that "Poland knows that France will never abandon her."[219] Wielopolski privately expressed his satisfaction with the Briand-Asquith note, regretting that "something of the kind was

[214] *Le Temps*, November 24, 1916.
[215] DRFP, December 13, 1916.
[216] Quoted in Bertie, II, 95.
[217] *Pis'ma imperatritsy*, II, 434.
[218] *Allied Press Supplement*, December 6, 1916, pp. 7-8.
[219] Paléologue, III, 84.

not done earlier in the war."[220] The *koło* members now urged
Russia to grant Poland broad rights "in concert with her
Allies,"[221] and Harusewicz openly decried Russian silence:
"None of our warnings were taken into account by the government. To our great regret, the government has shown a total
lack of comprehension of the immense international significance of the Polish question; it has placed all the aces in the
enemy's hand."[222]

THE LAST EFFORTS

Russia's total situation was rapidly worsening. The government and army were hindered by shortages and inefficiency
at every step. Scandal was followed by scandal, and the
government's impotence was more apparent every day. Even
reactionaries like Purishkevich ranged themselves irrevocably
against the Rasputin clique. It was in this atmosphere that,
on November 14, Miliukov made his famous attack on Rasputin and the Empress, in a speech unprecedented in the
Duma, and promptly censored. Ostensibly quoting from a
German-language newspaper, he hurled charge after charge
at the government, concluding each with the phrase "Is this
folly or treachery?" Touching on Poland, he asked:

When they, in spite of our unceasing pressure, stopped the
[solution of the] Polish question; when they hindered a wise
and honorable minister's attempt, even at the last moment,
to find a happy solution and instead forced his dismissal; when
they gave the enemy a chance to profit from our errors—was
this folly or treachery?[223]

General Alekseev, the Tsar's chief of staff, was compelled to
leave on a "prolonged vacation" to appease the right wing,
but he scored a final success in persuading the Tsar to dismiss
Stürmer.[224]

---

[220] Bertie, II, 61-62.
[221] *Novoe Vremia*, November 15, 1916.
[222] Fiłasiewicz, p. 78. See also *ibid.*, pp. 69, 98-99; and *Allied Press
Supplement*, November 29, 1916, p. 6, and December 6, 1916, pp. 7-9.
[223] English translation in DRFP, December 20, 1916, p. 3.
[224] Bazili to Neratov, December 10, 1916, *Krasnyi Arkhiv*, XXIX, 43;
Vasilii Gurko, *Memories and Impressions*, p. 180.

The new premier, Alexander Trepov, soon received a request for an audience from the Polish deputies and promised to speak on Poland in his first address to the Duma.[225] On December 2 he addressed it in a tumultuous session. Emboldened by Miliukov's speech, the Socialists sought to prevent Trepov from speaking; one by one, Chkheidze, Kerensky, Sukhanov and Skobelev were expelled from the hall. Finally Trepov was able to make his statement. As for Poland, he declared, "we still have to win back . . . the Kingdom of Poland, temporarily torn from us by force of arms. More than this—we must wrest from the enemies the age-old soil [of Poland that is now] outside her borders, and it is our wish to recreate a free Poland in her ethnic borders, in indivisible union with Russia."[226]

General Vasilii Gurko, who succeeded Alekseev as acting chief of staff—the son of a narrow-minded governor general of Poland and brother of a statesman who had written on the Polish question[227]—turned out to be an ardent advocate of concessions to Poland.[228] Soon after assuming his new duties Gurko submitted to the Tsar a detailed analysis of the Polish situation. The weak Nicholas again seemed to be shifting to the pro-Polish view; at least Gurko, like Sazonov half a year earlier, was "convinced that the Tsar agreed with my arguments."[229]

An unexpected opportunity for a proclamation on Poland occurred, when, on December 12, 1916, Germany made a peace offer to the Allies and, on December 18, President Woodrow

[225] *Russkoe Slovo*, quoted in *Allied Press Supplement*, December 20, 1916, p. 6.

[226] Quoted in Fiłasiewicz, p. 102.

[227] Vladimir Gurko, *Figures and Features of the Past* (Stanford, 1939), p. 386.

[228] "I desired," he wrote, "that Russia and Poland should only have one thing in common, a common frontier dividing these two independent countries. The remaining questions, which could only concern the Polish nation, should have been decided independently by the Polish nation itself without any foreign interference." Vasilii Gurko, *Memories and Impressions*, pp. 203-4.

[229] *Ibid.*, pp. 204-5.

Wilson volunteered to mediate the European war.[230] On December 25 Gurko handed the Tsar the draft of an Imperial Order of the Day containing an unequivocal promise of a "free Poland," and the next day Nicholas II signed it (antedated December 25).[231] It rejected the German peace offer:

The enemy has not yet been expelled from the areas he has seized. The achievement of the tasks which Russia faces as a result of the war—the attainment of Tsar'grad [Constantinople] and the Straits, as well as the creation of a free Poland out of all three of her presently dispersed parts—has not yet been assured. To conclude peace at present would mean to sacrifice the fruits of the unheard-of hardships which you, the heroes of the Russian Army and Navy, have suffered.[232]

At this late stage, the reaction in Paris and London was favorable, though unquestionably mixed with doubts and impatience.[233]

On January 25, 1917, Prince Nikolai Golitsyn, the new —and last—tsarist premier, submitted to Nicholas II a formal recommendation that a special commission on Poland be constituted, the membership to include various ministers, the chairmen of both chambers, as well as Gurko, Sazonov, Goremykin and Kryzhanovskii; some of the "Russian Poles" were to join in the discussions. Nicholas promptly approved the proposal, and on February 4 the commission was officially announced.[234] It met three times and heard Gurko expound

---

[230] The Wilson note was handed to the Russian foreign minister on December 20. U. S. Department of State, *Papers Relating to the Foreign Relations of the United States, 1916*, Supplement: *The World War* (Washington, 1929), p. 104.

[231] Vasilii Gurko, pp. 204-5.

[232] RPO, pp. 130-32; and Fiłasiewicz, p. 118. At the turn of the year the Tsar had authorized him to declare that "Poland must be united. Poland must be free, which means that she will receive her own state constitution, with her separate legislative bodies and her own army." See PTR, VI, 43-44; *Sprawa Polska* [The Polish Cause], No. 1 (1917), quoted in Fiłasiewicz, p. 118; and Miliukov, II, 262.

[233] Vasilii Gurko (*Memories and Impressions*, p. 206) cites Benckendorff's report of December 28 from London, where, he asserted, the order had produced expressions of "fervent and deep satisfaction" by the King as well as in the press.

[234] RPO, pp. 132-33; Fiłasiewicz, p. 136; and Vasilii Gurko, p. 251. Wilson's incongruous if circumspect phraseology in his "peace without

his ideas at length, advocating a free Polish state as the best and most expedient solution for Russia. The general was disappointed to find that he met with little support, except from the erratic Protopopov; even Sazonov was, characteristically, still opposed to Polish independence, favoring at the most a dual kingdom with a separate Polish army. At its third, and final, meeting the commission rejected the Gurko proposal.[235] There it rested at the end of February, without having completed its work.

Meanwhile the Polish question was once more commanding international attention in discussions of war aims. Just prior to his dismissal (in November), while working on the Russian reply to the Central Powers' proclamation of an independent Poland, Stürmer had approached Paléologue again urging that the Allies authorize disclosure of the secret agreements in which Britain and France had consented to Russia's postwar annexation of the Straits; the French envoy suggested that in return Russia might include a commitment regarding Poland in the draft of her war aims declaration.[236] The problem reemerged when the Allies consulted at the end of the year on their reply to Wilson's offer of mediation. While agreeing to a French draft, Russia apparently reserved the right to suggest slight amendments in the paragraphs referring to Poland and Armenia; her hesitancy was due to the chronic fear that an explicit statement on Poland would be interpreted as giving the Allies the option to "meddle" in Polish affairs.[237]

---

victory" speech, on January 22, 1917, regarding a "united, independent and autonomous Poland" produced the equally incongruous comment from Golitsyn that Wilson's statement "accords fully with the thought which our august Sovereign expressed in his latest Order of the Day"; Fiłasiewicz, p. 137.

[235] PTR, VI, 46; and Vasilii Gurko, pp. 256-58.

[236] On inter-Allied negotiations on war aims and future borders, see Malone, especially pp. 156-58. Stürmer had consistently urged a public pronouncement on Russia's war aims. including the Straits, as a morale boost. He was dismissed before the speech he was planning could be delivered. See also PTR, V, 182; Semennikov, ed., p. 148; and Paléologue, III, 86-87. Cf. Abrash, pp. 117-22 and 118, note 83.

[237] Paléologue, III, 121, 133-34.

In early 1917, during preparations for the Inter-Allied Conference to be held in Petrograd in February,[238] France and Russia (Britain was not kept informed of all conversations) were bartering about a quid pro quo by which they would each secure a free hand to expand at the expense of Germany after the war. But for the moment Briand objected to Izvol'skii's formula of a free hand. As he was to explain soon afterwards, he "realized the undesirability of thus leaving to Russia the question of the borders of Poland. He suggested that [Russia and France] limit themselves to stating that the two countries engaged to support each other in the claims they would raise regarding their borders, in the east for France, and in the west for Russia."[239] Despite such reservations, the French cabinet decided to accede. At the Petrograd conference Gaston Doumergue, as France's principal spokesman, gave his consent to the formula, while the Foreign Office informed Izvol'skii that the Russian government gave France a free hand to reannex Alsace-Lorraine and, if she desired, set up the left bank of the Rhine as a separate entity. On March 11 Izvol'skii replied that France had given formal assent: "The Government of the French Republic . . . recognizes Russia's full freedom in the matter of determining her western borders."[240]

By the time this message arrived in Russia, the revolution had broken out, and the Tsar was about to abdicate. First under the Provisional Government and later under the Soviet regime, the Polish question was to reemerge in an entirely different light. On March 30, 1917, the Provisional Government recognized the independence of Poland, but the actual establishment and recognition of the Polish state were to take another three turbulent years.

The tsarist government passed from the stage of history without having fulfilled its modest promises to Poland, without having satisfied the aspirations of those Poles who had been

---

[238] On this conference, see *Krasnyi Arkhiv*, XX, 39-55.

[239] Alexandre Ribot, *Lettres à un ami* (Paris, 1924), p. 225.

[240] Iurii V. Kliuchnikov and Andrei Sabanin, *Mezhdunarodnaia politika noveishego vremeni* (Moscow), II (1926), 69; see also Fiłasiewicz, pp. 138-41.

favorably inclined toward it, without having succeeded in keeping the Polish issue an internal Russian problem and without having made use of the issue to its own political advantage.

The Tsar himself had proved to be weak and ineffective, shifting his ground between the Sazoncv-Gurko wing, which advocated a modicum of "reconciliation" with Poland, and the "Russia-first" elements supported by Stürmer and above all by the Empress and her clique. More often than not the majority at the court and in the cabinet were to be found on the side of reaction. There were, to be sure, in the high command of the army and in the Foreign Office important individuals who, out of a sense of realism, were prepared to make "concessions" to the Poles. Sazonov was one, and his position became representative of those Western-oriented moderates who, staunch monarchists themselves, could be, and were, influenced on specific issues by more liberal men. Without himself becoming a "liberal," Sazonov could thus on occasion make common cause with, and become a convenient rallying point for, other, more principled and more progressive opinions.

Russian public opinion never seemed greatly concerned over Poland, perhaps less for historical reasons than because of limitations on knowledge imposed by censorship and preoccupation with serious domestic problems. Among those who concerned themselves with political affairs, attitudes ranged from sincere advocacy of Polish independence—often prompted by a sense of guilt combined with a measure of realism—to the prevailing support for Polish autonomy but not severance of all ties with Russia, and finally to well-financed but blind and biased obscurantism. As the war progressed, inevitably there took place a polarization of opinion for and against "concessions" to the Poles and, by 1916, a perceptible shift toward a more conciliatory position.

Polish opinion, or, rather, Polish pro-Entente opinion, after the early upsurge of optimism and loyalty in August, 1914, consistently developed "away" from the Russian side. In 1915 the inarticulate rank and file seems to have shed whatever loyalty it had for the Russian cause; and in 1916 even the "Tsar's Poles"—the narrow but influential stratum of Polish magnates and rather reactionary politicians who had steadfastly sided with Russia—were alienated by the inaction of Petrograd. Their hope, and that of more liberal Polish circles abroad, now lay in "internationalizing" the Polish issue, making it, like the Macedonian and Armenian problems, a matter of European concern and responsibility. Yet until 1916 France and especially Britain seemed content to consider Poland an internal matter of their Russian ally, much as they may have sympathized with Polish aspirations and much as they dreaded the prospect of a German-Austrian political warfare campaign to attract the support of the Poles.[241] Although by 1916 most Poles had abandoned all hopes with regard to Russia, they were not, it seems, taken in by the proclamation of Polish "independence" by the Central Powers in November, 1916.

One may argue that by 1916, when Sazonov's plan for Polish autonomy was pushed to the brink of acceptance in Petrograd, the time had passed for effective political action. As so often, political decisions crystallized too late—inertia and prejudice had caused too long a time lag between objective opportunity and requisite action. Once the crucial moment had passed, no reforms or proclamations could have stopped the growing alienation. In this sense, the failure of the Sazonov project was of little consequence. But it was important in that it was considered—by Poles and Western allies alike—a barometer of Russian attitudes and the acid test of Russian intentions. Its rejection and Sazonov's ouster provoked a somewhat more militant stand by France and Britain, foreshad-

---

[241] After the downfall of the monarchy, the Manchester *Guardian* accused the Western Allies, and especially the British Foreign Office, of having supported Polish reactionaries like Dmowski—who stood for "jingoism and reaction" and was "the father of modern Polish anti-Semitism"—rather than Polish liberals like Alexander Lednicki, who had been prepared to work with Russian moderates. Henryk Frankel, *Poland, the Struggle for Power*, 1772-1939 (London, 1946), p. 82.

owing insistence on an international solution of the Polish tangle. Yet the informal "internationalization" was, in effect, canceled by the agreement between France and Russia, on the eve of the revolution of 1917, by which France gave Russia a free hand in the west—France's own interests obviously took precedence over Poland's when Paris could secure, as a quid pro quo, a free hand for herself vis-à-vis the Second Reich.

Petrograd's treatment of the Polish question was symptomatic of the difficulties that beset the imperial regime in its last years and of the contradictory currents that swept through the capital. If the monarchy could not retain the support of its own people, it could not be expected to win the support of the Poles. The tsarist government forfeited its last opportunity to make a virtue of necessity and had no part in the eventual restoration of Polish independence.

MERRITT ABRASH

War Aims
toward Austria-Hungary:
The Czechoslovak Pivot

The two aspects of Russian war aims with which this article
is concerned are the intentions toward the Austro-Hungarian
Empire as a political entity and—inseparably connected—
the question of the Czech and Slovak lands. In the final
analysis, the disposition of these lands was the pivot on which
the future of Austria-Hungary turned.

The loss of Galicia, Bukovina, Transylvania, the South Slavic
lands and the Italian irredenta would have left Austria-Hungary still the most powerful state between Russia, on the
one hand, and Germany and Italy, on the other. Ethnic
Austria, ethnic Hungary (with Slovakia) and Bohemia would
have composed a state possessing a population of over twenty-
five million, good natural defensive frontiers facing Germany,
Italy and Poland, and—assuming a modus vivendi between
the Austro-Hungarians and the Czechs—a sound economic
balance based on Hungary's agriculture and Bohemia's industry.

But every war aim favorable to the establishment of a
Czech state, with or without the Slovaks, was necessarily
prejudicial to the maintenance of any sort of Danubian empire.
Without Bohemia, the truncated Austria-Hungary described
in the preceding paragraph could hardly survive; what remained of the Empire—Austria, Hungary and perhaps the
Ruthenian lands—would have counted fewer than twenty mil-

lion people in a state militarily indefensible as well as economically unsound.

This standing territorial threat to the very existence of the Habsburg Empire was intensified by the special political motives inherent in the movement for Czechoslovak independence. R. W. Seton-Watson, who during the war was as close to the makers of Czechoslovak independence as any Entente national, has pointed out that "none of the Czech leaders had pursued separatist aims before the war, if only because there was no Czech state outside the Monarchy toward which they could gravitate; they had always clung, though with diminishing hope, to the possibility of reconstructing the Monarchy on a federalist basis."[1] (Only those Croats who did not wish to become part of a greater Serbia were in an analogous position among the larger discontented national groups.) Lacking an established state to champion the cause of their independence, Czech nationalists—even Tomaš Masaryk—were forced to pursue as obvious a will-o'-the-wisp as the voluntary federalization of the Dual Monarchy; once the futility of this became clear, their only hope lay in the political destruction of Austria-Hungary. But to further this end they had neither an immediate strategic value to the Entente nor—until 1916— did they enjoy official British or French interest in their cause. Hence they soon found their national aims uncomfortably dependent upon a suspicious, irresolute Russia.[2]

FIRST RUSSIAN INTENTIONS

It is remarkable how little interest the Russian government seemed to take in war aims toward Austria-Hungary during

[1] Robert William Seton-Watson, A History of the Czechs and Slovaks (London, 1925), p. 285.

[2] For British and French ignorance of the Czech question and other Austro-Hungarian matters, see especially Izvol'skii to Sazonov, October 13, 1914, in Mezhdunarodnye otnosheniia v epokhu imperializma, Series III (Moscow, 1931-38), VI, Part 1, 395-96. (The abbreviation MOEI used hereafter refers to this title and series.) See also Merritt Abrash, "Entente Policy towards Austria-Hungary, August 1914-March 1917" (unpublished Certificate Essay, Russian Institute, Columbia University, 1958), pp. 34-38.

the period when Russian armies were advancing through Galicia and the war was expected to be short. Early in the war,
a proclamation to the "Peoples of Austria-Hungary" was issued
over the signature of the Commander in Chief, Grand Duke
Nikolai Nikolaevich. This document—presumably drawn up
in the Foreign Ministry, as was the Commander in Chief's
proclamation to the Poles—exemplified the aimless policy
and consequent evasiveness which imperial Russia displayed
toward the Habsburg Empire until the very end:

On entering Austro-Hungarian territory at the head of the
Russian army, in the name of the great Russian Tsar I declare
to you that Russia, which more than once in the past has shed
her blood for the deliverance of peoples from an alien yoke,
seeks nothing other than the re-establishment of right and justice.
To you likewise, peoples of Austria-Hungary, [Russia] brings
freedom and the realization of your national desires. . . .

Russia . . . seeks only one goal: that each one of you be able
to develop and prosper, while preserving the precious heritage
—language and faith—of your fathers, and that each one of
you, united with your brothers, may live in peace and harmony
with your neighbors, respecting their independence.[3]

The proclamation, issued in nine languages and warmly received by the dissatisfied nationalities in the Dual Monarchy,
bore only a superficial relation to war aims. It said nothing
at all concerning political matters, and by no stretch of the
imagination can the mention of "language and faith" be considered more than pious sentiments. (The Russian administration of Galicia quickly and thoroughly disabused the inhabitants of any illusions about their "emancipators'" respect for
their faith.) In addition, Masaryk found the Czech text substantially different from the Slovak.[4]

On September 14, 1914, "during a very friendly conversa-
tion" with the French and British ambassadors (respectively
Maurice Paléologue and Sir George Buchanan) Russian Foreign
Minister Sergei Sazonov set forth a war aims program of

[3] *Izvestiia Ministerstva Inostrannykh Del* (St. Petersburg), No. 6
(1914), p. 3.
[4] Tomaš Masaryk, *The Making of a State* (New York, 1927), p. 17.

thirteen points. They represented Sazonov's "unofficial ideas on the conduct which Russia, England and France ought to follow if the present success of their armies is crowned by a decisive victory."[5] In these thirteen points is found the most complete and orderly exposition of war aims produced by any important Entente statesman, at least before the fall of the tsarist regime, and the occasion was one of the very few when representatives of all three Entente powers met to consider war aims together.[6] Curiously, most historians who have examined Paléologue's report of the meeting—the only published first-hand record—have eliminated the clearly numbered point 13 (concerning reparations) and have made the "twelve points" a byword among students of First World War diplomatic history.

Besides the inevitable provision that Serbia should receive Bosnia, Hercegovina and Dalmatia,[7] two of the points affected Austria-Hungary:

3. Russia should annex the lower course of the Neman [Niemen] and the eastern part of Galicia. She should annex to the kingdom of Poland eastern Poznań [Posen], Silesia . . . and the western part of Galicia. . . .

8. Austria should constitute a triple monarchy, formed of the empire of Austria, the kingdom of Bohemia and the kingdom of Hungary. The Austrian empire should include only the "hereditary provinces." The kingdom of Bohemia should include Bohemia itself and Moravia (the Slovaks). The kingdom of Hungary would have to come to terms with Rumania in regard to Transylvania.[8]

[5] Paléologue to Delcassé, September 14, 1914, in MOEI, VI, Part 1, 247.

[6] Whether it was actually a discussion or merely a presentation of views by Sazonov is not known. Paléologue's report shows that he proposed certain procedures for establishing war aims and communicating them to other allies, but reveals nothing about what, if anything, he and Buchanan said in regard to the aims themselves.

[7] The future of Bosnia and Hercegovina was the one war aim concerning the Austro-Hungarian South Slavs which caused no controversy among the Allies. The heated diplomatic conflicts over the disposition of the other South Slavic lands under Habsburg rule are discussed elsewhere in this volume.

[8] Paléologue to Delcassé, September 14, 1914, in MOEI, VI, Part 1,

This program does not suggest that, in September, 1914,
Sazonov intended to dismember Austria-Hungary.[9] However,
point 2 ("Territorial modifications ought to be determined
according to the principle of nationality") admitted the most
efficacious means of producing that very result. This is the
more surprising in that the "principle of nationality" was
for obvious reasons rarely advanced by officials of the Russian
Empire as a general basis for territorial adjustments. After
presenting the points, Sazonov earnestly begged Paléologue
and Buchanan "not to attribute any official importance 'to
this sketch of a tapestry the woof of which is not yet woven.'"[10]
Perhaps so; Sazonov is not known ever to have mentioned
the triple monarchy idea again. But later in the month Paléologue reported that Minister of Agriculture Krivoshein had
reiterated Sazonov's program "on the modifications to be made
in the configuration of Europe" as his own views.[11] This raises
the possibility that the Russian Foreign Minister had revealed
to the ambassadors not just his own "unofficial ideas," but
a program which had some degree of backing from his colleagues.

The notion that there was no necessary contradiction between the maintenance of a Danubian empire and the principle
of nationality reappeared in a discussion on September 25,

247-48. Placing the Slovaks in Moravia is a striking example of Russian
haziness about the Czechs and Slovaks.

[9] A. J. P. Taylor interprets what is obviously point 8 thus: "The Habsburg monarchy would be dismembered into three Succession States—
Austria, Bohemia, Hungary." "The War Aims of the Allies in the First
World War," in *Essays Presented to Sir Lewis Namier* (New York, 1956),
p. 481. There seems little justification for attributing this meaning to
point 8; even if the term "Habsburg monarchy" is taken as something
different from the Austro-Hungarian state, the members of a triple monarchy would no more be "Succession States" to the Dual Monarchy than
Hungary was a successor state to pre-*Ausgleich* Austria.
    Eduard Beneš is in full contradiction to Taylor on the question of
exactly what point 8 signified for Austria-Hungary; discussing the thirteen
points, he wrote (*Souvenirs de guerre et de révolution* [Paris, 1928-29], I,
312, note): "This document, in my opinion . . . proves that Russia had
actually entered the war without any intention of destroying the Habsburg
Empire."

[10] Paléologue to Delcassé, September 14, 1914, in MOEI, VI, Part 1, 248.

[11] Paléologue to Delcassé, September 26, 1914, *ibid.*, p. 313.

1914, described many years later by Constantine Diamandi, the Rumanian ambassador:

"Russia," [Sazonov] said, "aims to put an end, once and for all, to the Austro-German intrigues which have poisoned relations between Russia and so many countries, for example, Rumania, Sweden, Turkey, Bulgaria. . . .
"She intends to create a stable state of affairs among the peoples of the monarchy, on the basis of the principle of nationality."[12]

According to Diamandi's account, Sazonov went on to invite Rumania to go right ahead and occupy "what is coming back to her"—Transylvania and Bukovina—without militarily assisting the Allies. (Russian documents fail to verify this report.) Diamandi concluded that the Foreign Minister intended to dismember Austria-Hungary: "One recognizes the desire of Russia to break the hereditary enemy, Austria-Hungary, into bits, and replace it with less populous national states; obviously, especially on [Russia's] frontiers, a Rumania of 15 to 20 millions was preferable to an Austria-Hungary of 60 millions."[13] But this was only Diamandi's opinion, and it hardly seems likely that Sazonov would have abandoned the idea of the triple monarchy in eleven days.

Point 8 stands in complete isolation among Russian war aims toward Austria-Hungary. A month earlier Sazonov had mentioned to Paléologue that it was essential "to free Bohemia,"[14] and several months later he was to emphasize the necessity of dismembering the Habsburg realm;[15] point 8 appears to be a substantial deviation from both statements. No judgment will be ventured here as to the influence of the thirteen points on Tsarist foreign policy; the evidence is so scanty that it would be guesswork to do more than note that

[12] Constantine Diamandi, "Ma mission en Russie—I," *Revue des Deux Mondes* (Paris), February 15, 1929, p. 810.
[13] *Ibid.* See also Alfred J. Rieber, "Russian Diplomacy and Rumania," in this volume, pp. 249 and 246, note 42.
[14] Maurice Paléologue, *La Russie des Tsars pendant la Grande Guerre* (Paris, 1921-22), I, 93.
[15] *Ibid.*, pp. 246-47.

they were propounded on a high official level at a time (shortly after the Marne) when a speedy Entente victory was considered possible. But in any case point 8 was never heard of again.

"A Certain Sympathy" for the Czech Cause

At the outbreak of war, any formulation of Russian policy toward the Czechoslovak question had to take into account two outstanding facts: official Russia's unwillingness to disturb the legitimist old order, and the Russophilism of the Bohemian Slavs. The Czechs' Russophile tendencies were restrained by religious differences, among other factors, but on balance were so strong that Masaryk could write in a 1915 memorandum intended solely for British eyes:

> The Bohemian people, that must be emphasized once more, are thoroughly Russophile. A Russian dynasty, in whatever form, would be most popular. At any rate, the Bohemian politicians wish the establishment of the kingdom of Bohemia in full accordance with Russia. Russia's wishes and plans will be of determining influence.[16]

Before the war the Russian government showed extreme hesitation about dealing with the Czechs on political matters. In 1914 the Russian consul in Prague, Zhukovskii, agitated among Czech politicians for a commitment to side with the Entente during "the impending events in Europe" but received no encouragement from St. Petersburg.[17] In February of that year, during a visit to Russia, Scheiner, head of the Czech Sokols (nationalistic physical-culture organizations), was told by members of the Duma, he later reported, that there was nothing for the Czechs to do but become Austrians, since no one in Russia was interested in them. V. N. Voeikov—identified by Scheiner as "Minister of Sports and Physical Education"—replied to Scheiner's mention of Czech prepara-

---

[16] Seton-Watson, *Masaryk in England* (Cambridge, England, 1943), p. 133.

[17] A. Popov, "Chekho-slovatskii vopros i tsarskaia diplomatiia," *Krasnyi Arkhiv* (Moscow), XXXIII (1929), p. 5.

tions for the coming struggle with a warning not to say such things and the statement that he (Voeikov) would not permit such ideas to be spread in Russia. Foreign Minister Sergei Sazonov told the Czech bluntly that Russia was not ready for war; when Scheiner protested that Russia might find herself in the war against her will, Sazonov continued: "You are an interesting people, but you hold no interest for us. Don't count on us, for you do not play any role at all in our military strategy."[18] Masaryk has stated that even earlier Sazonov had spoken in much the same vein to Klofač, a Czech member of the Austrian parliament.[19]

In striking contrast to these reports were the words, years later, of Sazonov himself:

Hardly any nation in Europe had as much right to independence as the Czechs. . . . When in the course of the war the opponents of Austria had to consider the possible changes to be made in the political map of Europe after the downfall of the Habsburg Monarchy, they were at once confronted with the restoration of the Czech state. Both the Emperor Nicholas II and I, who directed Russian foreign policy, were convinced that no doubts could be entertained as to the justice of such a restoration, and the public opinion of Russia was at one with us. I am speaking, of course, of the principle involved, i.e., of the union of all the Czechs into one independent state with a territory that would secure its free development.[20]

This categorical support for Czech independence not only is a far cry from the attitude described in Scheiner's report but also conflicts to a certain degree with Sazonov's presentation of Russian war aims in the "thirteen points"; yet no less a skeptic than Eduard Beneš conceded that at the beginning of the war Sazonov and the Tsar were sympathetic to the

---

[18] Beneš, "Les slaves et l'idée slave pendant et après la guerre," *Le Monde Slave* (Paris), No. 3 (March, 1926), pp. 331-32, note. A General Voeikov was commandant of the palace and in 1913 had been appointed Chief Supervisor of Physical Education for the Russian Empire.

[19] Masaryk, pp. 145-46.

[20] Sergei D. Sazonov, *Fateful Years, 1909-1916* (London, 1928), pp. 273-74.

Czech movement.[21] The Czech politician Karl Kramář plausibly reconciled this differing evidence by insisting that Sazonov, in his official capacity, "could not have answered Scheiner in any other way, even if we had been his one and only thought."[22] Kramář, who, it should be noted, was an unquestioning Russophile, also stated that in his own personal conversations with Sazonov, the latter had shown interest in the Czechs.

On August 20, with Russia and Austria-Hungary at war, the Tsar received a delegation of Czechs—Russian subjects—who wanted to organize a Czech unit to fight against the Dual Monarchy so that the "free and independent crown of St. Wenceslaus might shine in the rays of the Romanov crown."[23] Although Nicholas expressed earnest sympathy, he declined to commit himself. This was the same day on which Sazonov mentioned to Paléologue that it was essential "to free Bohemia"[24]—a clear statement as far as it went, but leaving open the crucial question of the political form in which Bohemia was to enjoy its freedom.

In September a more important Czech deputation—representatives of leading Czech societies in Russia—was received by the Tsar a few days after an interview with Sazonov. Nicholas listened to the deputation's requests, looked at a map on which a projected Czech state was outlined (including Vienna), and asked for a memorandum on Slovakia, all with the greatest sympathy but with that elaborate noncommitment at which he was so adept.[25] According to Masaryk, Sazonov had been notably cordial and said: "Should God grant decisive victory to Russian arms, the reestablishment of an entirely independent Czech kingdom would be in accordance with the intentions of the Russian government;

[21] Beneš, *Souvenirs de guerre*, I, 314.
[22] Karl Kramář, "M. Kramář et la politique slave," *Le Monde Slave*, No. 11 (November, 1926), p. 294.
[23] Vladimir Lebedev, "Chekhoslovatskaia politika tsarskogo pravitel'stva," *Volia Rossii* (Prague), No. 8-9 (May, 1924), p. 210.
[24] Paléologue, I, 93.
[25] Lebedev, p. 210.

this question was considered before the beginning of the war and decided in principle in favor of the Czechs."[26]

But this clear and definite statement, which gave promise of a fruitful concurrence of Russian and Czech objectives, never became the basis of Russian policy toward the Czechs and Slovaks. Just what the actual basis was, however, cannot be determined. There is no record of the prewar decision which Sazonov mentioned, and "an entirely independent Czech kingdom" is not easily reconcilable with the triple monarchy envisioned in the thirteen points.

What is suggested by the Tsar's vague responses to the Czech delegations and by the inconsistencies in Sazonov's Czech policy is that Beneš was right in ascribing to Nicholas and his foreign minister "a certain sympathy" with the Czech cause, although "the Petrograd government had nothing at all of a resolute plan or even of initiative and genuine action, and this resulted altogether naturally from the general concepts of Russian policy during the war."[27]

This analysis is reinforced by Sazonov's memoirs:

Russia left all details [concerning Czech independence] to the decision of the Czech people themselves, whose political maturity she did not call in question, reserving for herself, when the moment came, the privilege of actively helping them to realize their desires.[28]

The Russian government . . . knew little about the desires and needs of the population. It seems to me, therefore, that Russia was right in adopting the attitude she did. The Russian government had decided to confine itself to energetically supporting the aspirations of the Czech people and safeguarding their interests as defined by the Czechs themselves, against any outside interference hostile to their national aims.[29]

---

[26] Masaryk, pp. 143-44. There is a possibility that some nuance may have been lost in the multiple translation of this controversial passage; C. Jay Smith, Jr. (*The Russian Struggle for Power, 1914-1917* [New York, 1956], p. 17) considers it "highly probable that the phrase 'an entirely independent Czech Kingdom' does not convey precisely what Sazonov said at this time."

[27] Beneš, *Souvenirs de guerre*, I, 315.

[28] Sazonov, pp. 273-74.

[29] *Ibid.*, p. 275, note.

Thus was inaction transformed into a virtue.

DISMEMBERMENT AND ITS DANGERS

On November 21 Paléologue had an unusually long audience with the Tsar. There was a wide-ranging discussion of war aims, in the course of which Nicholas claimed Galicia (without reference to Poland) and the western half of Bukovina, for the purpose of enabling Russia to reach her "natural frontier," the Carpathians. The claim to Galicia and part of Bukovina, ethnically justified if Poland was to remain under Russian sovereignty, was the most extensive that Russia herself made to Austro-Hungarian territory during the war.

A little later in the same audience, the Tsar asked: "And what will become of Austria-Hungary?" Paléologue answered: "It will be difficult for Austria-Hungary to survive the territorial losses to which the unfortunate Emperor Francis Joseph will be forced to consent. The Austro-Hungarian partnership having gone bankrupt, I think the partners will no longer be able to go on together."

Nicholas agreed: "I think so, too. Hungary, deprived of Transylvania, would hardly be able to keep the Slavs dependent. Bohemia will demand at least her independence. Austria would therefore be limited to the ancient hereditary states, to the German Tyrol and to the district of [Salzburg]."[30]

Thus the Tsar, in his most important recorded statement of war aims, came out squarely for enforcing a settlement wherein the Habsburg Empire would in all likelihood disintegrate.

[30] Paléologue to Delcassé, November 22, 1914, in MOEI, VI, Part 2, 111. There are marked discrepancies between this account and the version in Paléologue's memoirs (La Russie des Tsars, I, 199-201), although quotation marks are used in both cases and there is a basic sentence-by-sentence similarity. The confusion is compounded in the English translation of the memoirs, notably when it renders "La Bohême réclamera pour le moins son indépendance" as "Bohemia will demand its autonomy at the least." An Ambassador's Memoirs (5th ed.; London, 1925), I, 194. The telegram to Delcassé is given preference in this article. The word "Salzburg," however, at the end of the quotation in the text here is supplied from the memoirs; the sentence is left incomplete in the telegram as published in MOEI.

His views differ considerably from the import of Sazonov's
point 8, ten weeks earlier, but they do sound very much like
Sazonov's views six weeks later, when, on January 1, 1915,
Paléologue initiated a discussion which revealed Sazonov's wartime attitude toward Austria-Hungary with greater clarity
than any other recorded statement or document.

The French ambassador (acting entirely on his own authority) asked if Russia would be willing to make a separate
peace with Austria-Hungary in return for the cession of Galicia to herself and of Bosnia and Hercegovina to Serbia.
Sazonov "made a face" and asked: "And Bohemia? And
Croatia? Would you leave them under their present form
of government? That's impossible." A moment later, after
Paléologue pressed his suggestion, Sazonov insisted with some
irritation that "Austria-Hungary must be dismembered." When
Paléologue persisted even then—mentioning that the Allies
could demand a large degree of autonomy for the Czechs
and Croats—Sazonov finally said, "As a matter of fact, this
calls for some thought," probably to end the ambassador's
importunities.[31]

After this episode there is an almost complete dearth of
first-hand information about Sazonov's plans and opinions
regarding Austria-Hungary. On March 27, 1915, he told
Paléologue that the Tsar had received a peace letter from
Prince Gottfried von Hohenlohe, Austro-Hungarian ambassador in Berlin, and added: "This letter shows how low morale
is in Austria; still, it won't be answered. Old Francis Joseph
is not yet disgusted enough with the war to resign himself to
the conditions we intend to impose on him."[32] (This was the
only unquestionably authentic Austro-Hungarian approach to
imperial Russia concerning a separate peace. There were no
proven Russian approaches to Austria-Hungary, and with
every rumor tracked down the conviction grows that there
was no possibility of a separate peace between Austria-Hungary

[31] Paléologue, La Russie des Tsars, I, 246-47.
[32] Ibid., pp. 334-35.

and the Entente before Francis Joseph's death in November, 1916. Great Britain showed interest in following up the separate-peace proposals made secretly by elements of Hungarian opposition parties, but Russia steadfastly opposed the idea.)[33]

Although in mentioning the Austro-Hungarian letter to Paléologue, Sazonov did not elaborate on the terms Russia "intend[ed] to impose," it is unlikely that he had dismemberment in mind at this moment, since "old Francis Joseph" could not possibly become disgusted enough to submit to the destruction of his Empire. In May, 1916, Pavel Miliukov, Cadet leader in the Duma, told Sir Edward Grey, British foreign secretary, that Sazonov considered it dangerous to dismember Austria because her Germanic peoples would then strengthen Germany;[34] but there is no other information to lend substance to this interesting remark.

From the evidence presented, Sazonov's war aims policy toward Austria-Hungary is hard to pin down. As has been related, he made one clear statement in favor of a triple monarchy and another in favor of dismemberment. The degree of contradiction between the two is a matter of interpretation (and perhaps of translation), but even at best they cannot both be related to one consistent policy.

Two relevant dispatches from Alexander Izvol'skii, Russian ambassador to France, merely deepen the uncertainty. On October 13, 1914, he reported: "I continually point out here on all occasions the necessity of putting an end to the Habsburg Monarchy—which is utterly anachronistic—and of calling on the nationalities which compose it (with the exception of the Poles) to enter upon independent political existence."[35]

It can be plausibly argued that the absence of any rebuke from the Foreign Minister for such outspokenly independent

---

[33] On the subject of a separate peace, see Wolfram W. Gottlieb, *Studies in Secret Diplomacy during the First World War* (London, 1957), pp. 296-300; and Abrash, "Entente Policy," pp. 57-83.

[34] "Dnevnik P. N. Miliukova," *Krasnyi Arkhiv*, LIV-LV (1932), p. 47.

[35] Izvol'skii to Sazonov, October 13, 1914, in MOEI, VI, Part 1, 395.

political activity on the part of an ambassador indicates the former's agreement. But on December 16 Izvol'skii made it clear that the question was still wide open:

> For my guidance it is important that I should know the Imperial government's fundamental opinion on this question. Will we insist upon the complete disruption of the Dual Monarchy and its final dismemberment, or, on the contrary, will we prefer to isolate Germany through the conclusion of a separate peace with Austria, taking from the latter some territories for ourselves and some for Serbia?[36]

If, after four months of war, and with Russian troops deep into Galicia, the Russian ambassador in Paris had no knowledge of his government's opinions on such fundamental and seemingly urgent questions, the surmise that no clearcut policy had been adopted gains in force.

The lack of policy was noted by prominent émigré leaders of the Czech and Croat nationalists—two groups which, lacking an established state to put forward their claims, were utterly dependent upon Entente support. Frano Supilo, the Croatian leader who had a good deal of experience with Russian diplomacy during his futile efforts in Petrograd in 1915 to block the Treaty of London, offered the Czech leaders his considered opinion that Russia simply had no Austrian or Slav policy at all.[37]

Masaryk discovered what appeared to him to be ignorance and apathy at the Russian embassies in Rome, Paris and London. He said of Count Benckendorff, in London, that he had never seen a racial map of Austria-Hungary and seemed to know little about the country, and of Izvol'skii, in Paris, that "it was quite clear that his government had not told him of any official Slav policy."[38] Masaryk concluded that Russia's only genuine war aims were embodied in the Entente

---

[36] Izvol'skii to Sazonov, December 16, 1914, *ibid.*, Part 2, pp. 225-26.
[37] Beneš, *Souvenirs de guerre*, pp. 213-14.
[38] Masaryk, *The Making of a State*, p. 98. For the situation in Rome, see Masaryk, *President Masaryk Tells His Story* (New York, 1935), p. 234; and for that in London, see Paul Selver, *Masaryk* (London, 1940), p. 255.

agreements giving Constantinople to Russia and in the 1917
treaty with France allowing Russia a free hand on her western
frontier. Insofar as "official Russia" wanted to reach Constantinople "without troubling about independent Slav peoples,"
her policy, he felt, was in effect anti-Slav.[39]

Beneš listed Russian diplomatic concerns, in order of priority,
as Turkish affairs, Galicia and Poland, the South Slavs and,
last, the Czechs. But in this respect he found no grounds for
either surprise or criticism: "All this was very natural, more
or less obvious and, from the Russian point of view, perfectly
proper and logical, since the imperial government had neither
a settled concept of a central European policy nor a clearly
established plan to follow in accordance with fixed principles."[40]

All the evidence justifies Supilo, Masaryk and Beneš in
their contention that Russia lacked a Slav policy. Masaryk,
who thought rather highly of Sazonov, wrote that even he
"had no positive Slav and Czech policy in the war."[41] Without
such a policy, however, war aims toward Austria-Hungary
were bound to be negative and inconsistent; nothing less than
unqualified support for the principle of nationality could have
clarified the Russian attitude toward Slavs and Austria-
Hungary alike, but this principle was one which had traditionally been handled by tsarist governments as the political
dynamite it was. As one Czech historian concisely put it,
"Russia, in particular, could not but be opposed to the principle
of nationality and of the right of peoples to determine their own
fate—principles in the name of which the dissolution of the
Dual Monarchy was called for—because this constituted a
precedent which could detach from Russia all of her hetero-
geneous ethnic populations."[42]

The other side of this coin, of course, was the ancient monarchic bulwark of "legitimism." Without a denial of the principle of nationality, legitimism in both Austria-Hungary and

[39] Masaryk, The Making of a State, pp. 144-45.
[40] Beneš, Souvenirs de guerre, I, 314.
[41] Masaryk, The Making of a State, p. 143.
[42] Ján Papánek, La Tchécoslovaquie (Prague, 1923), p. 33.

Russia was next to meaningless; and since legitimism and all that it signified became, if anything, an even stronger watchword for official Russia during than before the war, that clarification of policy toward the Slavs upon which so much else depended never took place.

A variety of lesser factors militated against such a clarification. For one thing, if Constantinople and the Straits indeed headed the list of Russian objectives, Sazonov was merely doing his ministerial duty by placing Slav matters in a subordinate position. Then, too, the formulation of a Slav policy in a war against Austria-Hungary and Germany was a far more delicate business than in a war against the Ottoman Empire. It was no longer a tidy matter of the Orthodox Serbs, Bulgars and Greeks; now there were also the Roman Catholic Poles, Croats, Czechs and Slovaks to be reckoned with. Masaryk maintained that there was a tendency for Russian officials, notably Izvol'skii, to concentrate their Slavic interests on the Orthodox Slavs, and related that, when Sazonov spoke to the Czech delegation in September, 1914, he "asked the Czechs for their idea of the relationship between an Orthodox dynasty and a Catholic people, and expressed doubts about it."[43]

Finally, Sazonov was faced with all varieties of emotional Pan-Slavism. A description by Anatolii Nekliudov, ambassador to Sweden, of the extreme Pan-Slav ideas prevalent in Russian society early in the war suggests the nature of the pressure to which Sazonov was subjected:

Once war had been declared and had led from the first months to startling successes on the Austrian front, that to us meant the complete triumph of the simplest political principles which had been preached for such a long time by our patriotic press, by our so-called Slavophiles, reactionary as well as liberal, and by the General Staff party. Austria-Hungary would be obliged by the force of circumstances to form a confederation, naturally under the auspices and presidency of Russia; this confederation extending from the Carpathians to Constantinople and from Danzig to the Adriatic, embracing Orthodox countries—

[43] Masaryk, *The Making of a State*, p. 143; see also p. 98.

because Russia is Orthodox; Slav countries—because Russia is Slav; and finally the Hungarians—because they could not exist otherwise. That was the program![44]

The program—despite its patent lack of realism—undoubtedly packed an emotional wallop both at court and in the nation at large.

Millennial Pan-Slavism of this kind rarely came to the surface in official circles, however, probably because liberals and reactionaries both feared the consequences (for entirely different reasons) of applying such doctrine to the Habsburg Empire.

The liberals, most of whom would have rejoiced in the dismemberment of ossified and oppressive Austria-Hungary, would hardly have been pleased to see it replaced by another autocratic empire such as Nekliudov described; the possibility of such a development may have lain behind Masaryk's statement that "the radical elements in the Russian intelligentsia— the Socialists in particular—who were in opposition to the government and its official nationalism and Slavophilism" were not well disposed toward the Czech independence movement.[45]

The reactionaries, most of whom naturally desired the maximum extension of tsarist domination, could not ignore the violation of legitimism involved in Austro-Hungarian dismemberment. It is significant that in November, 1914, the recommendations on Poland of the extremely reactionary minority of the Council of Ministers placed the "liberation of the remaining [non-Galician] Austrian Slavs" last in a list of six Russian foreign policy objectives.[46] The concern for legitimism was forcefully voiced to Paléologue in September, 1914, by Sergei Witte, former prime minister: "Let us suppose our coalition triumphs completely; let us suppose the Hohenzollerns

---

[44] Anatolii V. Nekludoff (Nekliudov), *Diplomatic Reminiscences before and during the World War, 1911-1917* (2d ed.; London, 1920), pp. 326-27.

[45] Masaryk, *The Making of a State*, p. 20.

[46] *Russko-pol'skie otnosheniia v period mirovoi voiny* (Moscow, 1926), p. 210. The minority report is discussed in detail in the article by Gifford D. Malone in this volume.

and Habsburgs are reduced to begging for peace and submitting to our terms. But that means not only the end of German domination, it means the proclamation of republics throughout Central Europe. And that very event means the end of tsarism !"[47]

At that time even Galicia failed to interest Witte. In January, 1915, however, he reportedly espoused an utterly different program. According to the Marchese Carlotti, the Italian ambassador, Witte and his followers—who, regardless of their actual numbers or influence, were taken very seriously by Britain and France because they favored an early peace with Germany—then supported the idea of vast Russian gains at Turkey's expense and a concurrent renunciation of all claims against Germany. Russia might "even favor the annexation to [Germany] of some of the Austrian provinces having an almost entirely German population." As for Austria-Hungary itself:

Here is the future lot which Count Witte and his friends have in store for Austria-Hungary, which from their point of view must be divided into separate states, among them in the first place an independent Hungary with . . . [sic] million people. Russia will get Galicia and part of Bukovina. Transylvania and the other part of Bukovina to Rumania. The Trentino and the western half of Istria to Italy. In the north a Bohemian state would be formed, and in the south a Yugoslav state including the Slovenes, the eastern half of Istria, Croatia, Dalmatia and part of Bosnia. Serbia would acquire the other part of Bosnia, and Hercegovina. Austria, with Vienna, would be reduced to six million inhabitants.[48]

This was a remarkably prescient description of the actual fate of Austria-Hungary, except for the postulate of separate Yugoslav and Serb states. Among important European political figures, only Greek Premier Eleutherios Venizelos and Masaryk displayed equal foresight at so early a date. But such a program was basically alien to official Russian policy,

[47] Paléologue, La Russie des Tsars, I, 120-21.
[48] Carlotti to Sonnino, January 19, 1915, in MOEI, VII, Part 1, 46-47.

which at all times placed the drastic weakening of Germany very high among its objectives. There is no evidence that Witte's outspoken advocacy of an early, conciliatory peace with Germany—whether involving the dismemberment of Austria-Hungary or not—ever found an echo in either Tsar or Cabinet; hence any scheme which would have left Germany untouched—to say nothing of giving her Austrian territory— had no connection with official policy.

One more set of war aims, reported by Masaryk, deserves mention, since its author was the Chief of Staff, General Mikhail Alekseev. At the beginning of the war "he had imagined that Austria-Hungary could be divided into states serviceable to Russia," and later informed Masaryk of an elaborate plan for such a division. The Czech referred to the General's views as an "indication of the way official Russia looked upon Slav questions," but any plan wherein the Czech state was to "extend to Trieste and Fiume on the Adriatic, and thus to take over a large part of German Austria, including Vienna, but [was] only to get a bit of Slovakia, as far as Kosičs, while being presented with a lot of Magyars,"[49] assuredly did not reflect any official word out of Petrograd.

THE CZECHOSLOVAK QUESTION: RUSSIAN FREEDOM OF ACTION

During 1915, general outlines of war aims toward Austria-Hungary vanished with the Galician front. Only the Czechoslovak question remained alive, not on its own merits but as a consequence of the persistent activities of the Czech societies which had gained access to Sazonov and the Tsar himself during the first two months of the war. These societies were primarily interested in obtaining an official promise that Czechoslovak national aspirations would be fulfilled after an Entente victory—although there was sharp disagreement among the Russian Czechs as to just what those aspirations were. Masaryk, in fact, had a rare kind word for Russian policy in connection with the Czech dissensions: "The Russians were

[49] Masaryk, *The Making of a State*, pp. 145-46.

estranged . . . by the haziness of our own people as to what they really wanted and by the unsavory quarrels between them. Frankly, I often wondered that the Russians had so much patience with us."[50]

Closely connected with the issue of the Czechoslovaks' political future was the complex subject of the Czech and Slovak prisoners of war. Tens of thousands of them had surrendered voluntarily and were obviously a valuable source of dedicated manpower against the Habsburg Empire. Although sheer manpower was not a major Russian military consideration, there was some support from Alekseev and Brusilov for the idea of utilizing the Czechs.[51] The issue became complex because of the many and varied efforts by the Foreign Ministry and reactionary officials elsewhere to prevent any organizing of the prisoners. These efforts were engendered by the fear that the formation of a unit composed solely of Austro-Hungarian Czechs would imply an acknowledgment of Czech independence and consequently of the principle of nationality, as well as by a reluctance to see within the ranks of the Russian army any element whose goals might conflict with tsarist aims. The prisoners-of-war dispute and the relations between the government and the Czech societies were essentially internal matters, but the intragovernmental communications on these subjects throw some light on larger issues.

In April, 1915, the legal section of the Foreign Ministry sent an unsigned draft—attributed to the legal adviser, Baron Nol'de—to Ivan Goremykin, chairman of the Council of Ministers:

As for the matter of the proposal by the Union of Czech Societies that the Imperial Government immediately announce its acknowledgement of future Czech independence, this liberating task, historically pursued by Russia in the relations of the Slav peoples, is sufficiently known to all. However, in the view

---

[50] Ibid., p. 153.
[51] For Alekseev's views, see "Neizvestnye dokumenty iz tsarskogo arkhiva," Volia Rossii, No. 8-9 (May, 1924), pp. 227-28; and for Brusilov's, see Lebedev, pp. 222-25.

of our government it is not possible to tie our hands with a formal declaration regarding the nationalist leaders, since their political interest to us does not warrant our hampering our future freedom of action with such an announcement.[52]

That same month there was an even more pointed draft, also unsigned:

But I do not see what purely political interests could impel us to carry out the wishes of the leadership of the Union [of Czech Societies]. Preliminary acknowledgment of future Czech independence, about which their report speaks, and the other purely political aspects of their proposal are so frivolous that they hardly merit detailed discussion.[53]

A year later, some remarks by Baron Maurice Schilling, a Foreign Ministry official close to Sazonov, demonstrated that Russian policy on the Czechoslovak question had become no less negative. Two assistants to the commander of the Czecho-slovak Rifle Regiment (the military unit of Czech subjects of Russia, requested by the Czech delegation on August 20, 1914) asked Schilling for an authoritative statement of the govern-ment's intentions regarding the future of the Czech and Slovak lands. He replied that such a statement could be issued only by the Foreign Ministry itself, but that Sazonov was not yet prepared to have this done. (The narrator of this episode, N. A. Bazili, the Foreign Ministry's representative at the Stavka, added that this was the same reply given to similar previous requests by various Czechs.) The Baron declared to his visitors that Russia would always help the Czechs as much as possible but that the future of Czechoslovakia de-pended to a large degree upon the circumstances at the end of the war. Besides, Russia did not know just what the Czech people wanted, a subject upon which the Czechs in Russia— none of whom could properly be considered representatives of the entire Czech people—were not in agreement. "Therefore it is necessary to wait until Czechoslovakia is occupied by Russian troops and is able to decide freely and clearly its

[52] Popov, XXXIII, 21-22.
[53] "Neizvestnye dokumenty," pp. 231-32.

desires. Only then will Russia, learning the Czechs' wishes to a certainty, be in a position to determine her relation to them."[54]

Russia's refusal to budge from her "freedom of action" position on the Czechoslovak question (partially explained by the steadily diminishing likelihood that Russian troops would ever actually reach the territory in question) cannot be clarified by reference to her larger policy toward Austria-Hungary. The fact is that there is no direct evidence at all of official Russian war aims concerning the latter after Sazonov's conversation with Paléologue on January 1, 1915, with the single, controversial exception of the Allied war aims note of January 10, 1917, to be taken up in due course. A tantalizing clue exists in Miliukov's diary of his 1916 trip to Britain and France as a member of the Russian Parliamentary Delegation. In the course of a long and detailed discussion with Sir Edward Grey, Miliukov made the significant remark (referred to earlier): "Sazonov is personally of the opinion that it is dangerous to dismember Austria; the Austrians . . . would strengthen Germany, and it would be better to tie them to the Slavs."[55]

The importance of this statement lies not in the supposed reluctance to dismember Austria-Hungary—it was, after all, only a casual remark by a man not close to Sazonov—but in the reasoning that after the war Germany would be strengthened as a result of such dismemberment. Such calculations had little in common with the bald territorial grabs and compensations envisioned during the first half-year of the war, but were in line with a similar change of attitude appearing at this time in Britain and France.[56] Hence Miliukov's comment suggests that Sazonov, following a general Entente diplomatic trend, was thinking more about Austria-

[54] "Dnevnik ministerstva inostrannykh del za 1915-1916," *Krasnyi Arkhiv*, XXXII (1929), 29-30.

[55] "Dnevnik P. N. Miliukova," p. 47.

[56] See Abrash, "Entente Policy," pp. 46-47, 53-55.

Hungary's role in *Mitteleuropa* and less about the disposition of each disputed segment of the empire.

But Sazonov's long tenure in the Foreign Ministry was almost over even as Miliukov spoke; in July Prime Minister Boris Stürmer, who lacked both imagination and dynamism, became Foreign Minister. Russian interest in war aims toward Austria-Hungary, slight enough under Sazonov, sank almost entirely out of sight. In fact, were it not for the memorandums about to be discussed, there might have been no Austria-Hungary at all as far as the known records of Stürmer's Foreign Ministry show.

A POLICY IN DRAFT, 1916

These three memorandums were drawn up between September 19 and October 30, 1916, in the political section of the Foreign Ministry.[57] The author was probably Priklonskii, prewar consul in Budapest and the Foreign Ministry expert on Czech—and presumably Austro-Hungarian—affairs, although not a high-ranking member of the Ministry. The scanty references describe him as anti-Czech and pro-Habsburg (pro-German, too), and as a "notoriously Magyarophile functionary."[58]

[57] See "La Russie tsariste et la question tchéchoslovaque," *Le Monde Slave*, No. 1 (November, 1924), pp. 123-38; and No. 2 (December, 1924), pp. 294-300. These memorandums were apparently first published in the Czech periodical *Narodni Osvobozeni* early in 1924, and later in the year were translated in full in *Le Monde Slave*. Except for references in Lebedev (pp. 218-19) and a few paragraphs translated in Popov (XXXIII, 25-26), the documents seem to have remained unutilized by Russian, British and French historians.

According to *Le Monde Slave*, the memorandums were copied in the Russian State Archives by Jaroslav Papoušek, of the Czech Ministry of Foreign Affairs (who had been Masaryk's secretary in Russia in 1917); Lebedev likewise credits Papoušek with obtaining them. Presumably both Lebedev and *Le Monde Slave* got their information from the same source, *Narodni Osvobozeni*. Interestingly enough, Popov, who might be expected to have had access to the Russian archives, gave the Czech publication as his source for the small segment he translated.

[58] Beneš, *Souvenirs de guerre*, I, 317. See also Lebedev, p. 317. Priklonskii is not mentioned in *Le Monde Slave*, but Lebedev called him the author, and Popov referred to him as the author of the majority of the reports on the Czechoslovak question.

There is a slight possibility that the memorandums may have been

Although these memorandums were written in the Foreign Ministry and sent to its representative at the Stavka, there is no reason to see in them an expression of actual policy; the extensive background material preceding the recommendations suggests, rather, a primarily advisory purpose. So do the last lines of the final memorandum:

Such a situation once created [the decision to dismember Austria-Hungary], new problems would present themselves: Which of the parts of the monarchy ought to be distributed to the profit of the existing states which are of the same nationality? Which new states ought to be created and what would their frontiers be? What should their political organization be? Should they be entirely independent and without ties with each other, or rather should they be grouped in one or several federations? A special note will be devoted to these different questions.[59]

Whether such a "special note" was ever written is not known, but this completely uncommitted approach to decisions of major importance does not suggest that the memorandums describe a policy already decided upon.

Although there is not the slightest indication that any of the recommendations were ever translated into actual policy, these lengthy and closely reasoned memorandums outlined a remarkably sound Russian policy toward Central Europe. Hence the chief value of the documents is the unparalleled insights they offer into the general framework and aims within which Russian policy toward that area had to operate at that time. They also prove that the indecision and negativism of wartime tsarist policy toward Austria-Hungary cannot be charged to a lack of expert information and analysis.

There are three separate memorandums; although the second is designated as an addendum to the first, it is dated two weeks later. The first (September 19, 1916) is called "Secret Note on

inspired by the letters of the Grand Duke Nikolai Mikhailovich to the Tsar suggesting that it was important to consider Russian war aims in detail and at once. See Malone, pp. 136-39, this volume.

[59] "La Russie tsariste," *Le Monde Slave*, No. 2 (December, 1924), p. 300.

the Czechoslovak Question."[60] The first section, headed "Interest Which the Czechs and Slovaks Hold for Russia," begins with a strictly historical review of the relations between Bohemia and Austria. Mention is then made of the fact that influential figures in all the Entente countries hoped to found "on the ruins of Austria-Hungary . . . organisms which might be of a nature to furnish a solid barrier against the development of Germanism toward the East."

The clearest exposition of German plans to set up an "economic protectorship (*tutelle*) of all Central Europe, the Balkan peninsula and the Turkish East—a plan which had begun to take shape in the form of the vast Hamburg-Bagdad railway"–was, Priklonskii believed, to be found in André Chéradame's widely known and influential book *Le plan pangermaniste démasqué*.[61] Chéradame thought that a "United States of Central Europe" would forever prevent such a development. As for the Hamburg-Bagdad railway in particular, Priklonskii observed, not only would it, if completed, "fatally perpetuate the violence done to Europe and to Asia Minor, but further it would erect an impassable barrier between Russia and the Anglo-Roman world and would drive back Russia's political influence toward the East."[62]

[60] *Ibid.*, No. 1 (November, 1924), pp. 124-31.

[61] André Chéradame, *Le plan pangermaniste démasqué* (Paris, 1916). Chéradame was a French political writer who, during the First World War period, wrote numerous books about a monstrous German plan to control the world. The books bore a strong resemblance to one another and contained numerous dramatic maps which were often exactly the same from book to book; nevertheless, the subject of Pan-Germanism was obviously of consuming interest in the Allied countries, since most of Chéradame's books were translated into English (one was aimed specifically at the United States market). To the extent that public opinion influenced the peace settlements, Chéradame undoubtedly had an effect on the latter. At any rate, the Central European territorial settlement was quite in accord with his proposals, although the political counterpart—the United States of Central Europe—never had a chance.

[62] A profound apprehension over the possible effects of the Berlin (or Hamburg)-Bagdad railway was in evidence among diverse elements of the Russian political scene. In terms even more emphatic than Priklonskii's, Sazonov wrote (although not specifically referring to the railway), "Should Germany and Austria-Hungary have established themselves on the Bosphorus and on the Balkans, Russia would have been cut off from

The crucial importance of the Czech territories was stressed by a reference to Bismarck's opinion that whichever state held them would control Central Europe. True, they were subject to Austria-Hungary rather than Germany, but the war itself demonstrated that this made no difference, since "Germany does not hide the fact that it considers Austria-Hungary as its vanguard in its march toward the Balkans and toward the East."

It was therefore not surprising that Russia's allies showed an interest in the independence movements within Austria-Hungary and among the émigrés. However, both Britain and France apparently wished to direct the Czechoslovak movement in a manner favorable to their own ends, since "it would be difficult to explain this unprecedented good will [British and French support for the movement] through any sentiments of sympathy for the Czech nation which has been struggling for its independence for so long a time." Neither ally had any serious ties, tradition of close contact, or common ethos with the Czechs. In particular, England was supporting Masaryk—whose unsatisfactory qualities (from the Russian point of view) were again catalogued—and France was reported to view the Czechoslovak question in the Chéradame manner. Furthermore, Izvol'skii had reported to the effect that "the secret inclinations of M. Chéradame, as expressed in his book *The United States of Europe*, include opposing that proposed

the sea altogether and [have] become once more of the same size as Muscov[y] in the seventeenth century." *Fateful Years*, p. 224.

Miliukov, referring to a map which showed Bohemia lying athwart the railway, wrote in 1916: "It is enough for one to glance at the map to understand the significance of the 'Slavic outpost,' which has been fortified by a ring of mountains, surrounded and already partly flooded by the tide of the German sea. The Slavic population of the Czech lands, together with their kin, the Moravians and Slovaks, will form a solid belt barring the German path to the southeast and preventing there, not only the execution of the nationalistic Berlin-Bagdad program, but even the creation of the first strong point in the achievement of that goal—the organization of a united middle empire." "Tseli voiny," in *Ezhegodnik gazety "Rech'*," *1916* (Petrograd, 1916), pp. 101-2. And Masaryk, generally anathema to official Russia, felt that his "opposition to the German Berlin-Bagdad scheme attracted attention" in Petrograd. *The Making of a State*, p. 148.

organization to the excessive strengthening of Russia which is bound to result if—as the Allies do not doubt—the war ends as we desire."

"The preceding considerations," Priklonskii concluded, "make it plain that Russia ought to exercise control over the Czechoslovak question—as events have defined it—without going so far as to prejudge the exact form which the Czechoslovak government will take." If nothing else, Russian direction of Czech affairs would prevent any manifestation of anti-Russian tendencies in that area. Russia was necessarily more interested in the Czech problem than were the other Allies, both because the Czechs were the "front line of Slavism" toward the West and because they could serve as the nucleus of a grouping which would check "the encroachments of militaristic Germanism on the lands where, in the course of history, the influence of Russia has been dominant."

As analyzed in this memorandum, the most compelling reason for Russia's particular involvement in the Czech question was the fact that the Czechs—an indispensable element of any anti-German arrangement in Eastern Europe—were Slavs. In addition, however,

Bohemia, because of its geographic location and the composition of its population, is of primary interest to us in connection with the Polish and Ukrainian questions. Finally, the Czech territory would also present for us a serious economic interest because of the important development of industry and industrial agriculture there.

The Ukrainian matter is raised in another of the memorandums, but the subject of economics never reappears. (Yet Bohemia was the most industrialized region of the Austro-Hungarian Empire.)

"It is therefore natural," the writer concluded, "that we should deem it necessary to exercise a decisive influence on the future organization of this country," and added the comment—so ironic in view of later events—that the means to do this were at hand in the persons of the Czech and Slovak prisoners of war. (The remaining two sections of this memorandum are concerned exclusively with the Czechoslovak groups in Russia and how they should be reformed.)

The second memorandum (October 3, 1916), headed "Addendum to the Secret Note on the Czechoslovak Question,"[63] goes on to the future political organization of the Czech and Slovak lands, explaining that detailed examination will be possible only after the war.

Three possibilities are envisioned: the Czechs and Slovaks might remain under the Austro-Hungarian monarchy, they might be annexed by Russia and enjoy territorial autonomy under a Russian viceroy, or they might become an independent state. In the first case (it is interesting that Priklonskii considered it possible), the Czechoslovak problem would obviously not be solved, but it would still be worth Russia's while to strengthen friendship with the Czechs by supporting a friendly Czechoslovak movement at this time.

The annexation of the Czech and Slovak lands "seems to us difficult to accomplish." It would dangerously provoke Russia's allies, both Chéradame's French adherents and those British statesmen whose eagerness to have all the Austro-Hungarian Slav groups establish headquarters in London indicated their desire for influence in Eastern Europe. Furthermore, the British had a particular interest in Hungary:

This interest was manifested (especially at the start of the war, at the moment of our success in Hungary) in connection with the efforts made by the Hungarians then to conclude a separate peace. New evidence of this interest toward Hungary will be found in the agitation periodically renewed by the influential newspaper *The Morning Post*, inviting the English to study the question of the frontiers and the role of the future Hungarian state among the peoples who surround it.[64]

[63] "La Russie tsariste," *Le Monde Slave*, No. 1 (November, 1924), pp. 131-38.

[64] For Hungarian approaches to the British, see p. 90, and work cited in note 33. Grey, who was playing the part of a good ally by relaying information about them, would surely have been dismayed to learn that the Foreign Ministry disregarded the courtesy but seized upon the efforts themselves as grounds for suspecting British "interest" in Hungary.

The Morning Post reports—supposedly from a correspondent in Buda-

Italy too had demonstrated an interest in Hungary and a
"certain tendency to become reconciled with her, naturally
on the condition that she quit the Germanic bloc."

All the foregoing leads us to think that the Western powers
would see [in a Russian annexation of the Czechs] a break in the
European balance which all are striving to conserve.

Besides, it would be difficult to maintain that such a combination would be advantageous for Russia, at least in the
present political circumstances. In reality she would find herself
joined to a population Slavic, to be sure, but Catholic, raised
in German culture, and never before connected with the Russian
state itself. Such a solution would only make the problem of
governing our country still more difficult.

The first of these two paragraphs is interesting because of
the deference expressed on Russia's part toward French and
British fears. Of course the Western powers would view Russian annexation of the Czechs as a "break in the European
balance"; but surely no statesman anywhere thought, in late
1916, that the war could possibly end (except through negotiation) without such a break. In fact, the 1915 agreements
about Constantinople meant no less a break than would the
annexation of the Czechs. (Although in theory Russian acquisition of the Straits—resting on general agreement of the
Entente powers—would cause no inter-Allied problems, in
the third memorandum Priklonskii acknowledged that there
might be trouble.) Priklonskii's reason for raising the "European balance" question might have been to anticipate objections by the Pan-Slavists, who would be outraged by the
real arguments (in the second paragraph of the above quotation) against annexation of the Czechs, but might be impressed
by the threat of great-power complications.

In any case, an official of the Russian Foreign Ministry
had voiced the unequivocal conclusion that Russia would
be better off without annexing Czechoslovakia, at least in

pest, stressing Hungarian interest in a separate peace—were exposed
as forgeries by R. W. Seton-Watson; see "Magyar Forgeries in England,"
The New Europe (London), January 18, 1917, pp. 16-23.

"the present political circumstances." Although he did not explicitly corroborate Masaryk's assertion that the Russians preferred an independent country, even in Masaryk's spirit, to annexation, Priklonskii unquestionably feared "our liberalism and our Catholicism," as Masaryk put it.[65]

The third possibility—creation of an independent state—would "suit Russia's true interests better." The Allies would approve, as would the Czech and Slovak leaders. The form of government, either monarchic or republican, should be left to the choice of the Czechs and Slovaks, provided all outside pressure was excluded. The Czech republicans, of course, would favor close ties with France, but the vast majority of the Czechs wished to restore the crown of St. Wenceslaus. Given the decision for such a restoration, the crucial question became that of the root of the new dynasty.

There were four possibilities: national, South Slavic, Russian and West European. The first would engender struggles between the aristocratic families desiring the honor and then between the one chosen and the "democratic spirit of the Czechs." The South Slavic ruling families were eliminated because they could offer no attractive candidate. Hence most Czech and Slovak politicians favored either an autonomous province under the Emperor of Russia or a kingdom under a Romanov.

However, the writer of the memorandum noted (somewhat inaccurately), some Czech politicians—a "tiny minority"—headed by Masaryk wished to establish a Czech kingdom under an English prince. They were probably influenced by Britain's mighty role in Europe's destiny and her current help to all the Austro-Hungarian nationality movements. At first glance the idea did not seem especially harmful to Russia, with which the English dynasty had such close relations, but upon more thorough consideration, this solution threatened to produce highly disturbing consequences.

The first result, of course, would be to put Masaryk in a strong position in Bohemia, and, however negligible his stand-

[65] *The Making of a State*, p. 155.

ing as a politician in his own country, as a professor he would
be quite influential in preaching a Western orientation for the
Czechs.[66] If Czech students were raised in English-style schools
and sent to England to finish their education, the antipathy
toward Russia now limited to Masaryk's group would become
widespread. True, the German milieu was never able to eradi-
cate Slavic ideas among the Czechs, but the effects of German
culture were counterbalanced by the Czech's hatred for their
political oppressors, whereas there would be no grounds what-
soever for serious friction between Czechoslovakia and Britain.
Hence "the progressive withdrawal of Bohemia" from Russia
might "lead to serious political wrangling because the Czech
territory borders on Poland, on the Hungarian-Russian territories which would be incorporated in Russia, and on Galician
Ruthenia."

The possibility of friction between Russia and Slav states
related to her was exemplified by Bulgaria, where Stambulov
was "a typical example of those Slav politicians who, sincerely
believing themselves nationalists but pursuing certain goals
without first adapting them to Russia's goals, cause considerable harm, sometimes irreparable, both to Russia and
to their own country." Slav politicians must work with Russia,
the "traditional protector of Slavism"; as long as they did
not oppose her outright, "Russia [would] show good will
equally to the Slav politicians of various parties in regard
to the internal organization of their country" and would not
interfere in such matters.

Should Masaryk's group gain the upper hand, the one question most likely to produce friction between Russia and Czechoslovakia was the Ukrainian movement, which the Czecho-
slovaks would encourage. Austria-Hungary has been the fore-
most agitator in this regard, but even if the Habsburg Empire disappeared, Czechoslovakia would become "one of the

[66] Because he had been the only member of the Realist Party in the
Reichsrat, Masaryk was not taken very seriously by Russia until his
audience with the French premier, Briand, in February, 1916. See Lebedev,
p. 215.

hotbeds of Ukrainian agitation" if the Masaryk group were in power. The frontiers which the latter had indicated it would seek were evidence of this. These frontiers went "well beyond the ethnic line where the Slovaks leave off, and that is to the detriment of Russians by ancestry; this would likewise have the effect of enlarging the possible sphere of action of Ukrainian agitation in a manner unacceptable to us."

Even if there were no Masaryk, Russia must object to an English dynasty. Because any Central European federation would have such enormous political importance and because Czechoslovakia "occupies a central position in the group of territories which would constitute the component parts of this federation" (geographically, Priklonskii was stretching a point), it would not be in Russia's interest to see a power like Great Britain dominant there. Great Britain and Russia might be on the best of terms now, but two great empires whose diverse interests "meet and intermingle" over so much of the world might easily find themselves involved in con-flicts—not necessarily reaching the point of armed conflict—even while still allies. Should this happen, it would be dis-astrous if Britain were able to turn Czechoslovakia—and through her, perhaps, the rest of Central Europe—against Russia.

To be sure, immediately after the war Czechoslovakia would work closely with Russia out of fear of the revengeful Germans, but when the new state became stronger and consolidated, it might look elsewhere. At the moment Britain appeared interested in federating the Czechs, South Slavs and Hungarians, under her auspices, to form a barrier against Germany, "but this barrier could equally well be turned against Russia."

Since neither a national, South Slavic or British dynasty was desirable, a Russian ruler would be "most fully in accord with our government's interests." The Czechs and Slovaks would probably choose just such a Slav prince, if allowed a free selection. "A unanimous plebiscite of this kind, if Russia guarantees, in addition, that she will not mix in any Czech affairs, could hardly meet justifiable opposition on the part of our allies."[67] But if a Russian ruler proved impossible, every effort should be made to defeat the candidate of any other great power and establish a dynasty from some small state, such as Belgium, which ordinarily had no concern with Slavic affairs.

In short, with respect to the Czechoslovak question Russia's objective should be to prevent the exercise of "any external influence which would not be in accord with the national inclinations of the Czechs and the interests of Russia—in other words, of Slavism."

Finally, Russia should refuse to work with Masaryk's adherents, but do nothing to split the Czech movement or hamper any Czech group in activity directed toward the national rebirth of Bohemia.

The last memorandum (October 30, 1916)—"Russia and Britain in Connection with the Question of a Czechoslovak State: Prerequisites to the Creation of This State"[68]—reiterated the danger of British influence in the future state and then examined the possibility of difficulties arising between Russia and Britain.[69]

In Priklonskii's speculations there were three sources of potential conflict between them: first, the reorganization of Central Europe (which threatened trouble because Britain and France apparently preferred to see there a Slavic federation independent of and opposed to Russia); second, the patterning

[67] The term "unanimous plebiscite," now reminiscent of Russian methods after the Second World War, of course carried no such connotation in 1916. However, the expression is puzzling in the context of these memorandums; after all, Priklonskii said over and over that the Czechs should be allowed to make their choice free from all foreign interference, and he was confident (with good reason, if Masaryk's own views are any indication) that they would favor a Romanov dynasty.

[68] "La Russie tsariste," Le Monde Slave, No. 2 (December, 1924), pp. 294-300.

[69] Priklonskii engaged in a bit of historical analysis to demonstrate that European nations had fallen out after fighting together in major wars. The absurdly far-fetched examples—for instance, that, although France and Britain were allied during the Crimean War, they almost arrived at a rupture during the Fashoda crisis—form the weakest section of the memorandums.

of new relations with the Balkan states, and the consequent accommodations between the Allies; and third, the long-standing conflict of interests in the Near and Far East.

Priklonskii devoted most of this memorandum to the first of these problems, undertaking "to study in its general framework the question in what measure the interests of Russia would be served by the dismemberment of Austria-Hungary, which seems to be the first condition and the essential condition for the creation of a state of this kind [Czechoslovakia]." One of the chief aims of Russia, Rumania, Serbia and Italy alike was to obtain territory from the Habsburg Empire on the basis of nationality, "and that aim could be achieved without completely dismembering Austria-Hungary." But there were other aims which mere weakening of Austria-Hungary would not satisfy.

> Our chief aim is to paralyze the offensive power of Germany in the future. An effective means of attaining this end would be to dismember Austria-Hungary, for in this case Germany would be prevented from using the total strength of this country for its military ends.[70]

The genius of Bismarck made of Austria-Hungary, Germanic power of the first order and hereditary enemy of Prussia, the docile vanguard of the latter in its advance toward the East; in that way, Austria-Hungary has been placed in irreconcilable opposition to the vital interests of Russia and the British Empire and has compelled those powers to view her complete dismemberment as one of the principal goals of the war.

Since half the population of the Dual Monarchy was Slavic, in its dismemberment the Entente powers would at the same

---

[70] Sazonov, too, adhered to this point of view—but, as far as the record shows, only in his memoirs: "The only way to weaken [Germany] permanently was to deprive her of the auxiliary forces she possessed in southeastern Europe by destroying the artificial system of alliances created by Bismarck and developed by his successors. The chief of these auxiliary forces was Austria-Hungary. . . .

"Austria increased the power of her ally as a nought increases the power of a number after which it stands. The surest way to deal a serious blow to Germany and to strengthen the Entente from the danger of her dominating the world was to destroy the tottering structure of the Habsburg Monarchy." *Fateful Years,* pp. 225-26.

time perform constructive work by bringing independence to
the oppressed nationalities. Austria-Hungary, threatening
less because of its power or population than because of the
brains at its disposal and its Germano-Jesuit spirit, would
be returned to its natural development ("in the domain of
the Germanic races") from the "course of least resistance"
(dominance over the South Slavs).

"To deliver from the heavy authority [of Vienna] peoples
which are foreign to it . . . to invite these to a new national
existence under the banner of their own national group . . .
such are the noble aims sought by Russia and its allies."
Such new states would be an automatic assurance against any
German advance toward the east:

> The political interests of Russia and Britain would be satisfied
> in large measure by this network of ancient national organisms
> delivered from the German yoke and summoned to a new po-
> litical life, which would dispel the German danger to the south-
> eastern part of Europe and, at the same time, to Asia Minor
> and Central Asia as far as India, and would also paralyze the
> offensive power of Germany—and that without anything coming
> into contradiction with the political aims of the other powers of
> the Entente.

Russia would gain a particular advantage in that Germany,
obstructed on the east, would most likely seek other outlets
"for its colonization, for its commerce and, in a general way,
for its politics," in areas where Russian interests would be slight.

Although there were definite disadvantages which the creation of the new states might incur for Russia, they did not
outweigh the advantages. The political evolution of the new
states, however, would require Russia's close attention:

> If it happened that, in spite of all the measures we take in ad-
> vance at the time of their creation, they display a troublesome
> attitude toward us, mighty Russia could always, without even
> resorting to the *ultima ratio* of nations—armed force—direct
> the political tendencies which these new members of the inter-
> national community might follow in this regard, in a way which
> would take account of her interests relative to [this community].

However, Priklonskii did not explain just *how* Russia could always exercise such political mastery without using armed force.

He summed up: "In short, the foregoing considerations show clearly that it is necessary to dismember Austria-Hungary and to organize new national states with what remains of her territory after the Allies have set apart the territories which they claim." This, of course, is the most important recommendation in the memorandums, but, once made, it sank without trace into the unknown depths of tsarist Foreign Office operations during the brief period remaining before the March revolution. Nor did the conclusion of second greatest importance—that Czechoslovakia should not be annexed but should have a Romanov king—have any apparent effect on dealings with the Czech societies in Russia.

Nevertheless, the memorandums demonstrate that, in weighing war aims in Central and Eastern Europe, the Russian Foreign Office was by no means preoccupied solely with German militarism and expansionism.

Priklonskii's emphasis on combating British influence in those areas was a manifestation of a long-range concern, hardly compatible with the Entente's often professed unity, but understandable enough when it is realized that at almost this very same time Sir William Robertson, Chief of the British Imperial General Staff, and Arthur Balfour, First Lord of the Admiralty, were drawing up memorandums stressing the importance of combating *Russian* influence in the same areas.[71]

Great Britain and Russia, standing staunchly as allies in a fraternity of arms while simultaneously scheming to keep each other out of Central Europe after the war, were caught in essentially the same dilemma—for each of the two powers, the exclusion of the other from Central Europe was a secondary objective not reconcilable with the primary aim of weakening the future potential of the Central Powers. Thus, Russia's

---

[71] For these memorandums in full, see David Lloyd George, *War Memoirs* (London, 1933-36), II, 833-43, 877-88.

desire to block British influence would have been best served
by the maintenance of an Austria-Hungary as little diminished
as possible; but this was out of the question because, if German
military, political, economic and cultural capabilities toward
the east were to be seriously weakened, it was necessary to
destroy her erstwhile southeastern spearhead. On Britain's
part, the desire to restrain Russia led Robertson and Balfour
to consider not only the preservation of Austria-Hungary but
the patently unacceptable continuation of a strong Germany
as well.

No doubt the deep-seated suspicion underlying all these
memorandums was the heritage of the century of Anglo-Russian
tension which had remained essentially unabated until 1907—
only nine years before Priklonskii and the two Britons set
down their ideas. Austria-Hungary might well have benefited
from the last hope of a vanquished state—a falling out among
the conquerors—except that she was too heavily tarred with
the Pan-German brush. And on the subject of the reorganization of Central Europe, Germany was the only factor the
Entente powers feared more than each other.

THE CZECHOSLOVAK QUESTION: FINAL POSTPONEMENT

The Russian interest in keeping British and French influence out of Central Europe did come to the surface in Russian policy during 1916 in one significant area, the Czechoslovak
movement. The Russian Foreign Ministry remained un-
shakably determined to leave the situation as vague as possible,
regardless of the effect on the political allegiance of the Czechs
and Slovaks. In July, Assistant Foreign Minister Anatolii
Neratov explicitly informed the Stavka that decisions about
the Czechs had been postponed in order to allow all Czechs
to express their political ideas first.[72] Bazili seemed to experience some doubt about this policy, so unsatisfactory to
independence-minded Czechs; he feared that too domineering
an approach to Czech affairs might completely alienate those

[72] "Neizvestnye dokumenty," pp. 238-40.

Czech groups inclined toward the West.[73] In August, however, he wrote Neratov what he had told Milan Štefánik, a Vice-President of Masaryk's Czech National Council: "Not wishing to interfere in internal Czech affairs, we still naturally expect [the Czechs] to be conscious of the natural ties with Russia above all."[74]

During the summer of 1916 the Tsar actually approved the release of Slav prisoners from captivity and the establishment of Czechoslovak military units, but execution of this program was obstructed and then (partly because of Rasputin) countermanded.[75] At the same time vigorous efforts were undertaken to transform the Russian Czechs' organizations into tools of tsarist policy (whatever that might turn out to be). Dissension was sown between Czechoslovak factions, and Joseph Dürich, the other Vice-President of the Czech National Council, actually fell so thoroughly under Russian influence (during a visit for the purpose of reconciling the Russian and Western Czechs) that he was set up as the head of the Czechoslovak movement in Russia.[76]

The Czech National Council was guided primarily by Masaryk, who, almost alone among the Czechs, had decided before the war that the Czechs and Slovaks should not look to Russia to fulfill their national hopes. He and Beneš coordinated the Czechoslovak movements in Britain and France—and, to a lesser degree, in Switzerland, the United States and other countries where there were Czech colonies—into a highly effective agency of propaganda and influence, under the name of the Czech National Council. Based on Western Europe and headed by Masaryk as it was, the National Council was viewed by official Russia with undisguised hostility. Štefánik and Dürich went to Russia largely for the purpose of bringing

[73] See Lebedev, p. 215.
[74] Quoted in Popov, XXXIV, 7.
[75] Lebedev, p. 220.
[76] Popov, XXXIV, passim; and Lebedev, passim. The devious government policy toward the Russian Czech groups was described in detail in a letter of May 19, 1916, from Priklonskii to Kudashev, Bazili's predecessor, in "Neizvestnye dokumenty," pp. 233-36.

the Czechoslovak movements everywhere into a modus vivendi acceptable to all, but none could be acceptable to the
tsarist government because Masaryk's organization had such
advantages of unity, independence and influence that it was
bound to dominate any combined movement.

This relatively minor rivulet of Czech politics flowed steadily
into the barely contained flood of inter-Entente competition
for Central Europe. Masaryk stated to a Russian newspaper
after the March revolution:

Stürmer offered us money and wanted to use us for Black Hundred
[a terroristic reactionary organization] propaganda against England and France, in order to keep these states from interfering
in Slav affairs. When we declined his offer, Stürmer began to
conduct a campaign of slander, accusation and foul play against
us. He asserted that I was a Westerner, living in London and
working for England on English money, etc.[77]

Yet even this energetic and—for once—clear-cut policy
was apparently not an expression of the concerted views of
official Russia; Masaryk mentions that, at the very time when
the Ministry of the Interior was turning Dürich against the
Czech National Council, the Tsar, through Štefánik, sent
friendly greetings and urged Masaryk to continue in his policy.[78] But by mid-1916 there was little question about the
Foreign Ministry's attitude. In the spring of that year Miliukov and Supilo told Masaryk and Beneš that "aller jusqu'au
bout" was not Sazonov's intention in either the Croat or
Czech question;[79] and Masaryk was convinced—correctly, as
far as can be judged from the published documents—that
the Russian ambassadors in Paris, London and Rome never
received instructions concerning the Czechoslovak movement.[80]

Tsarist policy toward the Czechoslovak movement was,
basically, one of obscurantism and obstruction. The Foreign
Ministry's formula for those Czechs willing to cooperate with

[77] Quoted in Lebedev, p. 215.
[78] Masaryk, *The Making of a State*, p. 101.
[79] Bèneš, *Souvenirs de guerre*, I, 304-5.
[80] Masaryk, *The Making of a State*, p. 148.

it was apparently simple and uncompromising: have faith in our wisdom, don't question our intentions and do what we say. The Russians seemed to feel that to be candid with the Czechs about Russian plans and motives would be a surrender of that freedom of action so stubbornly defended in respect to most Austro-Hungarian matters; but few Czechs outside Russia were willing to consign their hopes to a "freedom of action" policy the goals of which were equally unknown to friend, foe and Russia herself. Hence most of them looked to the Western members of the Entente for their national rebirth—and with their help, in the form of the Allied reply to Woodrow Wilson's peace note, found the first great step taken in that direction.

THE ENTENTE AND "LIBERATION OF THE CZECHO-SLOVAKS"

As the first official and public declaration of war aims by either coalition, the Allied reply to Wilson's peace note was one of the most important documents of the war. On December 18, 1916, the United States President had called upon the belligerents to state their war aims; the Central Powers brushed aside his plea on December 26, but on January 10, 1917, the Allies replied in a lengthy note which put teeth into the vague and unoriginal goal of a "reorganization of Europe" on a basis of "respect for nationalities" by specifying, among other things, "the liberation of Italians, of Slavs, of Romanians and of Czecho-Slovaks from foreign domination."[81]

Although it is possible to interpret "liberation" in the sense of autonomy rather than independence, the declaration more logically implied the destruction of the Habsburg Empire —an implication of which the French, at least, were well aware, to judge from the discussions which Beneš (instrumental in persuading the Allies to mention the "Czecho-Slovaks") had with French Foreign Ministry officials during the formula-

[81] *Official Statements of War Aims and Peace Proposals, December 1916 to November 1918*, ed. James B. Scott (Washington, 1921), p. 37.

tion of the reply.[82] Since Russia approved the note, her war
aims toward Austria-Hungary would seem to be quite clear
at this point. Unfortunately, the extent to which Russia
influenced the note is an almost complete mystery.

Paléologue has left a detailed description of the enthusiastic
reception which Pokrovskii, Stürmer's successor at the Foreign
Ministry, gave to a so-called Briand draft of the Allied reply
on December 23. According to the French ambassador's version, Pokrovskii was delighted with everything in the draft
(which included the reference to the Czechoslovaks), except
that he reserved the right to make changes concerning Poland
and Armenia. However, Paléologue was in error about the
date of this particular draft, since indirect evidence from
British, French and Czech sources proves it could not have
been drawn up until well after the twenty-third.[83] In addition
to this hopelessly confusing report, the only evidence concerning Petrograd's position that may even possibly be based

[82] Beneš, Souvenirs de guerre, I, 261-68.

[83] Briefly, Paléologue stated that on December 23 he showed Pokrovskii
a draft reply, just received from Briand, which contained numerous provisions—including the "liberation of Italians, Slavs, Rumanians and
Czecho-Slovaks"—virtually identical with the reply actually sent almost
three weeks later. Paléologue, La Russie des Tsars, III, 116-18. But
at an Anglo-French conference in London on December 26-28, a draft
by Briand was rejected by the British Cabinet as "too vague and too
evasive" (Lloyd George, III, 108), and Taylor describes "Briand's Note"
as limited to the generalities of "reparation, restitution and guarantees"
("The War aims of the Allies," p. 490). Paléologue's account is also in
total conflict with that of Beneš, who was told by the French Foreign
Ministry on December 27 that the Allies favored only a general statement
(Briand's draft?) concerning the liberation of the oppressed Central
European nations, and not until January 7 was told that the Czechs
would be mentioned in the reply to Wilson; Beneš, Souvenirs de guerre,
I, 261-68. Finally, it is almost certain that the singular inclusion of
both "Slavs" and "Czecho-Slovaks" was the result of a compromise between Italy, which was adamantly opposed to mention of the South
Slavs, and France, which argued that the mere word "Slavs" was much
too vague and seized the opportunity to rectify this by pressing the cause
of their protégés, the Czechoslovaks. Seton-Watson, A History of the
Czechs and Slovaks, p. 291; and Taylor, "The War Aims of the Allies,"
p. 490. These complex negotiations could not possibly have been initiated
and completed between December 18 and 23—an assumption supported
by Masaryk (The Making of a State, p. 124) and Seton-Watson (A History
of the Czechs and Slovaks, p. 291), who emphasize that the word "Czecho-
Slovaks" was inserted into an already completed draft at the last moment.

on inside information is the remark by the veteran Russian diplomat Baron Roman Rosen: "Russia assented to the collective replies of the Allies to the German and American notes."[84] This suggests that Russia did no more than approve replies drawn up by others.

Two other reports fall into the category of rumor. Beneš commented enigmatically that "in Vienna they know that Russia had no initiative in all this action against Austria-Hungary. This pleased them, and they supposed that the whole matter was due to the initiative of the English."[85] But he did not explain how Vienna could "know" this, and he himself knew little of affairs in Petrograd. Thomas Nelson Page, United States ambassador to Italy, reported in a dispatch after the Rome Conference (first week of January, 1917), at which the Allied reply was put into its final form, that he had heard—strictly as rumor—that Russia "was so to speak in opposition to the others nearly all the time." But he also stated what historians must sadly agree was the crucial fact: "It has been very difficult to learn with any precision what occurred in the Conference here."[86]

It is therefore impossible to assess the true significance of the Allied note in terms of Russian war aims. In view of the marked stiffening of Russian opposition to Masaryk after Sazonov's "resignation" in July, 1916, the "liberation of the Czecho-Slovaks" as a commitment undertaken jointly by the Western Allies and Russia is not consistent with the Russian attitude toward the Czechoslovak movement at this time, although it is in keeping with the earlier views of Sazonov and the Tsar. Still, the tsarist government did agree to the note and possibly helped draw it up. There may be no explanation of this paradox other than that at this moment the Russian

---

[84] Roman Romanovich Rosen, *Forty Years of Diplomacy* (London, 1922), II, 229.

[85] Beneš, *Souvenirs de guerre*, I, 267.

[86] U.S., Dept. of State, *Papers Relating to the Foreign Relations of the United States: The Lansing Papers, 1914-1920* (Washington, 1939-40), I, 747-48.

government was distracted by critical domestic troubles. It is worth noting in this connection that Rasputin was assassinated during the interval between the Anglo-French London Conference, at which the two participants prepared a draft reply, and the Rome Conference, at which the final draft was agreed upon by the Allies.

Perhaps the most curious fact about the Allied note was that within a few months all three Entente Powers nullified the provision concerning the Czechoslovaks. Great Britain did so by accepting President Wilson's offer (February, 1917) to sound out Austria-Hungary on the possibilities of a separate peace based on the latter's guaranteed retention of Hungary and Bohemia.[87] Russia and France negated their pledge of Czechoslovak liberation in a manner less complex but also less specific, in the secret agreement—resulting from French initiative—which allowed Russia a free hand on her western frontier in return for her support of drastic French plans for the future Franco-German Rhine frontier. This agreement and its bearing on Russian war aims toward Germany and Poland are discussed elsewhere in this book; its much slighter relation to Austria-Hungary will be dealt with here.

The telegram in which Sazonov notified Izvol'skii in March, 1916, that Russia would grant France and Britain a free hand in drawing up Germany's western frontiers in return for a corresponding Russian freedom on the east specified "our frontiers with Germany and Austria."[88] The treaty as finally concluded concerned only frontiers, and the raison d'être from the Russian point of view was the postwar frontier of Poland rather than those of Germany or Austria-Hungary as such; nevertheless, Russia certainly would have used this diplomatic carte blanche (reinforced by the dominant military position in Eastern Europe in which she would be placed by an Entente

[87] U.S., Dept. of State, *Papers Relating to the Foreign Relations of the United States, 1917*, Supplement I: *The World War* (Washington, 1931), pp. 40-43, 55-56.

[88] Sazonov to Izvol'skii, March 8, 1916, in *Konstantinopol' i prolivy* (Moscow, 1925-26), I, 298.

victory) to take the leading role in ordering the affairs of a defeated Austria-Hungary. It seems almost inevitable that, under circumstances such as these, Bohemia would have remained bound to Austria-Hungary if that empire was preserved or would have been granted an eastern-oriented independence under a Russian-sponsored king (à la Priklonskii) in case of dismemberment. Either way, Masaryk and Beneš would have written their memoirs in Paris or London rather than Prague.

But long before any of this could come to pass, fate intervened on a grand scale. France's assent to Russia's conditions for the frontier agreement was dated March 11, 1917. Within the week Masaryk's friend Miliukov became Foreign Minister of the Russian Provisional Government, and a new chapter began for all concerned—except Austria-Hungary, which had long since lost the power to rewrite the convulsive last chapter of an overlong book.

THE DILEMMA OF EMPIRE

Tsarist Russia's failure to adopt a definite policy of war aims toward Austria-Hungary was, at bottom, the outgrowth of the failure to solve two great problems: how to deal with the Slav peoples in general—an issue peculiarly Russian—and what to do with the Austro-Hungarian Empire as a whole—a problem shared with the other Entente powers.

Russia's perplexity over the latter question is more readily understandable if analyzed in the light of British and French reactions to the same issue. There is no evidence that, with the exception of Briand, any of the leading Entente statesmen were clear as to just where the interests of their respective nations lay in regard to Austria-Hungary. Sazonov and his successors seem—in common with Sir Edward Grey—to have been unable to reach a firm decision whether it was to their advantage to preserve the Habsburg Empire or to allow the principle of nationality to take its course. There was something to be said for both choices in connection with almost every desired goal in Central Europe, and Briand alone among Entente statesmen succeeded in making up his mind.

From this distance in time it can be hazarded that it was in the interests of all three Entente powers to maintain a diminished Austria-Hungary, on the condition—perhaps unrealizable—that there should be no possibility of Germany utilizing the Habsburg Empire to strengthen its own power position in Europe as had been the case since 1879. However, even a diminished Austria-Hungary would be of great usefulness to Germany if the two were allied; it was therefore understandable that, in the depths of an exhausting war, the Entente statesmen were reluctant to make any concessions, even on paper, which might have left such an alliance within the realm of possibility. This consideration carried most weight with Russians, who obviously did not see in a preserved Austria-Hungary the double advantage—so attractive to those Britons and Frenchmen who believed it feasible—of a barrier against both Germany and Russia. Furthermore, with normal luck and diplomatic skill Russia would have been able to turn to her advantage any drastic disruption of the Habsburg dominions more effectively than Britain or France, thanks to her ties with the Austro-Hungarian Slavs and the role she would have played as military liberator.

But the clear alternative—the dismemberment of Austria-Hungary—had its own dangers, which for Russia might have been even more menacing than those of preserving the empire. At least the Habsburg Monarchy was certain to be conservative and could be dealt with as a unit, whereas the small successor states would undoubtedly embody a variety of political complexions and would inevitably enmesh Russia in their own squabbles.

Had Russia been fighting Austria-Hungary but not Germany—regardless of the other allies on either side—her war aims would certainly have been clarified; but the overriding Entente preoccupation with "Prussian militarism" meant that the populous and strategic central Danubian lands were treated

for the most part as means to the end of an anti-Prussian reconstruction of Europe. From the point of view of both moral
feeling and national interest, tsarist Russia, and her allies
as well, must have come to feel that it was all the same whether
Austria-Hungary survived or not—an indifference equivalent
to no policy at all.

And, in fact, there was no consistent Russian policy toward
Austria-Hungary during the thirty-odd months from the outbreak of war to the revolution. Russian statesmen, like their
counterparts in Britain and France, speculated wishfully on
the postwar reorganization of a defeated Austria-Hungary,
but hesitated at facing up to the one real alternative to its
maintenance—dismemberment. The tsarist statesmen simply
did not know what they wanted to do with the Dual Monarchy,
and so they did nothing at all. The later dissolution of the
Habsburg Empire and the concomitant establishment of the
Czechoslovak state owed nothing to the wartime diplomacy
of prerevolutionary Russia.

GIFFORD D. MALONE

War Aims toward Germany

From almost the opening day of World War I war aims became a subject of investigation, controversy and recrimina-
tion, as, in the passions raised by the conflict, men sought
to prove responsibility for the war or to discover why they
fought. To many, both during the war and after, "war guilt"
and "war aims" seemed to be two sides of the same coin, and
Bolshevik publication of the secret treaties did nothing to
lessen the confusion. The connection between the two, as
is now obvious, was more apparent than real. Russia did not
start the war in order to gain Constantinople, nor did the
"imperialist powers" do battle in order to reapportion the
world. There is no longer any need to dwell upon such theories.
Most of the fog surrounding the question has been dispelled
—except in the Marxist-Leninist camp, where the simple
myth is still preferred—and one may now proceed more con-
fidently and directly to an examination of the facts.

Russia's war aims toward Germany during World War I
are, in one sense, of only academic interest, since the diplomatic
efforts and achievements of the imperial government were
completely nullified by the Revolution, Brest-Litovsk and
Russia's withdrawal from the war. On the other hand, these
aims do serve to illustrate the government's efforts—feeble
as they may have been—to come to grips with some of the
problems of long-range policy which were raised by the first
total war. The statesmen of the other great powers, of course,
were equally called upon to resolve problems which went far
beyond the scope of their previous experience. Analogies
between historical events of different periods can be mislead-

ing, but the reader, reflecting upon the aspects of the First World War presented here, may nevertheless find it useful to bear in mind some of the war aims adopted during the Second. One need not adhere dogmatically to the theory of unchanging and traditional characteristics in Russian foreign policy in order to recognize certain similarities which the nature of total war imposed upon the belligerents in both conflicts. In each case certain "permanent" factors produced questions which had to be answered in one way or another, by Stalin's regime just as by the tsarist government. What territorial compensations, if any, should Russia expect? How could Russia's security against Germany be ensured after the war, and, more specifically, what steps should be taken through territorial acquisitions or political arrangements, to see that Russia was not again attacked?

The time period covered in this study is limited to the wartime existence of the imperial government, but even this brief span of little more than two and one-half years is, in one respect, too long, for the documentary material is not adequate for the entire period. The chief source of information on the day-to-day diplomacy of the period is the series of diplomatic documents taken from the files of the Russian Foreign Ministry and published by the Soviet regime under the title *International Relations in the Period of Imperialism*. Publication of these documents was suspended with Volume X, and the bulk of the diplomatic correspondence after April, 1916, is therefore not available. Several collections of documents dealing with particular questions, for instance, the Straits or Asiatic Turkey, contain material for later months. But useful as these are, the information provided is still fragmentary. There is every reason to suppose that the remaining documents contain nothing startling about the question under consideration here, but a definitive answer must await the publication of the documents themselves. Despite this handicap, however, it seemed useful to continue this study through the remaining months of 1916 and to touch briefly upon the Russo-French Agreement of February-March, 1917. The agreement itself and the details of its negotiation have been described elsewhere.

Much has been omitted that is in one way or another relevant to the subject, for example, the attitude of Russian "society," political parties and the press to the question of war aims toward Germany—too large a question to be included in this context—and the problem of separate peace feelers. If it could be shown that the Russian imperial government initiated serious efforts to negotiate with Germany for a separate peace, this fact would have a significant bearing upon the question of war aims. The fact, however, has never been established, despite enthusiastic attempts to do so, and it is extremely doubtful that evidence will ever be uncovered to reverse the verdict. Whatever the hopes of certain groups in Russia may have been, the imperial government up to its last day remained loyal to the Allied cause and committed to the various war aims agreements into which it had entered.

It should be noted that Russia's aims toward Germany were only a part, and not the most important part, of the aims which she hoped to achieve from the war. While it is true that the realization of most of these aims was contingent upon the defeat of Germany, plans and negotiations regarding the future of the Balkans and Austria-Hungary, anticipated gains in Asia Minor and acquisition of the Straits and Constantinople were all major concerns of Russia's wartime diplomacy. For purposes of investigation, war aims toward Germany may be isolated from the total picture, but they are only one portion of a very complex story.

1

Russia, like her western allies, entered the First World War without any defined war aims other than the obvious aim of victory. Unprepared for the conflict from the military and material point of view, she was almost equally unprepared politically to define the tangible rewards which victory might bring. Certainly in Russia, as in most nations, there lay dormant a few "national grievances" and "historic tasks" which she might seize upon to remedy this deficiency, but for the most part these did not pertain to her most dangerous enemy, Germany. Russia's interest in the Balkans, her sympathy, such as it was, for fellow Slavs, and her special concern for Ukrainians under Austrian rule could be expected to supply certain aspirations realizable at the expense of the Dual Monarchy. And, from the point of view of war aims, Turkey's early entry into the war on the side of the Central Powers was unquestionably a windfall. But Germany was a different matter; she provided no such obvious possibilities for dismemberment, at least not from the Russian side, and the one major amputation which suggested itself, namely, Prussian Poland, was an operation of some delicacy, which was likely to result in complications of a serious nature. What then, if anything, could Russia expect to acquire from Germany? What aims toward Germany should she pursue? The problem presented difficulties, and it is not surprising that its solution was not in all respects adequate to the demands of the war.

Despite her general lack of preparedness, however, Russia was the first of the Entente powers to come forward with a list of war aims for the consideration of her allies. Understandably, such a list could not be drawn up overnight, and it was some six weeks after the commencement of hostilities before Foreign Minister Sazonov was prepared to outline his ideas on the matter to the British and French ambassadors in the Russian capital. But in the preceding weeks there had appeared a few indications of what some of these aims might be. The war was less than a week old when Prince G. N. Trubetskoi, a Foreign Ministry official, outlined briefly in a letter to the Russian ambassador in Constantinople the advantages which he thought Russia might wish to gain from the war. "What we can acquire on our western borders," he wrote, "is more a fulfillment of an unavoidable historic duty than an outright gain. Only the mouth of the Neman [Niemen] for us and of the Vistula for the Polish territory would be serious compensation." However, he added, indicating incidentally the relative importance which he attached to compensation from Germany: "Involuntarily one's thoughts turn first of all to the Straits."[1]

Trubetskoi, an advocate before the war of what has been described as "Russian liberal imperialism," was respected in the Foreign Ministry as a clear thinker, and his voice apparently carried considerable weight with Sazonov.[2] It is impossible to say how great his influence upon the general formulation of Russia's war aims actually was,[3] but his attitude was that of many thinking Russians who regarded the Straits as the greatest prize which the war could give.

Within a few days the government itself had taken a decisive step which established one of the aims to which it would henceforth be committed—the reunification of Poland. In the proclamation of the Grand Duke Nikolai Nikolaevich, issued on August 16, 1914, Russia announced her intention of reuniting the Polish people under the scepter of the Tsar, with "freedom of religion, language and self-government," and so made known the first of her war aims against Germany, the severance of Prussian Poland from the German Empire. In this decision immediate military considerations and overall needs of the war played a prominent part,[4] and it is question-

[1] Trubetskoi to M. N. Girs (Giers), in *Evropeiskie derzhavy i Turtsiia vo vremia mirovoi voiny: Konstantinopl' i prolivy* (Moscow), I (1925), 155; henceforth cited as *Konstantinopl' i prolivy*.

[2] Boris E. Nol'de, *Dalëkoe i blizkoe: Istoricheskie ocherki* (Paris, 1930), pp. 226-28. The Grand Duke Nikolai Mikhailovich also regarded Trubetskoi as an able planner, and in 1916 particularly requested him as a member of his proposed preparatory commission for the peace conference. See Vladimir P. Semennikov, ed., *Nikolai II i velikie kniaz'ia: Rodstvennye pis'ma k poslednemu tsariu* (Leningrad, 1925), pp. 89, 92.

[3] In his book *Dalëkoe i blizkoe* (p. 229), Nol'de feels that Trubetskoi's contribution was considerable and, upon occasion, "decisive." He does not say in which cases Trubetskoi was most influential but implies that Poland and the Straits were two such cases.

[4] A good deal has been written on this. See, for example, *The Cambridge History of Poland, 1697-1935* (Cambridge, England, 1951), pp. 482-85; C. Jay Smith, Jr., *The Russian Struggle for Power, 1914-1917* (New York, 1956), pp. 8-11; and Michael T. Florinsky, *Russia: A History and an Interpretation* (New York, 1955), II, 1323 ff.

able that the acquisition of Prussian Poland was generally regarded at this time as a reward or even a direct gain for Russia. Some, indeed, felt that it was a liability, and from this time on the Polish question became a subject of continuous and bitter dispute within the Russian government. This question is treated in detail elsewhere in this volume; suffice it to say here that in the main the controversy revolved about the issue of the future organization of the Polish state and the degree of autonomy which it should be accorded. In its relation to war aims against Germany, the Polish question was primarily a territorial one, and on this matter there was rather less difference of opinion. It was Polish "independence" which proved to be the real stumbling block, and the aim of reuniting Poland, once announced, was never discarded.

The perennial Polish question, however, was only in part connected with Russia's more direct war aims against Germany, which were made known in September, 1914. These were contained in Sazonov's general exposition of war aims, made to Buchanan and Paléologue, the British and French ambassadors, on September 14, and known subsequently to historians as the "Twelve Points." Sazonov had already mentioned a few of his thoughts on Allied war aims to Paléologue in August,[5] but the "Twelve Points" represented the first comprehensive statement of war aims that the Russian government put forth. The Foreign Minister took pains on this occasion to emphasize that the ideas expressed represented his own, "unofficial" opinions on the subject, but it was nevertheless understood that these "unofficial" views would be communicated immediately by the two ambassadors to their respective governments and that Sazonov hoped to learn what their reactions might be.

The principal Allied aim, in Sazonov's opinion, must be the destruction of the power of Germany and "her claim to military

[5] Sazonov saw the necessity of destroying "German imperialism" and of great political changes "if *Kaisertum* is not to rise at once from its ashes." Maurice Paléologue, *An Ambassador's Memoirs*, (5th ed; London, 1925), I, 96.

and political domination." This being understood, various
claims should then be made against the defeated Germany
and Austria-Hungary. From Germany, Russia would expect
to acquire the lower course of the Neman River while Poland
would receive eastern Poznań and Silesia. In the West, France
would recover Alsace-Lorraine and, "if she pleases," part of
Rhenish Prussia and the Palatinate, while Belgium would
receive an undefined but "significant increase in territory."
Britain and France, as well as Japan, would divide the German
colonies among themselves. The Kingdom of Hanover would
be restored, and Germany, in addition to paying a war indemnity, would be required to cede Schleswig and Holstein
to Denmark.

Curiously, Sazonov prefaced his remarks with the statement
that territorial modifications should be made "on the principle
of nationality." It is obvious that this did not necessarily
apply to territorial annexations by the Allies, though he seems
to have assumed that Austria-Hungary would be reorganized
more or less along these lines. Certainly, he envisaged a radical
territorial reorganization of the Habsburg Empire, including
the establishment of a tripartite monarchy composed of Austria,
Hungary and Bohemia, and the loss of a considerable amount
of territory to Serbia. To Russia proper, Austria-Hungary
would lose only eastern Galicia, while western Galicia would
go to Poland.[6]

These points, together with a few others relating to redistri-
bution of territory in the Balkans, constituted a general expression of Russian war aims as then conceived, hastily drawn
up and rather vaguely formulated. Territorial gains from
Germany, though limited in nature, were not precisely defined. It was not clear, for example, how much territory was

---

[6] *Mezhdunarodnye otnosheniia v epokhu imperializma: Dokumenty iz
arkhivov tsarskogo i vremennogo pravitel'stv, 1878-1917 gg.*, Series III
(Moscow, 1931-38), VI, Part 1, 247-48; the abbreviation MOEI is used
hereafter to apply to this title and series. See the article by Merritt Abrash
in this volume (pp. 78-123) for a detailed discussion of Sazonov's intentions toward Austria-Hungary in the so-called "Twelve Points."

encompassed by "the lower course of the Neman," nor was the extent of Polish gains in Silesia any more definite. These no doubt, were seen as tentative proposals, a basis perhaps for future negotiations among the Allies, and therefore not requiring any exact definition. The plans for the reconstitution of Germany were hardly more explicit. What was more notable was the emphasis placed upon Germany as the chief enemy— an obvious recognition of military facts, but nevertheless a contrast to the prewar attitude toward Austria.

It is obvious, moreover, that, while Sazonov had presented these ideas as his own, they did reflect accurately the aims of the Russian government at this time. Krivoshein, Minister of Agriculture, expressed the same views to Paléologue a few days later,[7] and in November they were repeated by Goremykin, Chairman of the Council of Ministers.[8] Finally, on November 21, the Emperor himself discussed this matter in an audience with the French ambassador, and indicated that his ideas coincided in all the essentials with those of his Foreign Minister. Paléologue, whose enthusiasm as a raconteur was apparently as great as his zest for conversation, has reproduced this dialogue in a form so lively that one may doubt that the shy Nicholas actually expressed himself in this way, but there is no reason to believe that the ideas themselves were other than those which the Emperor elaborated on this occasion.[9]

As Sazonov had done in September, the Emperor cautioned that his remarks should not be taken as an official statement, but the conversation nevertheless covered the question of Russian war aims in a fairly comprehensive fashion. Peace, he emphasized, must be dictated to Germany, and "German militarism" must be destroyed. "We must make it impossible

---

[7] MOEI, VI, Part 1, 313.

[8] *Ibid.*, Part 2, p. 84.

[9] Paléologue reported this conversation to Delcassé in three telegrams, of which the second was deciphered by the Russian Foreign Ministry. *Ibid.*, p. 111. The portion of the conversation reported in this telegram checks in its essentials with the version in Paléologue's memoirs.

for the German people even to think of revenge." Negotiation was not to be considered: "No Congress or mediation for
me !" The rewards which Russia would demand from a defeated Germany were essentially those limited gains already
stated by Sazonov. The reconstituted Poland would certainly
require Poznań (in addition to western Galicia) and possibly
a portion of Silesia. In East Prussia, Germany must accept
a rectification of the frontier, which, in the opinion of his General Staff, should extend to the mouths of the Vistula, though
he himself thought this a bit excessive. As for the Western
powers, "France will certainly recover Alsace-Lorraine and
possibly obtain the Rhine Provinces as well." Belgium would
receive "a substantial accession of territory in the region of
Aix-la-Chapelle," and France and Britain would divide the
German colonies as they saw fit. Schleswig and the Kiel
Canal zone should be restored to Denmark. And, to complete the
reconstitution of Germany, Hanover might be revived, a step
which, in the Emperor's mind, "should do much towards
putting the future peace on a solid basis." Whether or not such
changes meant the end of the German Empire was not important. Germany could adopt any organization she liked,
"but the imperial dignity cannot be allowed to remain in the
House of Hohenzollern. Prussia must return to the status of
a kingdom only."[10] Such were the Emperor's views on Russian
aims and the future of Germany.

Meanwhile the Russian government took the initiative in
attempting to get a statement of war aims from the other
Allies, while trying to learn what their attitude toward Russia's
own aims might be. Although no official request was made,
Russia evidently hoped that some sort of definite Allied agreement could be worked out. Sazonov had first suggested such
an agreement to Buchanan and Paléologue when he outlined
his "Twelve Points" to them in September,[11] and similar

[10] Paléologue, I, 191-95.
[11] The French historian Pingaud has pointed to a curious discrepancy
on this point in the German and French collections containing Paléologue's
report of September 14, 1914, to Delcassé regarding the "Twelve Points."

wishes were expressed by the Emperor and Goremykin two months later.

Why the Russians desired such an agreement is not entirely clear. Initially, it seems, they feared that Britain and France might not have the determination to push through to final victory after their immediate aims had been secured. In particular, as Sazonov wired "confidentially" on September 17 to Izvol'skii, the Russian ambassador in Paris, it was feared that France, once she had recovered the lost territories of Alsace and Lorraine, might be forced by the state of her army and public opinion to discontinue the offensive.[12] Although Britain, France and Russia had already bound themselves by the London Declaration of September 5, 1914, not to conclude a separate peace, perhaps (as Sazonov's message to Izvol'skii seems to imply), the Russians were as yet unsure that countries ruled by democratic governments possessed the fighting will that sustained war required; more likely they were simply displaying lack of trust in the good faith of their allies.

Whatever the reason, their fears were made known, in oblique fashion, to the Allied governments, who, in turn, took immediate steps to set their minds at rest. In Paris and London the Russian ambassadors received reassuring statements from Delcassé and Sir Edward Grey (on September 20 and 21, respectively),[13] and in Petrograd, meanwhile, Paléologue and Buchanan presented a joint note on the subject to the Foreign Minister. The Allied Declaration of September 5, the ambassadors affirmed, not only bound Britain and France not to conclude a separate peace but also clearly indicated that the

Pingaud takes as correct the German version (in the *Internationale Beziehungen*), according to which Sazonov said: "We must immediately convoke a congress." See Albert Pingaud, *Histoire diplomatique de la France pendant la grande guerre* (Paris, n.d.), I, 126-27. Actually, the French version (in *Un Livre Noir*) is the true one. In the latter, the French ambassador reported Sazonov's words as: "We must immediately draw up a plan" (*élaborer un projet*). This wording corresponds to that in the original Russian collection, which contains Paléologue's telegram in French, as well as a Russian translation. MOEI, VI, Part 1, 247.

[12] MOEI, VI, Part 1, 264.
[13] *Ibid.*, pp. 278-79 and p. 281.

two countries would not pursue their own special advantages and would continue the war until the forces of Germany and Austria-Hungary had been destroyed.[14] Whether or not the Russians were entirely reassured by these statements, there were other factors which no doubt contributed during the next two or three months to their desire for a political agreement. In the first place, the military situation, while not distinctly favorable to Russia, was not perilous enough to raise official doubts as to eventual Allied victory. Russia was opposed to any idea of a negotiated peace, as the Tsar emphasized in November, and a preliminary agreement on war aims among the Allied powers would have helped prevent such an eventuality. In November, also, Goremykin told Paléologue that Britain, France and Russia should agree beforehand on the conditions of peace, dictate these conditions to Germany at the appropriate time and convoke a peace conference only for the consideration of secondary questions. On this same occasion Goremykin quite frankly expressed the feeling that it would be well to reach an overall agreement at this time, while the Allies were closely united.[15] The obvious implication that they might not be so united later suggests a certain apprehension even at this time that Russia might be deprived of her just rewards after victory had been won. This fear, today, may seem more typical of recent Soviet history, but it is not a phenomenon confined exclusively to the Second World War. It was present, though to a much smaller degree and for quite different reasons, during much of the period under discussion here; it persisted even in 1916 when Russia had already extracted important concessions from her allies.

Russia's hopes for an overall war aims agreement during this early part of the war were disappointed, for both France and Britain regarded any agreement on war aims at this time as

---

[14] The note found in the Foreign Ministry archives is undated, but was filed immediately after a communication dated September 17, 1914. *Ibid.*, p. 260.

[15] *Ibid.*, Part 2, p. 84.

premature. As Delcassé told Izvol'skii in Paris in October, it was still too early "to sell the skin of the bear."[16] At the same time, however, Delcassé indicated his general approval of Russia's proposed aims for her western frontiers and for the future of Germany. France, he modestly added, would probably seek no territorial acquisitions in Europe except Alsace-Lorraine.[17] But, apart from generalities, the French displayed a reluctance to proceed further in the discussion of war aims.

In London Sir Edward Grey, adhering to the traditional British practice of avoiding absolute commitments for future contingencies, gave no opinion on war aims at all, and Benckendorff, the Russian ambassador, was forced to rely upon unofficial conversations with various members of the cabinet and government to get even a rough composite view of what British war aims toward Germany might be. In Benckendorff's opinion, Britain would certainly demand the destruction of the German fleet and neutralization of the Kiel Canal, perhaps by giving Schleswig to Denmark, and probably would demand cession of Luxemburg to Belgium and German Friesland to Holland. France should receive Alsace-Lorraine, and Russia, without question, all the Polish provinces of Germany and Austria, though, he added, it was hoped that Russia would live up to the promises contained in the Grand Duke's manifesto. According to Benckendorff—and his interpretation was later confirmed in a conversation with King George V[18]—Britain did not contemplate any direct interference in the future organization of Germany, though it was expected that German defeat would in itself put an end to Prussian hegemony in Germany. English sentiment, Benckendorff felt, was strongly in favor of territorial divisions on a strict ethnographic basis, and, while this certainly would mean a reorganization

[16] *Ibid.*, Part 1, p. 394.
[17] *Ibid.*, pp. 394-95. Izvol'skii also reported that the fate of Austria interested France much less than that of Germany, and that Frenchmen in general tended to sympathize with Austria. The same, he felt, was true in England. *Ibid.*, p. 396.
[18] *Konstantinopl' i prolivy*, I, 232.

of Austria-Hungary, it was hoped that France would not have aspirations to further German territory.[19] No mention was made here of East Prussia. Clearly its cession to Russia was not permissible on principles of ethnology, but there is no indication that Britain objected to it.

Despite the unsatisfactory nature of these replies, one thing is obvious from these and other conversations—all the Allies were agreed that their primary aim was the destruction of Germany's military might and "German imperialism." Germany was held to be the chief enemy; it was she who was responsible for the conflict which now raged, and it was she who must be prevented from aggression in the future. This reaction, as many have said, may indeed have been simply the rationalization of an irrational war, but statesmen are fully as capable as lesser men of believing sometimes in the irrational, and there is no reason to question the sincerity or strength of their views in this matter.

This shared conviction was not in itself sufficient, however, to bring about a general agreement on war aims, and after 1914 the Russian government abandoned any serious efforts along this line. There is some doubt, too, as to how great the Russians' desire for such an accord on overall war aims actually was. Certainly they wanted it, but their attempts to achieve it were cautious and indirect, and, one feels, halfhearted. Later they turned their attention, with greater directness and determination, to more specific goals.

In considering the war aims which Russia developed at this time, it would be useful to know whether widely divergent opinions existed on this subject within the government and what alternatives, if any, were suggested. The question of policy formation goes far beyond the scope of this article or the diplomatic documents upon which it is based, and information on the matter is quite inadequate for anything more than a tentative jugdment. Much has been written about pro-German sentiments in Russia and about the activities of

[19] MOEI, VI, Part 1, 327-28.

Germanophile elements within the government, although documentation of the latter point is scanty.[20] Of interest here, however, is not the existence of such sentiments, but the degree to which they may have affected the formulation of war aims against Germany. One outstanding example of the "pro-German" school is, of course, Count Witte, and there can be no question but that he looked upon the war as an enormous mistake. Further territorial expansion he considered to be not only absurd but actually dangerous to the Empire. Annexation of East Prussia, he told Paléologue, would simply bring in more German subjects, of whom the Emperor had too many already.[21] Witte, however, was not a member of the government, and the very vehemence of his remarks on proposed Russian aims indicates that he was probably in no position to influence the decisions taken. Stürmer, who became Chairman of the Council of Ministers in February, 1916, and replaced Sazonov as Foreign Minister in July of that year, was associated with the clique surrounding the Empress and was generally regarded as pro-German at the time. Still, there is no indication that his alleged sympathies with the enemy had any appreciable effect on Russia's war aims against that country. Other men in high governmental circles might also be mentioned in this connection, but if their Germanophile inclinations affected the war aims drawn up, the influence is not apparent from the material examined. This is not to say that such influence did not exist, but simply that it was not great enough to be obvious.

[20] Western writers are generally agreed on the existence of such elements. The Soviet historian Semennikov goes further, ascribing pro-German feelings to the Romanovs as a group and stating that, although they were bought off temporarily by the Allied promise of Constantinople, they worked consciously for a separate peace with Germany. Semennikov's evidence, however, by no means supports his statements and assumptions. See Semennikov, *Politika Romanovykh nakanune revoliutsii (ot Antanty k Germanii)* (Moscow, 1926).

[21] Witte also opposed annexation of Galicia and observed that no sensible man really cared about the Balkan peoples, who were only "Turks christened by the wrong name." He regarded annexation of the Straits and Constantinople as utter madness. Paléologue, I, 122-23.

On the other hand, certain members of the Council are on record as viewing the overall question of war aims in a way which diverged somewhat from the official formulation. Their opinions are clearly set forth in a memorandum which they submitted to the Emperor in November, 1914. During that month the Council of Ministers had met on five separate occasions to review the problem of Polish autonomy and to draw up recommendations on the subject, but so acute were the differences of opinion that three members of the group— Shcheglovitov, Maklakov and Taube[22]—rejected the findings of the majority and submitted their own recommendations concurrently. The majority statement, described elsewhere in this volume,[23] is of little interest in this connection, since, having admitted the necessity of Poland's unification, it concerned itself with her future organization. The minority memorandum, on the other hand, embraces a far wider field of interest, treating as it does the question of war aims as a whole. It was drawn up, at least in part, in order to prove that the reunification of Poland should not be a primary war aim for Russia, but in placing the Polish question in what they regarded as its proper perspective, the authors of the document presented a forceful expression of their views on varied aspects of the Russian national interest.

The memorandum is of interest not only because it relates to Russia's war aims against Germany but also because it appears to be the only available document which weighs the relative importance of war aims and establishes a priority of goals. Drafted, evidently, on the initiative of Shcheglovitov,[24] it represents the views of men regarded—with the possible

---

[22] Shcheglovitov was Minister of Justice, serving until July, 1915, Maklakov served as Minister of the Interior until June, 1915. Taube was acting in place of Kasso, Minister of Education, who was ill at this time and died soon afterwards.

[23] See Alexander Dallin, "The Future of Poland," pp. 12-15, this volume.

[24] M. de Taube, *La politique russe d'avant-guerre et la fin de l'empire des tsars, 1904-1917* (Paris, 1928), pp. 397-98.

exception of Taube—as profound reactionaries.[25] But their ideas, "reactionary" as they may have been in regard to Poland and various domestic issues, went further in certain respects than the official line in the matter of weakening and dismembering Germany. This point is not without significance, for it is sometimes assumed that "reactionary," "anti-Polish" and "pro-German" must invariably be taken as synonomous terms when describing public figures in Russia during this period.

There were, in the opinion of the minority, three general aims toward which Russia should strive. These were, in order of importance:

(1) The possible strengthening of Russia herself, in an ethnic, economic and strategic way.

(2) The possible weakening of Germanism as the chief enemy of Slavdom and Russia at the present time.

(3) The possible liberation of other Slavic peoples from the authority of Germany and Austria-Hungary (insofar as such liberation does not conflict with the direct interests of Russia).[26]

These general aims, it was recommended, should be realized through the accomplishment of corresponding "concrete tasks," which were to be placed in the following order of importance:

(1) Completion of the historic task of uniting all sections of the Russian people by reuniting eastern Galicia, northern Bukovina and Carpathian Rus' with Russia.

(2) Realization of the historic tasks of Russia in the Black Sea by the annexation of Tsar'grad [Constantinople] and the Turkish Straits.

(3) Rectification of the borders of the Russian state at the expense of East Prussia and also in Asiatic Turkey.

(4) The weakening of Germany internally in every possible way by means of her complete territorial reconstruction on a new basis, with a possible decrease in Prussian territory to the advantage of France, Belgium, Luxemburg, Denmark and

[25] Maklakov and Shcheglovitov may certainly be so described. Taube, who was a respected international lawyer and one-time legal adviser to Izvol'skii, does not fall so clearly into this category. He himself describes Shcheglovitov as "une intelligence hors ligne, quoique, hélas! profondément réactionnaire." *Ibid.*, p. 398.

[26] *Russko-pol'skie otnosheniia v period mirovoi voiny* (Moscow, 1926), p. 20; hereafter cited as RPO.

the smaller German states as well, and, perhaps, the restoration
of the Kingdom of Hanover, Hesse-Nassau, etc.

(5) Unification and liberation of Poland within as wide boundaries as possible, but, in any case, within limits which are ethnographic rather than historic (which would be contrary to the
basic interest and entire history of Russia).

(6) Liberation of the remaining Austrian Slavs.[27]

Territorial gains at the expense of East Prussia, therefore'
stood third in order of importance, while the internal weakening of Germany followed next. The unification of Poland
was clearly not regarded here as a measure by which German
power might be curbed. In fact the authors of this document
argued from the contrary view—Poles living under German
rule might prove useful to Russian national interests. "Leaving
within German borders a Slavic element which is hostile to
Germany and hates her," they suggested, "would plainly serve
more to weaken her internally than to strengthen her."[28]

Shcheglovitov, Maklakov and Taube partially succeeded in
achieving one of their ultimate desires—preventing a liberal
solution of the Polish question—but there is no evidence that
their suggestions had any great influence upon the formulation of Russia's war aims.[29] Many others no doubt agreed with
them that some of Russia's aims were more significant than
others, and Russia's "historic mission" in the Black Sea certainly carried greater popular appeal than the future reorganization of Germany. But it is impossible to tell whether the
government itself ever decided on any definite priority, and
the reunification of Poland remained an important, and explicit goal until the end.[30] In any case, Russia soon turned

---

[27] *Ibid.*, pp. 20-21.

[28] *Ibid.*, pp. 21-22.

[29] Taube maintains that the minority report was "not without result,"
since Sazonov soon secured Allied agreement for Russian possession of
Constantinople and the Straits. He admits, however, that this is only
a hypothesis on his part, and, of course, the three authors of this report
were hardly unique in suggesting this particular war aim. See Taube, p. 398.

[30] A different view of the minority report is held by the historian Komarnicki, who believes that the report "presented much more truly the
Russian views on the postwar settlement." Titus Komarnicki, *The Re-*

her attention to more specific agreements with her allies, and the consideration of overall war aims ceased to be of major diplomatic concern.

Thus, the end of 1914 provides a convenient dividing line in analyzing Russia's aims against Germany, nearly all of which, were conceived in this early period of war. Briefly summarized, they were as follows: Russia herself was to annex East Prussia, possibly, though not certainly, to the Vistula; Poland would receive, in addition to western Galicia, Poznań and perhaps part of Silesia. France would receive Alsace-Lorraine, and part of the Rhineland if she wished; Belgium would be given an undefined increase in territory; Britain, France and Japan would divide the German colonies. Germany herself would be reconstituted, through cession of Schleswig and at least part of Holstein to Denmark, and through the restoration of Hanover, and she would be forced to pay a war indemnity. These terms would be dictated to a prostrate Germany after her armies had been defeated, and by these means Prussian militarism would be destroyed and the threat of German imperialism eliminated.

These vague and hastily conceived plans for postwar Germany warrant a few observations. In the first place, Russia's expected acquisitions from Germany were rather moderate, particularly when compared with some of her other proposed annexations. Witte's warning about the absorption of large numbers of Germans into the Russian Empire had considerable merit, and no doubt the problem was equally apparent to members of the government. As for concessions to the Allies, Russia exhibited great generosity in her grants of German territory, and one can only assume that she simply offered them whatever she thought they might want. Later on she was to use some of these concessions as a bargaining point with France, but at this time she offered the Rhineland without strings attached.

birth of the Polish Republic: A Study in the Diplomatic History of Europe, 1914-1920 (London, 1957), p. 39

Secondly, Russia's limited territorial demands from Germany
seem to have been regarded primarily as a just reward for the
war effort, "historical tasks" notwithstanding. One does not
get the impression that security was an important motivation
at this time in the anticipated small territorial acquisition in
East Prussia. A united Poland, with her proposed increase
in territory, might have been expected to serve as a buffer
against Germany, and by 1916, it is true, the Emperor was
telling Sir George Buchanan that he had always looked upon
Poland this way.[31] But in this early period the security value of
a united Poland was not stressed. Later, when postwar prospects of a weakened Germany seemed less bright, Poland's
strategic significance became a subject of closer attention.

Thirdly, as one historian has pointedly observed,[32] one may
indeed wonder whether the reconstitution of Germany along
the lines indicated would have produced the result which the
Russians professed to seek. That this in itself would have
prevented a resurgence of "Prussian militarism" is unlikely;
that the Russians gave long or serious thought to this aspect
of the question is still more so.

It is possible also that the Russians at this time contemplated
one other means by which the threat from Germany could
be lessened. Sazonov, in his memoirs, has argued that the
only way to weaken Germany permanently was to deprive
her of her auxiliary forces in southeastern Europe. This meant,
first of all, Austria-Hungary, and, secondarily, Turkey and
Bulgaria. "The surest way to deal a serious blow to Germany,"
he asserted, "and to safeguard the Entente from the danger
of her dominating the world was to destroy the tottering
structure of the Habsburg Monarchy, which even in its decline remained a hotbed of European unrest."[33] There is, of
course, little question but that Austria-Hungary, through her
activities in the Balkans and by virtue of her close ties to

---

[31] George Buchanan, *My Mission to Russia and Other Diplomatic
Memories* (London, 1923), II, 26.

[32] Smith, pp. 49-50.

[33] Sergei Sazonov, *Fateful Years, 1909-1916* (London, 1928), p. 226.

Germany, had presented a real threat to the peace of Europe, although the history of postwar Europe throws considerable doubt upon the thesis that the destruction of the Dual Monarchy would guarantee the permanent weakening of Germany. But the question which arises is whether this argument, if explicitly advanced, was actually an important factor in Russian thinking at this time.

It is true that the Russian government evaded the question of a separate peace with Austria-Hungary when sounded out on this matter by Britain and France in December, 1914, and January, 1915, and Sazonov remained emphatic in demanding the dismemberment of the Austro-Hungarian Empire.[34] It is by no means clear, however, that in this insistence the Russians were primarily motivated by thoughts of the future weakening of Germany. Sazonov's memoirs, one must remember, were written some years after the event.

Finally, it is evident that, while the plans for Germany's reorganization might not have achieved the desired end, the proposed territorial annexations, when taken together, constituted a rather far-reaching scheme. War aims such as these could be achieved only through Germany's total defeat, a fact which Sazonov himself recognized. A negotiated peace, which Russia feared at this time, was in fact out of the question so long as these war aims were adhered to. It was not, as Paléologue put it, "the kind of war that ends with a political treaty after a battle of Solferino or Sadowa. It is a war to the death in which each group of belligerents stakes its very existence."[35]

2

After 1914 Russia made no significant efforts to define her overall war aims against Germany or to encourage a general

[34] France and Britain were from the start more sympathetic to Austria-Hungary than was Russia. They were unwilling to push the matter of a separate peace, however, in the face of Russian opposition. See Smith, pp. 120-24; and MOEI, VI, Part 2, 160. Izvol'skii strongly advocated dismembering Austria-Hungary. See, for example, his despatch of October 13, 1914, cited in F. Stieve, *Isvolsky and the World War* (New York, 1926), p. 248.
[35] Paléologue, I, 96.

Allied agreement on this question. A number of specific agreements were concluded in 1915 and 1916 for the settlement of
particular political or territorial questions. The Allies signed
treaties with Italy and Rumania, and, through concessions
required to entice these two nations into the war, Russia
made further commitments for the dismemberment of the
Austro-Hungarian Empire. In March and April of 1915, Russia
secured formal British and French agreement to Russian annexation of the Straits and Constantinople, and in the following year
she joined her two allies in staking out claims in Asia Minor.

From the time of the German offensive in the spring of 1915
Russia's military position deteriorated considerably, and under
such conditions the future reconstitution of Germany ceased
to be a matter of diplomatic discussion with her allies. In
1916, as will be shown, certain unofficial thoughts were directed
toward this question, but there is no evidence that the Foreign
Ministry displayed any real interest in the matter after 1914.
Indeed, Prince Kudashev, a prominent official in the Ministry
and Sazonov's chief representative at Army headquarters, was
writing to Sazonov in October, 1915, that all aims must be
subordinated to the single need of winning the war. Initially,
he said, the war had seemed to provide a favorable opportunity
for accomplishing certain political tasks, but aims themselves
necessarily depended upon the course of military events and
might have to be modified in relation to a changing situation.[36]
While Sazonov, at his post in the Foreign Ministry, may have
been somewhat less influenced by the immediate military situation, there is ample reason to believe he, too, no longer
concerned himself with vague plans for a future Germany.
Ostensibly, the destruction of "Prussian militarism" remained
a primary war aim, but, if there were hopes that Germany's
power and influence would be severely limited in the postwar
world, these hopes were not expressed in the diplomatic correspondence of the period.

[36] MOEI, IX, 13. Kudashev was also strongly opposed to Russian
acquisition of Constantinople and the Straits. See Florinsky, II, 1348-49.

On the contrary, it appears that, as the war dragged on,
the men in the Foreign Ministry gradually came around to
the view that Germany's position after the war might be
considerably stronger than they had once supposed and that
Russia's national interest should therefore be protected as
best they could against what now may have seemed to be a
long-range threat. One cannot assume that those responsible
for Russian foreign policy were especially farsighted or that,
caught up in the day-to-day problems of the war, they succeeded in forming a clear picture of the overall situation and
proceeded to take the rational measures which logic now tells us
the situation must have demanded. The historian often fails
to realize that there are times when men simply cannot see
things in perspective and that statemen frequently fall victim,
in thought as well as action, to their own slogans and earlier
misconceptions. It would probably be wrong, then, to suppose
that the period after 1914 produced any sharp turning point
or reappraisal of Russian war aims against Germany. Such
does not seem to have been the case. But apparently the
Foreign Ministry did begin to see the future in a somewhat
different light and, at least in certain instances, shifted its
diplomacy accordingly.

In his memoirs Sazonov, arguing of course with the benefit
of hindsight, has stated that, despite Allied agreement from
the autumn of 1914 on the necessity of rendering postwar
Germany "powerless to do mischief," it was clear that, in
view of her resources, population and geographical position,
even in defeat she could not but remain a great power.[37] This
sounds rather different from the easy optimism of the "Twelve
Points" and the ruminations of Emperor Nicholas in November, 1914, but it is a fairly accurate reflection of Sazonov's
views of 1916. Insofar as this new "realism" translated itself
into diplomatic action, Sazonov sought to provide for Russia's
security against Germany in two broad ways: security on the
western borders through settlement of the Polish question,

[37] Sazonov, pp. 223-26.

and strengthening Russia's position in the Far East through exclusion of Germany from that area.

In respect to the difficult problems presented by Poland, Sazonov, operating under considerable pressure, was compelled to pursue a dual policy, on the one hand, of preventing the matter from becoming a subject of international discussion and, on the other, of endeavoring to secure a relatively liberal solution of the problem. Both aspects of this policy are related to the question of war aims against Germany.

Sazonov's success in preventing foreign interference depended in part upon the forbearance of the British and French governments. But by March of 1916 indications were that their tolerance was wearing thin, and it seemed probable that the question of Poland might be raised at the high-level diplomatic conference scheduled to meet that month in Paris. Determined to forestall international discussion of the question, Sazonov now set forth the Russian position in terms rather more sweeping than those used in 1914. "In general," he instructed Izvol'skii on March 8, "it is necessary to remember that we are prepared to give France and England full freedom in determining the western borders of Germany, expecting that the Allies in their turn will give us equal freedom in the determination of our borders with Germany and Austria." In particular, he added, "we must insist on the exclusion of the Polish question from the subjects of international discussion."[38]

This statement, the contents of which Izvol'skii in turn communicated to Foreign Minister Briand,[39] thus foreshadowed the Russo-French Agreement of February-March, 1917. By this agreement France promised Russia full freedom in determining her western borders in return for a Russian promise that France might have equal freedom on the Franco-German frontier—a freedom in which she expected not only to acquire Alsace-Lorraine and the Saar but also to set up an "autono-

[38] MOEI, X, 351. For a fuller discussion of Russian apprehensions and efforts to prevent "internationalization" of the Polish question at this time, see Dallin, pp. 35-43.
[39] MOEI, X, 411.

mous" state on the left bank of the Rhine.[40] Sazonov's words of March, 1916, were, in fact, quoted in 1917 by the new Foreign Minister, Pokrovskii, as a basis for Russia's claim.[41] Doumergue, who initiated the negotiations for France, referred on his part to generous offers made to France by Emperor Nicholas in conversations with Paléologue on earlier occasions.[42] By the time of the 1917 negotiations, however, Russia had discarded her easy generosity of earlier days, and the French, who had expected merely tò receive Russian acknowledgement of their rights, were compelled to give something in return. While the agreement of 1917 is generally regarded as a bargain struck between the two powers, it actually implied no real concession on Russia's part. Russia had no particular interest in Germany's western borders, and, as the "Twelve Points" had revealed, she had originally been quite prepared to offer her western allies what she had thought they might want.[43] For France, however, the agreement meant at least a degree of concession, for in turning over the fate of Germany's eastern border to Russia she repudiated a long history of French interest in Poland.[44]

As a war aim for Russia, the demand for complete freedom in determining her frontiers with Germany may, taken out of context, be regarded as a radical revision of Russian war aims

[40] The agreement was concluded through an exchange of notes, February 14 and March 12, 1917. Notes and correspondence on this subject are printed in *Konstantinopl' i prolivy*, I, 449-62. The agreement is covered in some detail in Smith, pp. 459-66, and interpreted in larger context in A. J. P. Taylor, *The Struggle for Mastery in Europe, 1848-1918* (Oxford, 1954), pp. 556-57.

[41] *Konstantinopl' i prolivy*, I, 452.

[42] The conversations of the Tsar and Paléologue on the subject occurred on November 21, 1914, March 3, 1915, and March 13, 1916. See *ibid.*, p. 451; and Paléologue, I, 192, 194 and 297; II, 205-6; and III, 178 and 183.

[43] In 1917 the French argued that their agreement of 1915 to Russian acquisition of the Straits and Constantinople should be sufficient compensation, but were informed by Izvol'skii that Russia had paid for this already by agreeing to French claims in Asiatic Turkey. *Konstantinopl' i prolivy*, I, 453-54.

[44] The British were not informed of this agreement and apparently learned of it only when the Bolsheviks published the secret treaties. Smith, p. 459.

against Germany, a demand that Russia should be permitted
to take whatever portion of German territory she thought
fit in order to guarantee her security on the western frontier.
And certainly this right of full freedom was explicit in the
agreement finally concluded. Whether or not Russia would
have so interpreted the agreement had she emerged victorious
from the war it is impossible to say, but it is evident that this
was not Sazonov's intention when he first announced his position. There is nothing to indicate that Russia at that time,
or in March, 1917, had any designs on German territory other
than East Prussia and the German portion of Poland. The
overriding concern of Sazonov—and of the foreign ministers
who followed him—was that the Polish question be decided
by Russia alone. In this they temporarily succeeded.[45]

The second side of the Polish question bearing upon Russia's
war aims toward Germany, or, more precisely, her evaluation
of Germany's position in the postwar world, was the need to
decide in advance the future political organization of Poland.
Sazonov favored autonomy, though not complete independence,
for Poland, both as a matter of right and common sense; and
out of tactical considerations—both to forestall Allied intervention and to nullify any attempt by Germany to settle
the Polish question to her own benefit[46] (the Austro-German
proclamation on Poland in November, 1916 showed that this
apprehension had been fully justified)—he pressed for speedy
solution of this problem. In addition, by April, 1916, Sazonov
had begun to view the Polish problem as a factor in Russia's
long-term security against Germany. In a memorandum to
the Emperor dated April 30, 1916, he stated:

> For many decades we must be prepared to look upon Germany
> as our constant political enemy. The Polish problem, which
> formerly served as a guarantee of peace with her, will become
> both a weapon and a subject of Russo-German struggle. . . .
> A Russo-German demarcation on Polish soil is not simply a
> matter of drawing a strategically advantageous or topographi-

45 See Dallin, especially pp. 21-27.
46 RPO, p. 85.

cally convenient boundary line; it is rather a complicated political problem. . . .

I do not foresee any obstacles to an agreement with the Allies
on questions of a Russo-German boundary demarcation, but
I think we would create conditions favorable for resolving
[any possible difficulties] by convincing the Allies that we shall
draw our boundary with the German states correctly in the
political sense, that we shall create in Poland a line on which
Europe can be successfully defended from any new attempts
by Germany to establish her political hegemony.[47]

For Sazonov, therefore, the Polish question had acquired a
new dimension, and its resolution had become still more imperative. Assuming now that Germany would continue to be
a threat to Russia in the postwar world, he was convinced
that a united Poland, owing allegiance to the Russian tsar
but enjoying some degree of autonomy, would provide Russia
with a certain amount of security, and Germany would be
unable to utilize Polish nationalism as a political weapon
against her. The Foreign Minister's outlook was apparently
shared by the Emperor, who told Sir George Buchanan some
months later that he had always hoped "to create a united
Poland, under Russia's protection, as a buffer state between
Germany and Russia."[48]

Sazonov's thinking in this year provides an interesting contrast to the opinion expressed by Shcheglovitov, Maklakov and
Taube in November, 1914. Both views counted upon the
Polish people as an element in Russia's security against Germany, but the one depended upon Polish unification, and
the other on continued partition. The reactionary thesis, of
course, was never accepted; Sazonov's efforts, in the end,
proved of little practical value.

While Sazonov worried about Russia's western borders, he
also sought through diplomatic means to improve her position
in the Far East vis-à-vis that of Germany, and, if possible,
to ensure Germany's permanent exclusion from that part of

[47] *Ibid.*, p. 87.
[48] Buchanan, II, 26.

the world. Since he now assumed that after the war Germany was likely to remain a strong power, it was in Russia's interest to limit the extension of German influence in areas where such limitation was possible. In the Far East the war presented a favorable opportunity. Here, too, there were several factors in addition to fear of postwar Germany which entered into the calculations of the Foreign Ministry. Properly speaking, of course, Russian aspirations in this area were not "war aims," in the sense of rewards to be demanded upon surrender of the enemy, but were rather advantages to be seized during the course of the war itself. Nevertheless, the ultimate purpose was the same—the weakening of Germany's world position and the corresponding strengthening of Russia's.

Russian aims in the Far East with regard to Germany to some extent coincided with those of Britain and France, these aims having both an immediate and a long-term significance. It was generally agreed among the Allies that Germany's economic position in China should be weakened, if not eliminated, both as an aid to the war effort and as a means of preventing Germany from reasserting her interests in China after the war. Allied diplomatic activity toward this end included discussion of possible economic cooperation after the war in various parts of the world, including the Far East,[49] suggestions for the expulsion of German and Austrian citizens from China and proposals that China enter the war on the Allied side or, at the least, break off relations with Germany and Austria.

Important decisions involving China, however, required the agreement of the Japanese, who, after the acceptance of most of their "Twenty-One Demands" by China in May, 1915, exercised a steadily growing influence in that country,[50] and Sazonov's attempt in November, 1915, to induce a rupture between China and the Central Powers therefore ended in failure. Japan, intent at that time on preventing China from

---

[49] This could not amount to much in view of British unwillingness to make definite economic commitments for the postwar period. See MOEI, X, 52-53, 84, 374 and 596.

[50] *Ibid.*, pp. 571-74.

having a voice at the peace conference, rejected his proposals,[51] and it was not until much later, in August, 1917, that China was able to enter the war on the Allied side.

Sazonov was more successful in his efforts to expel Germany from the Five-Power Consortium which had been set up in China before the war. Britain in this instance was initially reluctant to proceed until the whole question of expelling German citizens from China had been settled, but Grey eventually came around to accepting Sazonov's view of the matter, and it was decided that a new Consortium would be formed, without the participation of Germany.[52]

In addition to such joint Allied endeavors, Russia moved separately to secure her own postwar position in the Far East at the expense of Germany. One means of achieving this aim was an agreement with Japan. Moreover, a Russo-Japanese treaty, it was believed, would provide additional insurance that Japan would not conclude a separate peace with Germany, something which the Russians had feared since the early days of the war.[53] For this reason, and with the hope that an alliance might increase the flow of war supplies from Japan to relieve Russia's acute shortage[54]—perhaps also with the hope that Japan might be persuaded to take a more active part in the war—Sazonov made various efforts to draw Japan more closely into the Entente, but by October, 1915, he had succeeded only to the extent of securing Japan's adherence to the London Declaration.[55]

Meanwhile Sazonov had begun to show an increasing interest in Russia's long-range security in the Far East. As he told

[51] Peter Berton, "The Secret Russo-Japanese Alliance of 1916," doctoral dissertation, Columbia University, 1956, pp. 108-10. Berton had an opportunity to study both the Russian and the Japanese documents covering this whole subject, and has discussed in detail the negotiations leading up to the treaty.

[52] MOEI, X, 85, 169, 189 and 610.

[53] Japan also feared that Russia would make a separate peace with Germany and that this in turn would lead to Russo-German cooperation against Japan. Berton, p. 256.

[54] Ibid., pp. 93-94, 255-56.

[55] Ibid., p. 104; and MOEI, VIII, Part 2, 351.

Goremykin in March, 1915, Russia would be obliged to concentrate her attention and her forces in the West for years
to come, and it was therefore wise to seek peace and friendship
in the Far East.[56] In the summer and fall of 1915 Sazonov
continued to think along these lines, stimulated perhaps by
Russian military defeats at the hands of the Germans, though
he did not at this time suggest a Russo-Japanese alliance.[57]
But in December, 1915, the goodwill tour of Japan by the
Emperor's uncle, the Grand Duke Georgii Mikhailovich, presented an opportunity for sounding out the Japanese on the
prospects for an agreement, and in February, 1916, Japan
finally agreed to enter into negotiations.[58]

The details of the agreement, which was concluded in July,
1916, need not concern us here.[59] What is of interest in this
context is the emphasis which Sazonov and the Foreign Ministry now placed upon the future threat of Germany and
their efforts to protect Russia against it. Such concern is
evident in much of the diplomatic correspondence of early 1916.

One of the men accompanying the Grand Duke in his mission to Japan was Kozakov, head of the Far Eastern Department of the Foreign Ministry, who was traveling under instructions from Sazonov to acquaint various influential figures
in Japan with Russia's views on future Russo-Japanese relations. The following excerpt from one of his conversations
in Japan serves as a good example of Russian thinking at
this time:

However the present war may end, Europe will long be divided
into two camps: in one will be the German states, in the other
the great powers of Europe. We would like to see Japan in

[56] Berton, p. 92. He expressed similar views to Buchanan in September.
MOEI, VIII, Part 2, 343.
[57] Berton, pp. 96, 105.
[58] Ibid., p. 255; and "Dnevnik Ministerstva Inostrannykh Del za 1915-
1916 gg.," Krasnyi Arkhiv (Moscow), XXXII (1929), 9-10.
[59] Complications were introduced by the question of increased arms
deliveries to Russia and Japan's desire to acquire from Russia a sector of
the Chinese Eastern Railway in Southern Manchuria, and the negotiations
offer a splendid example of diplomatic bargaining in its most delicate
form. See MOEI, X, 206, 259-61, 271, 397, 555 and 567.

our camp, and we think that this is advantageous for her because Germany is also a danger to Japan in China.[60]

And in February, 1916, in an *aide-mémoire* to the Japanese ambassador, Motono, Sazonov stated, speaking of the danger of German activity in China:

It is with the aim of combating this danger that the Russian government seeks to unite its efforts with those of Japan. . . . The present moment, when Germany is isolated in Europe and deprived of all communication with the Far East, appears to be particularly favorable for dealing her a blow on Chinese territory which will prevent her from making the latter a base of intrigue during the war and from establishing her influence there after the peace.[61]

These and other statements of a similar nature[62] leave no doubt that Russia clearly envisaged a postwar threat from Germany and saw an agreement with Japan as one means of counteracting it. The public convention signed in Petrograd on July 3, 1916, bound the two countries not to enter into political combinations against each other and to confer on measures to be taken if any of their territorial rights in the Far East should be threatened. The attached secret agreement, however, designed to prevent China from falling under the domination of a "third power," was clearly directed against Germany,[63] and provided for mutual armed assistance by the signatories in the event of war.[64] Thus, in theory at least, Russia protected her immediate and postwar interests against Germany in the Far East and the same time freed herself

[60] *Ibid.*, p. 259.

[61] *Ibid.*, p. 270.

[62] *Ibid.*, p. 206, 243 and 290.

[63] The Bolsheviks, when they published this treaty, claimed that it was directed against Britain and the United States. This is false. Not only was Britain kept informed of the negotiations, but the text itself (Art. II), upon Russian insistence, prevented the signatories from taking armed action as contemplated unless they received assistance in turn from their allies. This made armed action against Britain impossible and action against the United States highly improbable, to say the least. See Berton, p. 216, as well as the treaty text.

[64] The text of both the public and secret agreements is printed in J. V. A. MacMurray, *Treaties and Agreements with and concerning China 1894-1919* (Washington, 1929), II, 1327-28.

to concentrate her attention upon the primary source of danger on the western frontier.

At a time when official Russian policy was directed toward securing specific advantages or safeguards such as those mentioned above, one prominent individual, the Grand Duke Nikolai Mikhailovich, focused his attention on the larger question of the peace. The planning which he initiated and carried on, evidently with the Tsar's permission,[65] lay outside the main stream of foreign policy formation and seems to have had little, if any, impact upon the activities of the Foreign Ministry. His thoughts, nevertheless, have a certain historical interest and deserve brief mention in this context.

The Grand Duke, who saw himself as a leading Russian delegate at the future peace conference, developed his ideas in a series of letters which he wrote to the Emperor during the period from May through October, 1916.[66] Fearing that Russia might arrive at the conference table unprepared to defend her interests,[67] both against her enemies and her present allies, he suggested that, whether the war ended in Allied victory or in stalemate, she should be in a position to define her demands when the moment came. Although he made no definite proposals regarding priority of aims, he recommended that all Russian war aims, in their totality, be given careful advance study.[68]

---

[65] Taube (p. 406) regards this as one of several "vague gestures" made at this time by the Tsar, who, he believes, was dreaming of a general peace or at least a peace concluded by Russia with the consent of her allies. However, he offers no evidence for this view.

[66] It is possible that his letters continued after October, but none of subsequent date have been published, and Semennikov mentions no further correspondence in his editorial commentary; see Semennikov, ed., *Nikolai II i velikie kniaz'ia*, pp. 17 ff. Selected portions of the letters are conveniently translated in Frank A. Golder, ed., *Documents of Russian History, 1914-1917* (New York, 1927), pp. 63-77.

[67] Semennikov describes the Grand Duke as being motivated solely by thoughts of his role at the peace conference. Semennikov, ed., *Nikolai II i velikie kniaz'ia*, p. 18. However, a more charitable—and more likely —assumption is that he was also genuinely concerned about the question itself.

[68] *Ibid.*, pp. 63-65.

Interestingly enough, the Grand Duke inclined to the dismemberment of Germany rather than of Austria-Hungary, arguing that the existence of a weak, multiracial empire in the center of Europe would be more to Russia's interest than the existence of a powerful Germany. And, though admitting that Austria's dismemberment would be justified as punishment for her past behavior, he preferred to see some German territory from Bavaria and the Saxon part of Silesia transferred to Austria, and certain other portions of German territory distributed to France, Denmark, Belgium, Holland and Poland.[69] Such changes, he realized, depended upon total victory on the part of the Allies. He did not, however, exclude the possibility that this might not occur, apparently believing that Russia should be prepared to settle for something less if necessary. Reverting, in effect, to Sazonov's policy of 1914, the Grand Duke also suggested that a general war aims agreement be drawn up with the Allies.[70]

As has already been indicated, no agreement of this sort was ever made, nor did the Grand Duke's well-intended efforts lead to practical results in any other respect. In October, 1916, he was still discussing the possibility of a preliminary study commission,[71] and his remarks throughout the period of correspondence provide strong evidence that the Foreign Ministry was paying no great attention either to him or to his ideas. Continuing on the general course followed by Sazonov since early 1915, the Ministry—insofar as it did anything about war aims at all—pursued the path of special agreements. Sazonov's dismissal, which occurred soon after the signing of the Russo-Japanese Treaty in July, 1916, shook the confidence of the Allies in Russia's good intentions,[72] but produced no

[69] He suggested that Schleswig-Holstein go to Denmark, Alsace-Lorraine to France, Luxemburg to Belgium, part of the mouth of the Rhine to Holand and Poznań to Poland. *Ibid.*, pp. 76-77, 85-86.

[70] *Ibid.*, p. 77.

[71] *Ibid.*, pp. 88-92.

[72] See Paléologue, II, 305-6; Buchanan, II, 18-19; and communications from Benckendorff, in Semennikov, ed., *Monarkhiia pered krusheniem, 1914-1917: Bumagi Nikolaia II i drugie dokumenty* (Moscow, 1927), pp. 14-17.

striking change in Russia's foreign policy. Although documentary material is rather scanty for this later period of tsarist Russia's diplomacy, one may assume with some reason that Sazonov's two successors, both lacking in experience in foreign affairs and enjoying only a brief stay in office amid conditions of increasing governmental chaos, had neither the time, the wisdom nor the inclination to think deeply about the general question of war aims against Germany.

The incompetent Stürmer, for all his pro-German reputation, held to the general line already laid down, and emphasized Russia's determination to fight through to final victory.[73] The famous Stockholm conversations between Protopopov and Warburg had taken place early in the summer of 1916, and in the fall of that year rumors of secret Russo-German peace negotiations abounded. But there is no evidence that such negotiations actually took place, nor is there any conclusive proof that Stürmer was actively associated with such endeavors.[74] On the other hand, one of Stürmer's chief concerns during his four-month tenure in office was to secure Allied agreement to a public announcement of Russia's aim—and of Allied permission—to acquire the Straits and Constantinople after the war, a declaration which he and others felt would raise public morale and make any announcement of future Polish autonomy more palatable.[75] There is no reason to

[73] Semennikov, ed., *Monarkhiia pered krusheniem*, p. 17; and Paléologue, III, 308.

[74] Semennikov, *Politika Romanovykh*, pp. 52, 56. Paléologue was unable to uncover any real evidence of "treachery." Paléologue, III, 48. Buchanan felt that Stürmer was simply too clever to advocate a separate peace, since he knew the Emperor would never approve it. Buchanan, II, 19. Baron Rosen, who regarded the war as a calamity, said he knew of no evidence that Stürmer carried on separate peace negotiations. On the contrary, he criticized Stürmer for not having raised with the Allies "the question of the earliest possible conclusion of a *general* peace," a course which he, Rosen, had personally urged upon him. Roman Rosen, *Forty Years of Diplomacy* (New York, 1922), II, 206.

[75] Semennikov, ed., *Monarkhiia pered krusheniem*, pp. 147-48, 297; *Konstantinopl' i prolivy*, I, 416-21, 423-27. Stürmer later began to hesitate because of the adverse military situation in Rumania, and the announcement was finally made by Trepov in a speech in the Duma in December; see the discussion in Smith, pp. 438-42, 444-49.

think, however, that he made any attempt to reformulate Russia's war aims against Germany; in fact, it seems reasonable to accept Paléologue's opinion that Stürmer appeared to have only the vaguest notions on that subject.[76]

There was some indication in November that the Emperor who never flagged in his determination for victory over Germany, was losing faith in Russia's ability to acquire German-held territory for Poland. Discussing this matter with Buchanan, he told the Ambassador that he no longer hoped to include Poznań in a united Poland, since a Russian advance into Germany (which he apparently believed necessary to achieve this aim) would result in too heavy Russian losses.[77] If, however, he had indeed lost his determination to take from Germany her Polish lands, he recovered it in the following month. His Order of the Day to the Russian army on December 25, 1916, announced Russia's intention of continuing the war until the aims of uniting Poland (including German Poland) and securing the Straits and Constantinople had been achieved.[78] The message was apparently drafted by Pokrovskii, who had now succeeded Stürmer as foreign minister.[79]

The Emperor's declaration was intended as a public answer to the recently received German peace proposals, which were followed almost immediately by President Wilson's request to all belligerents to state their war aims.[80] In answer to the latter communication, the Entente powers prepared a joint statement, which they presented on January 10, 1917. Having already rejected the German proposals, the Allies had no in-

[76] Paléologue, II, 308.

[77] Buchanan, II, 26.

[78] Paléologue, III, 125. For the relevant portion of the text, see Iurii V. Kliuchnikov and Andrei Sabanin, eds., *Mezhdunarodnaia politika noveishego vremeni v dogovorakh, notakh i deklaratsiiakh* (Moscow, 1925-29), II, 60-61.

[79] Paléologue, III, 117. Stürmer was dismissed on November 23, 1916. Pokrovskii became foreign minister on December 13.

[80] The Germans published a note on December 12 expressing their willingness to enter into peace negotiations with the Allies. For the text, see U. S., Department of State, *Papers Relating to the Foreign Relations of the United States, 1916*, Supplement: *The World War* (Washington, 1929), p. 85. For Wilson's request, see *ibid.*, pp. 97-99.

tention of concluding peace except on their own terms, and
their reply was drafted so as to convey this impression without
at the same time antagonizing the American president. Their
efforts resulted in a skillfully worded document, moralistic in
tone, seeming to answer in some detail, yet reserving to the
future or obscuring in vague generalities much that was relevant
to the war aims question. It affords little insight into Russian
intentions toward Germany, except as an indication of Russia's
determination to continue the war and adhere to her public
pronouncements on Poland. The language of the note ("the
restitution of provinces or territories wrested in the past from
the Allies by force or against the will of their populations")
would cover the separation from Germany of Alsace-Lorraine
and Prussian Poland and possibly of other territories. At the
same time, the note specifically denied that the Allies were
planning" the extermination of the German peoples and their
political disappearance."[81] In any case, it was generally recognized that the Allies expected nothing to come of this
exchange.[82] Their attention was focused on the preparations
for the Allied conference scheduled for February in Petrograd;
here France and Russia initiated the discussions which led to
their agreement on Germany's western and eastern borders.

After 1914, then, a change had occurred in Russian war
aims toward Germany as seen through the diplomatic correspondence of the imperial government—a change in emphasis
if not in substance. None of the aims announced in 1914
was explicitly dropped,[83] though Russia made no further efforts to reach a general agreement and concentrated hence-

[81] U. S., Department of State, *Papers Relating to the Foreign Relations
of the United States, 1917*, Supplement I: *The World War* (Washington,
1931), pp. 6-8.
[82] See for instance, Charles Seymour, *American Diplomacy during the
World War* (Baltimore, 1934), pp. 189-91.
[83] Belgium may be regarded as a partial exception. In February, 1916,
Britain, France and Russia presented a joint statement to Belgium guaranteeing her political and economic independence and indicating their
intention of continuing the war until this independence had been achieved.
Many Belgians felt that an increase in territory should also be guaranteed,
but the Allies were apparently unwilling to make such a statement.
MOEI, X, 105, 116, and 203-4.

forth upon concluding specific agreements for securing what she regarded as her own particular national interests. Concerned as she was with the prosecution of the war and with certain political goals which now, in time of war, seemed immediately attainable, she gave correspondingly less attention to the overall question of the peace. Plans for the future reconstitution of Germany evidently ceased to interest the Foreign Ministry and were most certainly not a matter of diplomatic concern.

But, while Russia remained stubbornly committed to the decisive defeat of Germany, Sazonov, and no doubt other members of the Foreign Ministry, recognized that even in defeat Germany was likely to remain a powerful nation and to pose a long-term threat to Russia. The question of security, therefore, took on greater significance, and, to the extent that the problem was understood and that diplomatic opportunities presented themselves, the Russians made efforts to provide for their postwar defense against Germany. That these steps would in fact have brought security is doubtful, and it might well be maintained that the time had come for more, rather than less, attention to the future organization of Germany and the overall questions of the peace. To say this, however, is to argue with a logic not likely to be found in a nation whose very existence is at stake and where visions of ultimate victory are increasingly darkened by signs of impending catastrophe.

3

Imperial Russia's war aims against Germany have been analyzed and enumerated in the foregoing pages and require no summary here. A few very general observations on the nature and overall significance of these aims may, nevertheless, be useful.

Russia's territorial claims for herself against Germany were relatively modest in scope when compared with some of her demands in other areas. The moderation was due not to the

haste with which these claims were drawn up but to the fact that
Russia's primary territorial ambitions lay elsewhere. Outside
of Poland and East Prussia she had no great interest in large
annexations of German territory; and to others she offered
more than she asked for herself.

The realization of her proposals for territorial changes and
for Germany's reconstitution would probably not have contributed greatly to the announced purpose of weakening Germany in the future and preventing the restoration of German
militarism. But, to judge from the evidence, the Russians
never devoted to this aspect of the question the thoughful
consideration which an adequate solution would have required.
Their ideas on the subject, such as they were, had been formulated hurriedly in 1914, and, failing to achieve a general
Allied war aims agreement at that time, they apparently lost
interest in them.

Meanwhile, as the war dragged on and the country labored
under conditions of growing hardship, realism demanded that
the men in the Foreign Ministry look beyond the immediate
situation and take what practical steps they could to advance
or protect Russia's interests for the future. And the future,
as they now saw it, seemed to include a Germany whose power
though perhaps temporarily curbed, could not be eliminated.
Thus, in addition to pursuing her own private advantages
through agreements such as those on the Straits and Asia
Minor, Russia commenced to look to her postwar security
against Germany. The agreement with Japan was concluded
in part for this purpose, and concern about the future drove
Sazonov to intensified efforts for solving the Polish question.

Still, despite the modest extent of Russia's territorial claims
against Germany and the inadequacy of her plans for the
elimination of German militarism, these aims could not be
achieved without decisive German defeat. This was obvious
from the start. In 1914 Russia was adamant in insisting
that peace be dictated to Germany, and throughout the period
covered a negotiated peace was probably out of the question.

In any case, despite undercover efforts on both sides, the imperial government never accepted the idea of a separate peace. Total war, in fact, implied total destruction of the enemy, and therefore in the last analysis it was perhaps not of decisive importance what specific aims against Germany were chosen. If for the Allies as a whole, as has often been said, victory was expected to provide the policy, the statement is equally valid for Russia in particular. This is not to say that she made no effort to define her aims; certainly she did. But considering the nature of the conflict in which she was involved, her aims against Germany were, on the one hand, insufficient for the ends in view and, on the other, meaningless without total victory.

MICHAEL BORO PETROVICH

The Italo-Yugoslav Boundary Question, 1914-1915

With the outbreak of the First World War it was apparent
to South Slavs and Italians alike that fundamental changes
were due that would have a direct bearing on their conflicting
aspirations. Both were intent from the outset on obtaining
the maximum benefits to be derived from these changes.
The prize which both Italy and Serbia claimed was the eastern
Adriatic coast.

Serbia could pay no higher price than the bloody sacrifice
she was already being forced to make in fighting the invading
armies of Austria-Hungary, and then she could offer this price
only to her allies and would-be protectors. Italy could afford
a more profitable game. Though a signatory of the Triple
Alliance, Italy proclaimed her neutrality from the outset and
dangled the promise of her military aid before both the Central
Powers and the Allies. This study is not immediately concerned with the negotiations which took place between Italy
and the Central Powers; however, it must be borne in mind
that knowledge of these negotiations served to goad the Allies
into a quicker and more favorable consideration of Italy's
demands. The ensuing negotiations culminated, after ten
months of double-dealing, in the Treaty of London, which
was signed on April 26, 1915, and in which Britain, France
and Russia sacrificed the aspirations of the Yugoslavs to
the ambitions of Italy.

Though Italian diplomacy held all the belligerents in the vise of their own exigencies, none felt the squeeze more than Russia. On the one hand, Russia was bound by powerful considerations to support Serbia. Serbia had succeeded Bulgaria as Russia's most promising base for enlarging her influence in the Balkans. Besides, there were the then no less compelling emotional bonds of Slavic kinship, Orthodox intercommunion and comradeship-in-arms. On the other hand, Russia's devastating losses on the eastern front forced her to cast about for whatever additional military assistance she could muster. Italian participation on the Allied side promised to relieve Russia of considerable pressure from Austria-Hungary.

It is this dilemma, so evident in the published documents of the Russian Foreign Ministry, that makes a study of Russian diplomacy concerning this particular problem an especially instructive one. It involves the conflict between a long-term national interest coupled with moral considerations and an immediate national interest, based on survival, which had to be pursued in accord with the general war aims of all the Allies acting in concert.

From the outbreak of the Sarajevo crisis, Austria-Hungary and Germany failed to consult Italy, though this strategy violated the terms of the Triple Alliance. Their decision was not effected without a penalty. On July 31, 1914, the very day Germany presented France and Russia with its ultimatum, the cabinet in Rome revenged itself by a decision to proclaim Italy's neutrality. Although the announcement was not made public until August 3, the news was officially allowed to leak out the same day, not without a purpose.[1]

RUSSIAN INITIATIVE

No sooner did the powers of the Triple Entente learn of this decision than they sought to entice Italy into the war as an ally. Subsequent developments were to lend irony to the circumstance that it was initially Russia which demonstrated

---

[1] Antonio Salandra, *Italy and the Great War*, (London [1932]), p. 67.

the most aggressive interest in securing Italy's aid, and at a price it was long to regret. On that first day of August, however, the day on which Germany declared war on an inadequately prepared and militarily isolated Russia, the St. Petersburg Foreign Office thought primarily to divert as many enemy forces as possible from the eastern front. The decision of the cabinet in Rome seemed to present an ideal opportunity.

On the same day that Foreign Minister Sergei Sazonov received the news of Italian neutrality, he received a dispatch from Ambassador Izvol'skii in Paris relaying the alleged opinion of French President Raymond Poincaré that "it would be advisable to undertake to attract Italy. . . ." The attraction suggested was Italy's annexation of Valona (Vlonë) and freedom of action in Albania.[2] Sazonov immediately approved, adding, however, that France should undertake the necessary negotiations, since, as a Mediterranean power, it was naturally more interested than Russia.[3]

Now that Italy had suddenly become the object of unusual solicitude on the part of both the Triple Alliance and the Triple Entente, "sacred egoism"[4] allowed no course but to take full advantage of an extremely profitable situation. Nor was any time lost. Immediately following the official declaration of Italian neutrality, the Italian ambassador to St. Petersburg, the Marchese Carlotti, informed Foreign Minister Sazonov that his country desired "a preponderant position" on the Adriatic Sea, to which end it required the annexation of Valona; it also wished to retrieve the Trentino from Austria.

---

[2] Izvol'skii to Sazonov, August 1, 1914, in *Mezhdunarodnye otnosheniia v epokhu imperializma: Dokumenty iz arkhivov tsarskogo i vremennogo pravitel'stv, 1878-1917 gg.*, Series III (Moscow, 1931-38), Vol. V, Doc. No. 411. The abbreviation MOEI used hereafter refers to this title and series.

[3] Sazonov to Izvol'skii, August 2, 1914, *ibid.*, Doc. No. 453.

[4] The Italian principle of *sacro egoismo* was well defined in Premier Salandra's observation in October, 1914, upon assuming the duties of foreign minister pro tempore: "We must be bold in deeds, not words, without prejudice or preconception, and uninfluenced by any sentiment but that of an exclusive unlimited devotion to our country, a sacred egoism for Italy." Salandra, p. 153.

On the other hand, Italy would not object to certain territorial acquisitions on the Adriatic coast by Serbia and Greece. Since Franco-Italian relations were traditionally not the best, Carlotti finally suggested that Russia act as intermediary in the ensuing negotiations. The Russian foreign minister immediately instructed Izvol'skii in Paris to inform the French government of Russia's approval of these terms and to obtain the opinion of the French government.[5]

The reaction in France appears to have justified Italian fears of French antipathy. President Poincaré felt the Russian proposal to be "inopportune" and "extremely ill-advised," for he saw in the Italian demands a possible threat to French territorial aspirations. An unconditional commitment in favor of these demands, the veteran statesman feared, might in some way mean giving priority to Italian claims before the restitution to France of its own lost provinces.[6] The French government accordingly approved the project only on the condition that any future territorial disposition be effected "without prejudice to the national aspirations of France,"[7] and further emphasized its understanding that Serbia and Greece would obtain territorial satisfaction on the Adriatic coast. Having obtained France's consent—Great Britain was not yet in the war—Russia now felt able to continue negotiations with the Italian government with the greatest possible dispatch.

The Russian government's eagerness to expedite Italy's intervention in the war is not to be explained entirely by immediate military necessity. Torn between the urgent need of obtaining an ally to engage Austria-Hungary and the fear of encouraging an Italian advance into the Slavic East, Russia desired to present the government in Rome with a definite

[5] Sazonov to Izvol'skii, August 4, 1914, in MOEI, Vol. V, Doc. Nos. 521 and 529.

[6] Raymond Poincaré, *Memoirs of Raymond Poincaré* (London, 1926-30), III, 9.

[7] Izvol'skii to Sazonov, August 5, 1914, in *Tsarskaia Rossiia v mirovoi voine* (Leningrad, 1925), p. 236. This title is hereafter abbreviated as TRMV.

proposal from the start. By offering a precisely defined reward and by hurrying Italy to accept, St. Petersburg hoped
to obtain immediate Italian aid at a minimum price. There is
likewise evidence that, until Great Britain became involved in
the war, France also participated in these tactics. The French
ambassador in St. Petersburg, Maurice Paléologue, so in-
sistently urged his Italian colleague to avail himself of the
opportunity while it lasted that Carlotti complained to Rome
of "a certain nuance of a threat," which he likewise detected
in the tone of the Russian foreign minister.[8]

With Great Britain's entry into the war on August 4, 1914,
the negotiations suffered a new turn although they remained
Russia's responsibility. The active participation of British
arms in the war naturally lent significant weight to any opinion
advanced by the London Foreign Office. This opinion was
expressed by Sir Edward Grey, the British foreign minister,
only two days later in reference to Sazonov's conversations
with the Italian ambassador. As the Russian ambassador in
London, Count Alexander Benckendorff, reported, "Grey gives
[them] extraordinary importance. He believes that it is absolutely necessary to add Trieste as the most important point
for Italy and one which more than anything else will satisfy
Italian public opinion."[9] All available documents thus point
to Britain as the first to offer Italy a definite region on the
Italo-Yugoslav ethnic boundary. There is no evidence that
Grey's offer was solicited by the Italian government. The
increasingly clamorous campaign of the irredentist press in
Italy, however, left no doubt that the British foreign minister's
appraisal of Trieste's value for Italy was correct.

By August 7, therefore, the Russian foreign minister had
the full concurrence of France and Great Britain to offer Italy
the now enlarged prize of the Trentino, Valona and Trieste
with a preponderant position on the Adriatic Sea. At the
same time Sazonov gave Italy to understand that its reward

[8] Carlotti to San Giuliano, August 6, 1914, *ibid.*, p. 244.
[9] Benckendorff to Sazonov, August 6, 1914, *ibid.*, p. 236.

THE EAST COAST OF THE ADRIATIC IN 1914

From *Studies in Secret Diplomacy during the First World War*,
by W. W. Gottlieb (London, Allen & Unwin, 1957)

would be in proportion to the dispatch with which it entered the war.[10]

Anxious to conclude an agreement before Italy's price rose again, Sazonov urged the British and French governments to exert further pressure on Italy.[11] It was suggested that both governments officially inform the cabinet in Rome of their adherence to the following two proposals advanced by Sazonov :

(1) The Italian army and navy will immediately attack the Austro-Hungarian army and navy;

(2) After the war the region of the Trentino and the ports of Trieste and Valona will be annexed to Italy.

This declaration was to include the hope that Italy would expedite its acceptance.[12]

These Russian tactics met with the serious disapproval of both France and Great Britain. An official representation such as Sazonov suggested would, they believed, place the Italian king and cabinet in an extremely difficult position. The Italian public could not be expected to take action against the erstwhile allies of Italy without proper preparation. Meanwhile a démarche by the Triple Entente in Rome would certainly assume the character of pressure which could only affect the sensitive Italians unfavorably.[13] It was feared that the Central Powers would make the most of such pressure by assuring Italy that the Triple Entente was attempting to lead it into a war against its own interests.[14] Under the circumstances the Allies feared that they would only expose themselves to the risk of an Italian refusal which they could ill afford.[15] In view of Italy's "great susceptibility" and "amour-

---

[10] Sazonov to Krupenskii, August 7, 1914, in MOEI, Vol. VI, Part 2, Doc. No. 24.

[11] Sazonov to Izvol'skii and Benckendorff, August 7, 1914, ibid., Doc. No. 25.

[12] Sazonov to Izvol'skii, Benckendorff and Krupenskii, August 10, 1914, ibid., Doc. No. 54.

[13] Benckendorff to Sazonov, August 9, 1914, ibid., Doc. No. 42.

[14] Doumerge to Paléologue, August 24, 1914, in TRMV, pp. 246-47.

[15] Carlotti to San Giuliano, August 12, 1914, in MOEI, Vol. VI, Part 2, Doc. No. 74.

propre," prudence rather than pressure seemed advisable.[16] Thus the Western allies urged that Italy be given to understand that it alone was to decide where its self-interest lay. The Allies would only offer separate and discreet expressions of their goodwill and satisfaction should Italy decide to join them on the basis of guaranties already made.[17] The impatient Russians were reminded that meanwhile Italy's uncertain neutrality was only beneficial to the Triple Entente since Italy's vacillation in itself served to neutralize a part of the Austrian forces.[18] The Italian foreign minister had given his assurance that, although Italy's joining Austria was "unthinkable," the possibility of joining the Allies was not excluded.[19] Thus the Allies had nothing to lose and much to gain by a policy of patience and caution. Sazonov accordingly instructed his ambassador in Rome to limit himself "to an expression of satisfaction to the foreign minister at Italy's decision to maintain neutrality" with the addition that, "if Italy should desire further to arrange its policy in accord with the states of the Triple Entente, it would find a grateful reception and readiness to grant considerable satisfaction to its national aspirations."[20]

Obviously this delicacy on the part of the Allies served Italy's purposes admirably. The negotiations of the Foreign Office in Rome with both contestants were secret enough to avoid arousing public opinion at home and sufficiently rumored in diplomatic circles to make the bidding brisker. Besides, the informality of Italy's conversations with Russia made it possible for the Italian government to disavow them should the need arise. As Poincaré observed, "Italy has given no mandate to her ambassador to negotiate with Sazonov, and anything the former says is of a purely personal character."[21]

By the middle of August there was general dissatisfaction on the part of both the Western allies and Italy with the

16 Doumerge to Paléologue, August 12, 1914, *ibid.*, Doc. No. 79.
17 Benckendorff to Sazonov, August 12, 1914, *ibid.*, Doc. No. 77.
18 Benckendorff to Sazonov, August 9, 1914, *ibid.*, Doc. No. 42
19 Krupenskii to Sazonov, August 13, 1914, *ibid.*, Doc. No. 81.
20 Sazonov to Krupenskii, August 13, 1914, *ibid.*, Doc. No. 86.
21 Poincaré, III, 36-37.

course of the negotiations with Russia. To the French president, Sazonov was "always a little bewildering with his multiplicity of ideas" and "plethora of proposals and projects."[22] According to Poincaré's information, Sir Edward Grey was also "less and less favorable to the hurried and rather ragged proposals which Sazonov is piling up for the Balkans. . . ."[23] Needless to point out, the Italians were growing increasingly irritated at Russia's clumsy attempts to push them into a deal faster than they were willing to be pushed without the proper incentive. And the idea of what would constitute proper incentive was, as the Russians feared, unmistakably growing. Poincaré noted on August 11, 1914, "The Marchese Carlotti has been at no pains to conceal that, besides Trentino, Trieste and Valona, his country will require the Dalmatian littoral. . . ."[24] It was becoming apparent that St. Petersburg was no longer a suitable market for such trade. The Italian foreign minister, San Giuliano, accordingly informed the Russian ambassador in Rome that any negotiations for Italian collaboration must be held "in the most absolute secrecy and must take place in London, exclusively in London" (on the grounds that the British Foreign Office did not make statements to the press, and the treaties for the Balkan peace were made in London). One of the main Italian conditions was that the British, French and Italian fleets should act jointly. Russia, Britain, France and Italy must commit themselves not to conclude a separate peace.[25]

The Italian foreign minister emphatically and repeatedly declared that his government insisted on absolute secrecy, that it would be forced to withdraw from negotiations and deny the reports in the event of any disclosure. Above all, as San Giuliano instructed the Italian ambassador in St. Petersburg, "I repeat that my condition *sine qua non* is that

[22] *Ibid.*
[23] *Ibid.*, p. 41.
[24] *Ibid.*, p. 37.
[25] Krupenskii to Sazonov, August 15, 1914, in *L'Intervento dell'Italia nei documenti segreti dell'Intesa* (Rome, 1923), pp. 27-28.

the negotiations do not take place at Rome, where ambassadors
of Germany and Austria are currently stationed. I also beg
you to request Sazonov to have instructions issued to Krupenskii and Sir Rennell Rodd [the Russian and British am-
bassadors] not to speak to me any further of this affair for
I do not wish to have too lengthy and too frequent conversations with them."[26]

Thus a proposed draft of a treaty with Italy based on negotiations with Russia as intermediary was to lie unsigned
and undated in the files of the Russian Foreign Office. This
draft, marking the progress of the negotiations until August 14,
contained the following provisions:

(1) Italy commits herself to join immediately, on land and
sea, in common action with England, France and Russia against
Austria-Hungary. The General Staffs of their respective armies
and navies will be charged with establishing without delay
the means of Italian collaboration with the English, French
and Russian armed forces.

(2) England, France and Russia commit themselves to grant
to Italy the possession of Trieste and all the territories of the
Trentino which may be occupied by Italian troops at the time
of the signature of the peace treaty, as well as a preponderant
situation on the Adriatic Sea, with the provision that Serbia
be conceded an access to the sea within limits to be established.[27]

Italy was satisfied neither with these terms nor with the
treatment it had received in the capital of the Tsar. Only
London displayed tact, understanding and amenability. By
the middle of August, 1914, it was officially understood by
the Triple Entente powers and Italy that further negotiations
were to take place on the Thames. Russia had lost its initiative.
There was to be neither immediate help nor a small price.
Italy was to gain eight months of peace and compensation
such as only its more imaginative irredentists could have hoped
for.

[26] San Giuliano to Carlotti, August 15, 1914, *ibid.*, p. 33.
[27] MOEI, Vol. VI, Part 1, Doc. No. 95.

HOPES AND FEARS

The negotiations which took place from mid-August, 1914, to March 4, 1915, were particularly marked by a divergence in aims between Russia on the one hand and Great Britain and France on the other. Having lost the initiative in bargaining with Italy, Mother Russia now began to demonstrate unmistakable alarm over Latin inroads into the Slavic Balkans. As early as September, 1914, in a statement of Russian war aims, Sazonov informed the Entente governments that he supported the cause of a Greater Serbia which would include Bosnia, Hercegovina, Dalmatia and northern Albania.[28] Russian ambassadors in all the capitals of the Entente and Italy were clearly instructed to commit their country to no definite provisions concerning Italian demands in Dalmatia.[29] Russia's Balkan policy was well summarized by Ambassador Izvol'skii in October, 1914, when he wrote to Foreign Minister Sazonov, "I venture to suggest here the idea that a strong and unified Serbo-Croatian kingdom which included Istria and Dalmatia would constitute the necessary counterweight to Italy, Hungary and Rumania."[30]

While the Russians were making their plans for a dim future, Italian officials were likewise engaged in formulating their country's war aims. On September 25, 1914, the Italian foreign minister, San Giuliano, sent Ambassador Carlotti in Petrograd a program of sixteen conditions to provide a basis for negotiations with the Entente. Although garbled in transmission, the message clearly indicated that, as part of its compensation, Italy desired "the Italian provinces of Austria with a frontier which would follow the watershed of the Alps to the Quarnero" and Italian entry into Dalmatia. San Giuliano himself expressed doubt as to which Dalmatian islands Italy should occupy. As a sop to the South Slavs, Italy offered

[28] Paléologue to Delcassé, September 14, 1914, *ibid.*, Doc. No. 256.
[29] Sazonov to Izvol'skii and Benckendorff, August 24, 1914, *ibid.*, Doc. No. 154.
[30] Izvol'skii to Sazonov, October 30, 1914, *ibid.*, Doc. No. 386.

Montenegro and Serbia (as well as Greece) all of Albania, provided the coast were neutralized and Valona remained in Italian possession.[31] Carlotti's reaction two days later was full of confidence: "As England, France and Russia have no direct interests in the Adriatic, once the necessary concessions to the economic needs of Serbia have been assured, no obstacle will remain on the part of the three powers in the way of the Adriatic becoming an Italian sea. As for Serbia's presence on the other coast, one cannot see what serious concern this should cause in Italy."[32]

Meanwhile the Serbs, uninformed of the negotiations between their allies and Italy, were also eager to register their war aims. On September 21, 1914, the wily premier of the Serbian kingdom, Nikola Pašić, informed the Russian Foreign Office of Serbia's territorial aspirations. In tracing the future boundaries of his country, Pašić became very vague in his plans for the northwestern regions. With reference to the line southward from Slovenia into the Istrian peninsula, Pašić merely declared, "The latter could be divided with Italy should it immediately join against Austria-Hungary."[33] Irredentist claims in the noisy Italian press and discomforting rumors of official Italian territorial aspirations stirred Pašić to a more definite statement. He sent a warning to his Russian colleague on September 28, 1914, through Serbian Ambassador Spalaiković. "Dalmatia desires to be united with Serbia," Pašić declared. "Italy will be satisfied if it obtains Trieste, Trent, Pola, and Istria with Pulj [Pola]."[34] Thus the prime minister of the Serbians added his country's assent to an Italian annexation of the western strip of the Istrian peninsula with Trieste. In the light of later developments, this was to seem an unjustifiably excessive offer to many South Slavs, particularly to the Croats, Slovenes and Serbs of Austria-Hungary.

[31] San Giuliano to Carlotti, September 25, 1914, pp. 49-50.

[32] Carlotti to San Giuliano, September 27, 1914, ibid., pp. 52-53.

[33] Memorandum of the Serbian Mission in Petrograd, to Sazonov, October 3, 1914, in MOEI, Vol. VI, Part 1, Doc. No. 351.

[34] Memorandum of the Serbian Mission in Petrograd to Sazonov, October 3, 1914, ibid., Doc. No. 352.

The disposition of the eastern Adriatic coast land was of more vital concern to the seven million South Slavs of Austria-Hungary than to their four million fellow Slavs of Serbia. For the land-locked Serbians an outlet to the sea was a necessity which constituted one of their most urgent war aims. To the Croats, Slovenes and Serbs of the Dual Monarchy, however, the Adriatic question directly concerned their very freedom from centuries of Habsburg rule.

The anti-Slav purge which swept across the entire Dual Monarchy following the tragedy at Sarajevo necessitated the speedy flight of many distinguished leaders of the Slavs. Unlike thousands of their compatriots who fled for refuge to the Serbian kingdom, a certain number of proscribed Croatian, Serbian and Slovenian leaders felt that the cause of Yugoslav unification could best be served from safer neutral ground. An Austrian invasion of Serbia was imminent. They desired a base from which they could more readily influence the governments of the Entente through direct contact and still not lose touch with their homeland.[35]

It is ironical that it was Italy that, through its declaration of neutrality on August 3, 1914, should have afforded these Yugoslavs just such a base, for more than any other country, Italy now threatened to succeed Austria in its role of preventing the unification of the Serbs, Croats and Slovenes by annexing their lands. An Italian base offered several advantages to these Slavic refugees. Neighboring Italy provided a bridge between the Slav-inhabited territories of Austria-Hungary, Serbia and Montenegro on the one side and France and England on the other. The fact that many of the most distinguished of these political refugees—among them Ante Trumbić, Frano Supilo and Josip Smodlaka—were Dalmatians whose acquaintance with Italy and fluency in Italian were almost native rendered Italy a natural choice for refuge. The

---

[35] Unless otherwise specified, material pertaining to the so-called Yugoslav Committee has been taken from Dr. Milada Paulová's work *Jugoslavenski Odbor: Povijest jugoslavenske emigracije za svijetskog rata od 1914-1918* (Zagreb [1925]), Chapters 1 and 2, *passim.*

early outbreak of a vigorous irredentist campaign in the Italian press aimed against South Slav aspirations made imperative the presence of qualified observers able to counteract Italian claims.

It was from press clippings, scraps of conversations in diplomatic circles and rumors that both this group in exile and the Serbian government had to obtain their first news of Italian maneuvers to gain Slav-inhabited territory. In keeping with the way of big powers, neither Britain, France nor even Russia had any intention of complicating an already unsavory situation by informing the victims of their fate. By September, 1914, nevertheless, both the Serbian government and the South Slav exiles in Italy were painfully aware of Italian intentions.

The most alarming rumor of that moment involved the formation of an Italian volunteer expedition which would supposedly without the official knowledge of the Italian government, stage a surprise attack on the Dalmatian coast. Upon receipt of this news the exiled South Slav leaders who had initially gathered in Venice hurriedly transferred their base to Rome. Their situation was desperate. It was not difficult for them to perceive that Britain and France particularly would favor an Italian coup in Dalmatia for several reasons. By this attack on Austrian soil Italy would almost certainly provoke a conflict with the Dual Monarchy which would make Italian intervention in the war inevitable. Whatever coastal bases the Italian expedition might capture would eventually assure the Anglo-French fleet of a strategic position in the Adriatic. The South Slav leaders in Italy, on the contrary, were not only appalled by the prospect of an Italian occupation of Dalmatia, which was likely to be a permanent one; they were even more horrified by their conviction that their compatriots would support Austria-Hungary against the detested Italians and thus irreparably discredit the cause of Yugoslav unification.

On September 28, 1914, a delegation of three Croats from Austria-Hungary set out to call on the French, British and

Russian ambassadors to Italy. This delegation consisted of Dr. Ante Trumbić, former member of the Austrian Reichsrat and Croatian leader in the Dalmatian Diet; Ivan Meštrović, world-famous sculptor; and Frano Supilo, former Croatian deputy to the Hungarian Parliament. Their purpose was to warn the Entente against the consequences of an Italian attack on Dalmatia as well as to refute Italy's claims on Dalmatia, Istria and Trieste and the Julian March. This group's concern over the territories at the head of the Adriatic, in contrast to the Serbian government's apparent willingness to bargain away these more remote regions, was symptomatic of the serious rift between these two bodies. The mediocre results of the interviews with Barrère (the French ambassador in Rome), Rodd and Krupenskii convinced the delegation of Croats that more direct contact with the Entente governments was urgently needed.

Frano Supilo was immediately delegated to travel to Bordeaux, temporary seat of the French government. With the aid of the Serbian diplomatic representative there, he succeeded in conferring with both French Foreign Minister Delcassé and Russian Ambassador Izvol'skii. Although Supilo's conversations with the former are not available, his four memorandums to Izvol'skii have been published. The first, sent to Petrograd on December 14, outlined the main arguments in favor of South Slav unification from the Russian point of view. In it Supilo significantly referred to Gorizia, Gradisca, Trieste and Dalmatia as Slavic territories, though admitting Italian majorities in the cities and coastal towns. Choosing to take these regions as a whole, however, Supilo claimed a Slav majority of 70 percent. The memorandum further included a veritable ode of homage to Mother Russia as the protectress of the Slavs.[36]

---

[36] The text of this memorandum may be found in Friedrich Stieve, *Iswolski im Weltkriege: Der diplomatische Schriftwechsel Iswolskis aus den Jahren 1914-1917* (Berlin, 1925), Doc. No. 242. For the French text see Paul-Henri Michel, *La Question de l'Adriatique (1914-1918): Recueil de Documents* (Paris, 1938), pp. 30-36.

Following his journey to Bordeaux, Supilo made two trips to London, unaware that he was at last in the capital where the fate of his compatriots was then being decided. The negotiations between Italy and the Entente had by that time been transferred from Petrograd to London. It was on his second trip, in November, 1914, that Supilo gleaned the first hint as to the extent of Italy's demands. In the course of a conference with Prime Minister Asquith during an intimate luncheon, Supilo happened to draw a map of Dalmatia in an attempt to supplement his inadequate command of French. Suddenly Asquith took Supilo's pencil and himself sketched a line on the map asking whether Italy's demand for the territory thus indicated would be unbearable for the Slavs. Supilo, whom Asquith once subsequently described to Count Sforza as a "boiling Stromboli," assured the British premier in unequivocal terms that such an arrangement would be catastrophic for his people.

The Croatian emissary returned to Rome on January 23, 1915, convinced that the cause of Yugoslav unification was desperate in the face of Italy's strong position with the Entente Powers. Upon his return, therefore, the now enlarged group of Yugoslav leaders in exile resolved to constitute itself into a "Yugoslav Committee" which would represent abroad the Croats, Serbs and Slovenes of all the Yugoslav provinces under Austria-Hungary. A motion proposed by Dr. Ljuba Leontić in December, 1914, that the Committee organize Yugoslav volunteer units to fight against Austria-Hungary and to seek funds and recruits from the Yugoslavs of America, was now adopted with enthusiasm. Supilo was authorized to confer on behalf of the Yugoslav Committee with Premier Pašić in Niš, the temporary seat of the Serbian government, and thence to travel to Petrograd.

Following a series of conferences with members of the Serbian government into which the conflict between Yugoslav federalism versus pan-Serb centralism introduced a disturbing note, Supilo left Serbia for Petrograd. No sooner had he arrived in February, 1915, than he felt that his was a lost cause in Russia. He had come in the midst of a campaign in the Russian press urging Italian participation in the war against the Central Powers. Editorial references to Trieste as an Italian city and an open discussion in favor of Italian compensation in Gorizia, Istria and northern Dalmatia were disheartening. Supilo was even more discouraged by the ignorance not only of the Russian public but of Russian officialdom regarding the Balkan Slavs and the territories they inhabited. Another distinguished member of the Yugoslav Committee, Dr. Ante Mandić, had reason to observe seven months later: "We are not known here. They know absolutely nothing about us, and we are of no concern to them."[37]

If the task of influencing Russia in favor of Yugoslav aspirations as defined by his Committee appeared to Supilo a virtually impossible assignment, there was good reason. Russia's immediate interests demanded the aid which Italy could furnish by throwing over a million fresh soldiers into the field against Austria-Hungary. The Russian government sadly realized that such assistance was to be bought dearly and at the expense of the South Slavs. Hindenburg's successes concerned Russia far more than the maintenance of ethnic principles in distant unknown provinces, the ethnology of which was at best confusing. Furthermore, what pan-Slavic sympathies Russian circles had for the Balkan Slavs were almost exclusively reserved for the Orthodox Serbs and Bulgars. The centuries-old hatred for the Roman Catholic Poles was easily expanded under wartime stresses to include a distrust of all the Roman Catholic Slavic subjects of the Dual Monarchy. Foreign Minister Sazonov said to an unofficial Serbian delegation which came to Petrograd not long after Supilo's mission, "I can tell you nothing about the Croats and Slovenes. They are fighting against us, and I tell you now that, if the Russian people had to fight under arms for only half a day

---

[37] Paulová, p. 149.

for the liberation of the Slovenes, I would not agree to it !"[38]
Official Russian circles were plainly against a unification of
the Roman Catholic westernized Slovenes and Croats with
the more backward Orthodox Serbs. They saw in this union
only a weakening of Russian influence over the Serbs.

Armed with a letter from Pašić, Supilo called on Sazonov
during February, 1915, but was quickly referred to a Foreign
Office official on the Near East desk, Baron Maurice Schilling.
In the course of a conference Baron Schilling suddenly asked
Supilo, as a Slavic subject of the Austro-Hungarian empire,
what conditions he would deem necessary to safeguard Polish
national rights should Austrian Poland be ceded to Russia
after the war. Struck by the strangeness of this request,
Supilo's active mind realized that it was not irrelevant to
the fate of his own people. Recalling Premier Asquith's fatal
line on his map two months ago, Supilo grasped the horrifying
thought that Russia had already decided to sacrifice the
Yugoslavs of the Adriatic to Italy and now merely sought
to ensure their national rights. The fiery Croat sought an
immediate audience with Sazonov and accused the Russian
foreign minister of having acceded to Italy's claims. Sur-
prised by Supilo's exact references to the geographic division
then under discussion by Italy and the Entente, Sazonov
admitted the truth of the charge, offering as justification
Russia's deteriorated military situation. Supilo at once wired
this discouraging news to both Premier Pašić and the Yugoslav Committee in Rome.

Thus the leaders of the Serbs, Croats and Slovenes discovered
in this roundabout manner the main provisions of the secret
Treaty of London before it was signed.

RUSSIA VERSUS ITALY

If the Russian foreign minister deserved the protestations
of his Balkan friends, he did not deserve to bear alone the
burden of their resentment. After all, at no time had Russia

[38] *Ibid.*, p. 54.

offered Italy more than the Serbian government, the largest single free voice of the South Slavs, itself was willing to see Italy receive. Committed to a policy of support for a stronger Greater Serbia, Russia applied itself to the task of influencing its Western allies to obtain Italian aid at the earliest possible time at the smallest possible price. With each successive day of waiting, however, Russian interest in Italy as an ally diminished, and in early 1915 evolved into downright discouragement of Italian intervention. In a memorandum drawn up in Petrograd on March 2, 1915, the Russian foreign ministry actually declared:

Sazonov could not but view with alarm Italy's entry on the scene at a time when its military and naval assistance has lost the better part of its value. . . . If a fourth power were to mix into their concert [of the Entente], would there not be reason to fear that it was seeking to disunite them for its own personal advantage? Sazonov therefore thinks that, if the Italian government offers us its assistance, we should decline in a most friendly manner.[39]

In a somewhat more realistic frame of mind Sazonov told the French and British ambassadors in the Russian capital five days later:

the advantages which the Allied powers could offer Italy [in exchange for its co-operation] should be in proportion to the military and political assistance which Italy's entry would constitute. With this aim it would be useful to re-examine the proposals the powers were disposed to make to Italy six months earlier in order to conform to the current situation.[40]

Sazonov's telegram of the next day (March 8) to Izvol'skii and Benckendorff repeated his fear that Italy's aspirations would prove to be out of proportion to the actual help which her intervention would afford Russia. He was especially insistent in his demand that Italy should fight not only Turkey but Austria-Hungary as well.[41]

[39] MOEI, Vol. VII, Part 1, Doc. No. 276.
[40] Memorandum of March 7, 1915, in TRMV, p. 259.
[41] MOEI, Vol. VII, Part 1, Doc. No. 331.

Even as Italy was carrying on negotiations with the Central Powers, negotiations between the Entente and Italy came to a head on March 4, 1915. On that day Italian Ambassador Imperiali read to Foreign Minister Grey in London a document of sixteen articles comprising Italy's conditions for joining the Entente. The first three articles dealt in general with an Allied pledge not to conclude a separate peace, Italy's declaration of war on Austria-Hungary and Turkey (though not Germany) and a provision for the cooperation of the Anglo-French and Italian fleets. The articles which dealt with Italy's territorial claims in the Adriatic region stated:

IV. In the Treaty of Peace, Italy will obtain the Trentino and the Cisalpine Tyrol, following the geographical and natural frontier (the Brenner frontier) with Trieste, Gorizia, Gradisca, and the whole of Istria as far as the Quarnero including Volosca, besides the Istrian islands of Cherso, Lussin[o] and the smaller islands of Plavnik, Unie, the Canidole, Sansego, the Oriole, Palazzuoli, San Pietro di Nembi, Asinello, Gruica and the neighboring islets.

V. The province of Dalmatia will also fall to Italy, according to its actual administrative boundary, including, on the north, Lisarica and Tribania, and proceeding south as far as the Narenta River, with the peninsula of Sabbioncello and all the neighboring islands lying to the north and west of Dalmatia itself, from Premuda, Selve, Ulbo, Maon, Pago and Puntadure to the north, as far as Meleda to the south, including Sant'Andrea, Busi, Lissa, Lesina, Curzola, Cazza and Lagosta with the neighboring rocks, besides Pelagosa.

VI. Valona, with the entire coast surrounding the bay, including the island of Saseno, with sufficient territory for their defense, will devolve on Italy in full sovereignty (from the Voiussa [Vijosë] on the north and east as far, approximately, as Chimara [Himare] on the south).

VII. Should Italy obtain the Trentino and Istria (according to Art. IV), Dalmatia and the Adriatic islands (according to Art. V) and the Bay of Valona (Art. VI), and should the central part of Albania be reserved for the constitution of a small autonomous neutralized [Moslem] State—she will not object to the rest of northern and southern Albania, should England, France and Russia so desire, being divided between Montenegro, Serbia and Greece; that is, provided the coast be neutralized from the Bocche di Cattaro inclusive as far as Cape Stylos [Stilo].

VIII. The islands of the Dodecanese, at present occupied by Italy, will remain in her possession.

IX. In general the parties agree to recognize that Italy has an interest to guard the equilibrium of the Mediterranean, so that in case of the dismemberment of the Ottoman Empire, she ought to have her appropriate share. . . .[42]

The succeeding articles included Italy's demand for Libya, a share in the reparations, a guaranty of Yemen's independence, a share in Germany's colonies and regulation of Italian Eritrea, Somaliland and Libya's borders with French and British colonies, the receipt of a British loan of 50 million pounds sterling, an allied pledge to prevent a papal representative from attending the peace conference, and a pledge to hold the treaty secret.

This Italian memorandum constituted the first concrete results in seven months. Six days following its first reading to Sir Edward Grey on March 4, it was read to the French and Russian ambassadors in London, Cambon and Benckendorff, both of whom chose to reserve their opinion at the time. It was the British Foreign Office, therefore, which first committed itself regarding the Italian demands. A British memorandum of March 11 contained the following evaluation : "Certain of the conditions seemed excessive, but without doubt, in order to purchase her neutrality, considerable offers had been made to Italy by Prince Bülow. Sir E. Grey considered therefore that the conditions proposed by the Italian government should not be rejected, but should, where excessive, be met by a counterproposal or with criticism."[43]

The French reaction to the Italian memorandum was largely one of disapproval. Specific objections were raised against these three Italian demands: (a) the Italian occupation of Dalmatia, (b) the neutralization of coastal territory to be awarded to Serbia and Montenegro and (c) the founding of

[42] Text in Salandra, pp. 268-70.
[43] Memorandum of the British Embassy in Petrograd, to Sazonov, in MOEI, Vol. VII, Part 1, Doc. No. 348.

a Moslem Albanian State. "Nothing could be better than to encourage Italy," Poincaré observed, "but let us not discourage Serbia, which is fighting so wearily over there for its national existence."[44]

Russia's views were transmitted to London by Foreign Minister Sazonov on March 15, 1915. Finding himself in agreement with most of Italy's demands, including the annexation of Trieste, Istria and the Quarnero Islands, he urged that Serbia be given the Dalmatian littoral with the offshore islands from the mouth of the Krka (Kerka) to the Montenegrin border, which would run, probably, somewhat to the north of Dubrovnik (Ragusa). The Croats were to get the remainder of the coast, from the mouth of the Krka to the Italian frontier near Volosca, with the adjacent islands. As for the Italian demand for neutralization of certain parts of the littoral, the Russian foreign minister declared, "Russia would find it possible to agree to this with respect to the coast of a future independent Albania and also to the Greek coast between Chimara and Cape Stilo, but does not believe to be admissible the application of this principle to the Bay of Cattaro and the rest of the littoral which will be awarded to Montenegro."[45]

Sir Edward Grey briefly summarized these alterations in a note handed to the Italian ambassador in London on March 20 in the name of the Triple Entente. "The three Powers," Grey wrote, "would ask the Italian government to review their claims in this direction and if possible to find some means of ascertaining the *desiderata* of the Yugoslav leaders. In other respects the three Powers accept generally the Italian proposals subject to agreement on points of detail."[46]

The Italian government forwarded its reply to the British Foreign Office on March 24. The following document, written

---

[44] Mario Toscano, *Il Patto di Londra* (Bologna, 1934), p. 88.

[45] Sazonov to Izvol'skii and Benckendorff, March 15, 1915, in TRMV, p. 263. In this volume the document (Foreign Office telegram No. 116) is incorrectly headed "telegram to the [Russian] ambassador in Rome." (The error is noted in MOEI, VII, Part 1, 485, note 3; the document itself does not appear in MOEI.)

[46] Grey to Imperiali, March 20, 1915, in MOEI, Vol. VII, Part 1, Doc. No. 402.

by Sonnino himself, affords the best indication of Italy's aspirations at that time:

The principal motive which determined us to take the field on the side of the Entente was the wish to liberate ourselves from our present intolerable situation of inferiority in the Adriatic over and against Austria by reason of the great difference, from the point of view of military offense and defense, between the physical and geographical conditions of the two shores—a difference made more serious by modern methods of warfare. No doubt Italy could obtain the greater part of the national *desiderata* by a simple undertaking to maintain neutrality without exposing the country to the terrible risks and hardships of a war. It would not be worth our while to go to war for the purpose of freeing ourselves from the overbearing Austrian domination in the Adriatic, if we were obliged immediately to fall back into the same conditions of inferiority and constant danger, owing to the Yugoslav League of young and ambitious States.

For the same reasons we must insist upon the neutralization of the coast from Cattaro down as far as the Voiussa.

To Croatia, whether it remains united with Austria-Hungary or not, will remain the coast from Volosca as far as Dalmatia, with the nearest islands of Veglia, Arbe, Pago, and so forth. She will have as her principal port Fiume, together with other lesser ports in the Morlacca Channel.

The shores of the Narenta, as far as the Drin, will remain in the possession of Serbia and Montenegro, who will probably soon merge and consolidate, as also the important ports of Ragusa and Cattaro, together with the smaller ports of Antivari, Dulcigno, San Giovanni [di] Medua and the Mouths of the Bojana. . . . As for Bosnia-Hercegovina, it will presumably become Serbian, together with all the Serbo-Montenegrin hinterland. . . .

Even Sazonoff, last August, admitted that Dalmatia "from Zara to Ragusa" (he did not say "from Zara to Sebenico") must fall to Italy if she took the field on the side of the Entente.[47]

Finding itself between Italy's and Russia's cross-purposes, Britain felt constrained to talk both contenders into a compromise. Upon receiving Sonnino's memorandum, Sir Edward

[47] Salàndra, *L'Intervento* (*1915*): *Ricordi e pensieri* (Milan, 1930), pp. 167-68.

Grey, backed by Lloyd George and Herbert Asquith, requested Italy to lower its demands. Rome replied by renouncing all claims to the port of Spalato (Split). In his memoirs
Premier Salandra complained with noble eloquence, "It fell
to our lot to abandon Spalato, seat of our glorious civilization
and of a fervid Italian patriotism."[48] The reminder seems
hardly necessary that this seat of a fervid Italian patriotism
was overwhelmingly Slavic.

While attempting to limit Italy's demands, Britain simultaneously tried to influence Russia not to cause further delay
in the negotiations. In relaying Sonnino's demands to the
Russian foreign ministry, the British ambassador, Buchanan,
expressed the views of his government. Stressing Italy's entry
into the war as a "turning point," he strongly urged Allied
acceptance of Rome's demands on the following three conditions: (a) that Italy sign the treaty of alliance immediately
though unable to declare war until the end of April, (b) that
Italy declare war on Germany as well as Austria-Hungary
and (c) that Italy guarantee Spalato as a free port accessible
to Serbia.[49]

The Russian foreign minister clearly indicated his displeasure
with this formula on March 25 in a memorandum addressed
to the British and French embassies in the Russian capital.
Reminding them that both Grey and Delcassé had at one
time or another admitted that Italy's demands were exaggerated, the Russian foreign ministry insisted on maintaining
its former reservations concerning the Adriatic coast. Counter-
ing Italy's apprehension of Slavic hegemony in the Adriatic,
Russia warned its allies against providing the cause of a future
war by substituting Italian for Austrian domination over the
Slavic Balkans. Finally, Sazonov denied ever having offered
Italy more than the coast down to, but not including, Spalato.
As a final concession, however, Sazonov offered the coast

    [48] *Ibid.*, p. 169.
    [49] Buchanan to Sazonov, March 24, 1915, in MOEI, Vol. VII, Part 2,
Doc. No. 419.

from Zara (Zadar) to Cape Planka (Rt Ploče) including the port of Sebenico (Šibenik).[50]

Russia was, however, handicapped in this diplomatic struggle. The failure of the Russian army on the German front had weakened Russia's bargaining power considerably, while Italy's bargaining power was steadily increasing as the German pressure on the western front became more acute. That same evening of March 25, Prime Minister Asquith recorded the prevailing view of the British government on the pages of his diary: "The great thing for the moment is to bring in Italy."[51]

The negotiations from the last week in March through April, 1915, centered on a discussion between Russia and Italy via London regarding the legitimacy of Italy's desire for hegemony in the Adriatic and the means with which to achieve it. Sir Edward Grey appeared to be swayed by the contention that Italy would have reason to fear a Slav-dominated eastern coast as a potential naval base. The Russian government, in turn, maintained that the Yugoslavs had more reason to fear an actual Italian fleet than the Italians had to fear a potential Yugoslav fleet which had little chance of materializing. Nevertheless, in reply to Grey's constant needling, the Russian foreign ministry came out with another "final concession" on March 28. According to this new compromise, Italy was to be given the Adriatic coast down to Cape Planka including the ports of Zara and Sebenico. Serbia was to be awarded the Dalmatian coast from Cape Planka to Montenegro with the adjacent islands and the ports of Spalato, Metković and Dubrovnik (Ragusa). Cattaro (Kotor) would be neutralized. Finally both Italy and Serbia were to neutralize their respective sections of the coast from Zara to the Narenta (Neretva) River. Sazonov reminded the British that Italy had never demanded neutralization of the coast south of that river.[52]

---

[50] Memo of Russian Foreign Ministry to Paléologue and Buchanan, March 25, 1915, *ibid.*, Doc. No. 423.

[51] Herbert Henry Asquith, *Memories and Reflections, 1852-1927* (Boston, 1928), II, 68.

[52] Sazonov to Benckendorff, March 28, 1915, in TRMV, p. 267

Sazonov received word of Italy's willingness to relent on March 30, when British Ambassador Buchanan informed him that Italy would agree to let Serbia have the coast from Cape Planka to the Montenegrin border including Spalato. As for the islands, however, Serbia would be awarded only five— Zirona Grande (Veliki Drvenik), Zirona Piccola (Mali Drvenik), Bua (Čiovo), Solta and Brazza (Brač). The remaining islands and the peninsula of Sabbioncello (Pelješac) were to go to Italy. The British urged acceptance of this alternative on the condition that Italy neutralize the islands and the peninsula. Sazonov refused. "Public opinion in Russia," he declared, "can never be reconciled to a solution which would place Serbia materially and morally in a state of absolute inferiority vis-à-vis Italy."[53]

Having reached an impasse with the professed inability of Britain or France to obtain further concessions on behalf of Serbia, Russia offered still another "last concession" on March 31, revising its proposal of the previous day as follows: (a) Serbia to be given the entire Dalmatian coast from Cape Planka to Montenegro including Sabbioncello peninsula and all the islands except Lissa (Vis), Busi (Biševo), Cazza (Sušac) and Lagosta (Lastovo); (b) all the islands, Sabbioncello peninsula, and the coast from Zara to the mouth of the Narenta as well as Cattaro to be neutralized by both.[54]

As a result, on April 1 Asquith delivered to Imperiali a memorandum containing the following points: "(a) Italy to receive the islands of Lissa, Busi, Cazza, Lagosta and Pelagosa; (b) Italy to receive the Adriatic coast, with adjacent islands, from Cape Planka to the Dalmatian frontier; (c) the rest of the Dalmatian littoral, including Sabbioncello Peninsula, from the Montenegrin border to Cape Planka, with the offshore islands, to go to Serbia; (d) all the offshore islands from Zara

---

[53] Sazonov to Benckendorff, March 30, 1915, in MOEI, Vol. VII, Part 2, Doc. No. 450.
[54] Memo of the Russian Foreign Ministry to Paléologue and Buchanan, March 31, 1915, ibid., Doc. No. 455.

to the mouth of the Narenta, and also the Bay of Cattaro, to be neutralized."[55]

Sonnino and Salandra regarded this proposal as quite unacceptable as it deprived Italy of islands considered necessary for its security. At this point Italy adopted the tactics of a disappointed and hence no longer interested client. Sonnino wired Ambassador Imperiali in London the following instructions:

It is not possible to accept the changes presented by Asquith in the name of the three Powers. Should the hostilities have a fortunate issue, our situation in the Adriatic would remain such as to make it incomprehensible why we had gone to war and shouldered an immense burden and danger. Your Excellency will explain to said Government the reason why, if the three Powers hold to their emendation, we shall be compelled, to our regret, to withdraw our proposals and to regard them as not having been made.[56]

On April 4 the British ambassador in Rome reported Sonnino's direct expression of dissatisfaction with the compromise proposal of April 1. Sonnino complained about the disposition of the islands, the question of neutralization of the Dalmatian coast and the awarding of Sabbioncello Peninsula to Serbia. If the Italian foreign minister's conditions regarding these points were not accepted, Rodd reported, Italy would drop the whole matter and remain neutral.[57] Worse still, there was always the threat that Italy would yet look to the Central Powers to satisfy its ambitions. This threat lent ur-

---

[55] Memo of Buchanan to the Russian Foreign Ministry, April 3, 1915, ibid., pp. 81-82, note 2.

[56] Salandra, L'Intervento, p. 171.

[57] L'Intervento dell'Italia, pp. 138-39; also Salandra, L'Intervento, p. 172. As Carlotti informed Sazonov at the same time, Sonnino had actually telegraphed the Italian ambassador in London that since the Allies had rejected Italy's demands, "Italy would probably have to break off negotiations and seek to ensure her interests by other means" (italics added). Apparently such a possibility so disturbed Carlotti that, in a subsequent conversation with Baron Schilling of the Russian Foreign Ministry, Carlotti, although himself of Jewish origin on his mother's side, exclaimed, "Sonnino is nothing but a little Jew out to make a big deal." See Daily Report of the Ministry of Foreign Affairs, April 4, 1915, in MOEI, Vol. VII, Part 2, Doc. No. 479.

gency to a feverish week of negotiation during which each side demonstrated almost equal apprehension that the other would withdraw, much to Russia's amazement.

Meanwhile Sazonov himself was to comprehend fully the significance of Russia's strategy against Italian ambitions if carried to extremes. If Russia discouraged the alliance with Italy, then obviously Russia would be expected by its allies to make up for the loss of a million fresh soldiers. The Russian ambassador in London, Benckendorff, wrote to his chief on April 1: "To me it is clear that if France and England are made to renounce the Italian alliance because of us and then take all the consequences possibly ensuing, it would have an effect on our joint morale for which I can foresee no good, and our interests will thereby most certainly suffer a great deal."[58] Sazonov likewise felt the pressure of the army. On April 6, Grand Duke Nikolai Nikolaevich, commander in chief of the Russian armies, urged immediate Italian intervention out of military considerations. At the same time, however, in the interests of Russia he advised against the neutralization of Cattaro.[59] The Montenegrin seaport was much too good a naval base to give up.

On April 8, 1915, Sonnino transmitted to Austria the final counterproposals of the Italian government. The Italian government demanded the following settlement in return for its benevolent neutrality: (a) cession of the Trentino with the borders of 1811; (b) rectification of the eastern Austro-Italian frontier in favor of Italy to include Gradisca and Gorizia ; (c) establishment of a free city of Trieste and surroundings; (d) cession of the Archipelago of Curzola, including Lissa, Lesina (Hvar), Curzola (Korčula),Lagosta, Cazza, Meleda (Mljet) and Pelagosa (Palagruža); (e) occupation by Italy of the ceded territories and evacuation of Trieste by Austria-Hungary; (f) recognition of full Italian sovereignty in Valona and Saseno

[58] Benckendorff to Sazonov, April 1, 1915, in MOEI, Vol. VII, Part 2, Doc. No. 462.
[59] Grand Duke Nikolai Nikolaevich to Sazonov, April 6, 1915, ibid., Doc. No. 493.

(Sazan) Bay in Albania; (g) Austro-Hungarian renunciation of interests in Albania; (h) amnesty for political and military offenders from the ceded regions; (i) Italian payment of 200 million lire to Austria-Hungary for property in the ceded regions; (j) Italian friendly neutrality; and (k) mutual renunciation of further compensations during the war.[60]

Two days later Italy received Britain's final counterproposals as advanced by Prime Minister Asquith himself in Grey's absence. This last British proposal included the following four points: (a) the territory from Zara to Cape Planka (not neutralized) to be ceded to Italy; (b) the territory from Cape Planka to Cattaro, including Sabbioncello and the islands of Brazza, to revert to Serbia and to be neutralized (with the exception of that section of the littoral defined in point d); (c) the Curzolari group of islands and Lissa (none to be neutralized) to go to Italy; and (d) the coast from Sabbioncello to Castelnuovo (Hercegnovi) not to be neutralized.[61]

By now Italy was ready—especially because of the unpromising silence in Vienna—to agree to Asquith's formula with one exception. As was reported to Sazonov on April 15, Italy wished to fix the southern limit of the non-neutralized zone at a point ten miles south of Ragusa rather than at Castelnuovo, since Castelnuovo was very close to Cattaro.[62] Sazonov agreed to extend the neutralization of the Montenegrin coast northward to twenty kilometers north of Cattaro, particularly since Italy agreed to renounce its claims to Sabbioncello. He repeated his government's insistence, however, that Italy join the war by the end of April, as previously promised.[63]

[60] Sonnino to Avarna, April 8, 1915, in *Diplomatic Documents Submitted to the Italian Parliament by the Minister for Foreign Affairs (Sonnino): Austria-Hungary*, Session of May 20, 1915 (London [1915]), pp. 82-84.

[61] Memorandum of Buchanan to the Russian Foreign Minister, April 10, 1915, in TRMV, pp. 275-76.

[62] Memo of the British Embassy in Russia to the Russian Foreign Ministry, April 15, 1915, in MOEI, Vol. VII, Part 2. Doc. No. 535.

[63] Memo of the Russian Foreign Ministry to the French and British Embassies in Russia, April 16, 1915, *ibid.*, Doc. No. 537.

Only a day later, however, on April 17, Sazonov revealed his true dissatisfaction with the course of the negotiations to Ambassador Benckendorff in London:

It is impossible for me to share Delcassé's opinion that "the most important thing at the moment is to sign the treaty as soon as possible," because this treaty assures Italy of many and large gains in exchange for its promise to declare war only after a month. I persist in entertaining no great hopes of the military aid of Italian troops, which have never offered proof in the past of fighting qualities. I find that Italy's participation is important solely for morale. . . .[64]

Sazonov's low opinion of Italian military prowess was not shared by the commander in chief of Russia's armies, the Grand Duke Nikolai Nikolaevich, nor by the Tsar himself. The Grand Duke unequivocally agreed with his colleagues in France and Britain, Marshal Joffre and Lord Kitchener, that Italy's active participation in the war was of paramount interest to the Allies. In answer to Poincaré's plea that Russia not impede the final stage of negotiations with Italy, Tsar Nicholas assured his "very dear and great friend" of his co-operation: "Conscious of the usefulness which Italy's participation might have for us—perhaps shortening the duration of the war—I have authorized my government to make large concessions to Italian demands even though these demands were very considerable and, on numerous points, in contradiction to the aspirations of the Slavic peoples."[65]

When a final draft of the proposed agreement with Italy was submitted to the Russian foreign ministry on April 17, Sazonov could only repeat the protests he had already made, and even these had to be quickly dropped in the face of a pointed reminder from the now impatient British. In an unusually blunt telegram sent to Ambassador Buchanan on April 20, Sir Edward Grey observed: "After the complaisance we have shown toward Russia in the question of Constantinople, it seems to me that it would be unjust on the part of Mr. Sa-

---

[64] Sazonov to Benckendorff, April 17, 1915, *ibid.*, Doc. No. 545.
[65] Nicholas II to President Poincaré, April 21, 1915, *ibia.*, Doc. No. 571.

zonov to insist. . . . Read this telegram to Sazonov and transmit to him my request that he study the situation from this point of view."[66]

Upon studying the situation not only from this point of view but from that of Tsar Nicholas, the Grand Duke Nikolai Nikolaevich, the French government, the allied chiefs of staff, and the threat of an Italian withdrawal, Sazonov wrote to Benckendorff on April 20, 1915: "I am forced to accept the signing of the treaty with Italy in a form which, in my opinion, is very unsatisfactory."[67] At the same time he complained that the terms of the treaty had been drawn up by Grey and Cambon without his participation and that he had only been presented with accomplished facts. However, in his communication of the following day to Ambassador Benckendorff, Sazonov observed stoically: "Now that the signing of the Treaty of London has been decided upon, this is no longer the moment to complain, even though the complaints are justifiable."[68]

THE SECRET TREATY OF LONDON

On the afternoon of April 26, 1915, the representatives of the Triple Entente and Italy—Sir Edward Grey, M. Paul Cambon, Count Alexander Benckendorff and the Marchese Imperiali di Francavilla—affixed their signatures to the Treaty of London. This treaty consisted of an Italian memorandum, which constituted the major part of the treaty, an agreement pledging the signatories not to conclude a separate peace, and a pledge to keep the treaty secret for the duration of the war.

The Italian memorandum of sixteen articles had the following to say regarding the Italian frontier in the region of the Balkans:

Article 4. Under the Treaty of Peace, Italy shall obtain the Trentino, Cisalpine Tyrol with its geographical and natural

---

[66] Buchanan to Sazonov, April 20, 1915, *ibid.*, Doc. No. 563.
[67] Sazonov to Benckendorff, April 20, 1915, *ibid.*, Doc. No. 564.
[68] Sazonov to Benckendorff, April 21, 1915, in TRMV, p. 286.

frontier (the Brenner frontier), as well as Trieste, the counties
of Gorizia and Gradisca, all Istria as far as the Quarnero and
including Volosca and the Istrian islands of Cherso and Lussin[o], as well as the small islands of Plavnik, Unie, Canidole,
Palazzuoli, San Pietro di Nembi, Asinello, Gruica and the neighboring islets.

   Article 5. Italy shall also be given the province of Dalmatia
within its present administrative boundaries, including to the
north Lisarica and Tribania; to the south as far as a line starting
from Cape Planka. . . . She shall also obtain all the islands
situated to the north and west of Dalmatia . . . with the exception of Greater and Lesser Zirona, Bua, Solta and Brazza.[69]

   Italy further obtained the neutralization of the entire Adriatic coast from Cape Planka on the north to the southern base
of Sabbioncello Peninsula in the south, as well as the portion
from a point ten kilometers south of the headland of Ragusa
Vecchia down to the Voiussa River in Albania.

   Italy's gains by the secret Treaty of London by no means
corresponded to maximum irredentist claims.   Nevertheless,
when the leaders of the Italian government compared their
newly obtained gains with their initial demands, they had
reason to be pleased with their efforts.   The Trentino, the
southern Tyrol, all of Venezia Giulia with Trieste, the lion's
share of the Dalmatian islands, a third of Dalmatia itself,
outright posession of Valona and the Bay of Saseno as well as
a virtual mandate over Albania, possession of the Dodecanese
Islands, a promise to get a substantial area in Turkey, all of
Libya, compensation in East Africa and a loan of 50 million
pounds sterling from Great Britain constituted Italy's final
price for intervention in the war on the side of the Entente.
Italy's initial request from Austria had been for the Trentino
alone, its first demand from the Entente for the Trentino
and Valona.   Now, after ten months of neutrality during a
savage world war, Salandra's government could well afford to
be satisfied.   In his report to the Italian foreign minister,
Sonnino, on the signing of the Treaty of London, Ambassador

   [69] For a complete text of the Treaty of London, see British White
Paper, Misc. No. 7, 1920, Cmd. 671.

Imperiali could write in all sincerity: "Will you allow me, as a patriotic Italian, to add my fervent wish that the treaty just concluded will, by divine aid and the strength of Italian arms, secure to our beloved country the full realization of her exalted destiny. . . . My most devoted gratitude for the particular honor you have paid me in allowing me to append my modest signature to this historic document."[70]

David Lloyd George recalled in his *Memoirs of the Peace Conference*: "Sir Edward Grey's defense of the treaty was characteristically simple and direct: 'In war you will have secret treaties. Many things regarded as criminal are regarded as inevitable in time of war.'"[71]

While congratulations were being exchanged in Rome, and while British and French statesmen were shrugging their shoulders in resignation, a far different atmosphere hung over the Russian and Serbian capitals as well as over the Balkan domains of the tottering Austro-Hungarian Empire. Had not Sazonov warned: "Should the excessive aspirations Italy nurtures regarding the eastern Adriatic coast be realized, a conflict might certainly be predicted in the not too distant future between Italy and the Serbs and Croats. . ."?[72] Not even Sazonov could imagine how truly prophetic his words were. This prophecy was to hang over two generations.

[70] Salandra, *Italy and the Great War*, p. 284.
[71] David Lloyd George, *Memoirs of the Peace Conference* (New Haven, 1939), II, 502.
[72] Sazonov to Izvol'skii and Benckendorff, March 15, 1915, in TRMV, p. 263, Doc. No. 89. (In regard to the addressees named, see note 45 above.)

JAMES M. POTTS

The Loss of Bulgaria

After the outbreak of the World War in 1914, neutral Bulgaria acquired an importance to each of the two major alliances far greater than was justified by her military power, size or resources alone. Were she to join the Central Powers, Bulgaria was in a position to deal Serbia a death blow from the rear. Furthermore, she occupied a highly strategic position relative to the Turkish Straits, the closure of which isolated Russia from her more industrialized allies, Britain and France, and prevented a mutually beneficial exchange of resources for waging war, with particularly damaging results for Russia. One of the causes of Russia's ultimate collapse was her dire want of munitions and supplies, with which her allies could have better supplied her had a secure, all-weather route for their transport been available. Turkey blocked that route, and Bulgaria lay in the direct path along which assistance to Turkey from Germany and Austria-Hungary had to pass. If Bulgaria joined the Central Powers, Serbia might be doomed, and Turkey reinforced. If she joined the Entente, Serbia's rear would be secure, and Turkey would be cut off from Germany and Austria-Hungary and vulnerable to Allied attack. To Bulgaria's strategic position were added the strength of her battle-tested army and the weight her entry would carry with her neutral neighbors, Greece, Rumania and, for a brief period, Turkey. For these reasons Bulgarian neutrality or Bulgarian participation in the war was regarded in some quarters as a decisive factor in turning the tide of battle. Immediately after the Sarajevo crisis and for the next fifteen months both the great power groupings therefore made vigorous efforts to obtain Bulgaria's pledge of assistance or at least to hold her neutral. On the Entente side, Russia was usually in the forefront in this effort, Britain and France often lagging behind because of their greater emphasis on securing Italian and Greek cooperation.

BULGARIA IN 1914

By the Treaty of Bucharest of August 10, 1913,[1] the victorious allies of the Second Balkan War imposed terms on defeated Bulgaria. Although Bulgaria emerged with a one-fifth increase in territory over her pre-1912 size, Greece and Serbia had each nearly doubled in area, and Rumania with little sacrifice had gained the Dobruja region. Bulgaria felt their expansion had been at her expense, believing as she did that the Macedonian Slavs were predominantly Bulgarian. Sullen and estranged from her neighbors (Bulgarian ill feeling was exemplified in a popular song entitled "Allies-Robbers"), she awaited a revision of the treaty which each of her neighbors had a stake in maintaining.

Bulgaria's political leaders distrusted all the great powers. They felt Russia had left them in the lurch by not backing Bulgaria's claim to a strict interpretation of the Serbo-Bulgarian Treaty of 1912.[2] They blamed Russian Foreign Minister Sazonov for encouraging rather than checking the Rumanian attack on their rear on July 10, 1913. They were resentful of Austria-Hungary's failure to intervene in the Second Balkan War in view of the Austrian Foreign Minister's previous declaration of support,[3] overlooking their own failure to meet one of his conditions, that Bulgaria compensate Rumania for

---

[1] For the text see *The Eastern Question* (London, 1920), pp. 134-38 (British Foreign Office *Peace Handbook* No. 15).

[2] The text is given in *Sbornik sekreinykh dokumentov iz Arkhiva byvshago Ministerstva Inostrannykh del*, Vol. II (Petrograd, 1917).

[3] Berchtold to Tarnowski, June 28, 1913, in *Österreich- Ungarns Aussenpolitik von der Bosnischen Krise 1908 bis zum Kriegsausbruch 1914: Diplomatische Aktenstücke des Österreichisch- Ungarischen Ministeriums des Äussern* (Vienna, 1930), VI, 761; quoted in H. N. Howard, *The Partition of Turkey* (Norman, Oklahoma, 1931), p. 30.

her neutrality. During the deliberations at Bucharest both
Germany and France supported the Greek claim to Kavalla,
and reservations on this point by Austria-Hungary and Russia
were weak and ineffective. Even Turkey gained lost ground
by a separate treaty of September 29, 1913. Thus the end
of the Balkan wars saw Bulgaria alone of the Christian Balkan
states without a champion among the great powers.

Despite a liberal constitution, King Ferdinand was absolute
master in Bulgaria. He appointed and dismissed ministers
at will, he was commander-in-chief of the army, and a constitutional amendment of 1911 had empowered him to conclude
secret treaties and alliances. He could summon or prorogue
the National Assembly. Though a German prince with an
Austrian and German background, Ferdinand was motivated
mainly by personal ambition, and it centered on the aggrandizement of Bulgaria, to which his own fortunes were tied.
Friends and enemies alike regarded him as cultured, intelligent
and well grounded in European diplomatic history. Those
who disliked him described his intelligence as shrewdness,
and his diplomacy as a specious form, marked by cunning.

His chief minister, Minister-President Vasil Radoslavov,
before his appointment had (in an open letter to the King)
urged a break with Russia and with ideas of Slav solidarity,
favored reconciliation with Rumania and demanded revenge
on Serbia and Greece, suggesting that Bulgaria exploit the
hostility of Austria-Hungary to Serbia and of Turkey to Greece.[4]
But even after Ferdinand placed Radoslavov at the head of
the government, Bulgarian efforts to draw closer to Austria-
Hungary met with cautious reserve. Austria-Hungary was
dependent upon Germany, and William II disliked Ferdinand.
He thought it "more important for Austria-Hungary to win
Serbia than Bulgaria, whose king was untrustworthy and

---

[4] For excerpts from the letter see Howard, p. 35. A Russian translation of the text is given in *Mezhdunarodnye otnosheniia v epokhu imperializma*, Series III (Moscow, 1931-38), III, 56, note 1; the abbreviation
MOEI used hereafter refers to this title, Series III.

always inclined toward intrigue." If Ferdinand came to Berlin he would be told to "get his engine's steam up for departure."[5] William II did not want to jeopardize his alliance with King Charles (Carol) of Rumania. But the Transylvanian problem impeded understanding between Austria-Hungary and Rumania, and, moreover, Austria-Hungary apparently feared that, if she ignored Bulgaria's overtures,[6] Bulgaria might be forced into a bloc with Serbia and Russia against Austria-Hungary.

At home the Radoslavov government was in political and economic trouble. Ferdinand had dissolved the National Assembly in July, 1913, and in the December elections of that year the Radoslavov government received only two-fifths of the votes cast. The opposition, with a majority in the legislature, refused to approve the government's budget. The budget was nevertheless put into effect, and the National Assembly dissolved. Ferdinand's success in retaining Radoslavov was facilitated by the antagonisms among the seven parties in opposition.

In new elections in March, 1914, Radoslavov's government gained a scant majority, his margin being provided by thirteen Moslem deputies from the newly acquired (formerly Turkish)

---

[5] Report of the Austro-Hungarian chargé d'affaires at Munich to Berchtold, December 16, 1913, on an interview with William II; quoted in R. W. Seton-Watson, "William II's Balkan Policy," *Slavonic Review*, VII, No. 19 (June, 1928), 19-20, 26-29.

Savinskii, Russian minister to Bulgaria, reported to Sazonov on February 6, 1914, that Ferdinand had told him that "Emperor William hates me as he has been pro-Greek since the time when his sister became their Queen. Still, one can reach an understanding with William, but with Austria it is impossible." MOEI, Vol. I, 368, Doc. No. 291 (the document numbers cited in this article are the editorial numbers used in the source).

Tschirschky reported Francis Joseph's personal antipathy for Ferdinand in a telegram to Bethmann-Hollweg, July 2, 1914: "Although he, the Emperor, certainly didn't think much of King Ferdinand, nevertheless Bulgaria was a great country" and should be supported. K. Kautsky, ed., *Documents on the Outbreak of the World War* (New York, 1924), p. 65.

[6] Ferdinand was in Vienna in November making such overtures; a memorandum of a meeting on November 6, 1913, between Ferdinand and Berchtold appears in *Österreich-Ungarns Aussenpolitik*, Vol. VII, Doc. No. 8934.

territory in Thrace, to which he had just granted the franchise
in violation of the Constitution.

Bulgaria was also undergoing severe financial strains. Just
before and during the First Balkan War, French banks had
advanced 75 million francs,[7] and Russian banks 45 million
francs. In November, 1913, a Bulgarian emissary, Gennadiev,
was sent to Paris to negotiate a long-term loan to cover the
repayments to the French banks soon to fall due and to miti-
gate the after-effects of the heavy expenditures of the Balkan
Wars. The Russian ambassador in Paris, Izvol'skii, to whom
Gennadiev denied any Russophobe inclinations, did not at first
propose to hinder Gennadiev's work,[8] but Sazonov instructed
him to warn the French government against the loan and to
bring to its attention the anti-Russian "calumnies" and "intrigues and coquetting" with Austria of the Radoslavov government.[9] Gennadiev went home empty handed. Nor were efforts
to raise money in Berlin and Vienna more successful. Austria-
Hungary advised Bulgaria to bring about a rapprochement
with Rumania in order to overcome Germany's objections to
Bulgaria's adherence to the Triple Alliance. The Radoslavov government found this impossible.[10]

RUSSIAN POLICY OF ALOOFNESS TOWARD BULGARIA

Since the Treaty of Bucharest in 1913, it had been Russia's
aim to dissipate the rancor between Serbia and Bulgaria and
to bring these two together under Russian influence as a
means of blocking Austro-German expansion southward and,
if necessary, of exerting pressure on Turkey. However, Sa-

[7] Jacob Viner, "International Finance and Balance of Power Diplomacy,"
Southwestern Political and Social Science Quarterly, IX, No. 9 (March,
1929), 440; and *Entente Diplomacy and the World: Matrix of the History
of Europe, 1909-14*, trans. B. de Siebert, ed. George Abel Schreiner (New
York, 1921), p. 452.

[8] Izvol'skii's telegram and dispatch to Sazonov both dated November 6,
1913, in *Un livre noir: Diplomatie d'avant-guerre et de guerre d'après les
documents des archives russes* (Paris, 1922-34), II, 167-72.

[9] Sazonov to Izvol'skii, November 7, 1913, *ibid.*, pp. 178-79.

[10] Tarnowski to Berchtold, December 11, 1913, in *Österreich- Ungarns
Aussenpolitik*, Vol. VII, Doc. Nos. 9080 and 9136.

zonov regarded the government of Radoslavov as Austrophile
and not to be trusted. The Russian press was violently hostile
to the Bulgarian government ; a British report from St. Petersburg observed that "the Bulgarian Minister of Foreign Affairs
has been reminded almost daily that, in view of his former
malpractices, his proper place is the felon's dock."[11] Nor was
King Ferdinand himself spared, and talk of his abdication,
voluntary or otherwise, was common in St. Petersburg.[12] Nevertheless Sazonov assured Buchanan, the British ambassador,
that the Russian government was supporting Ferdinand, "for
were he to go, Bulgaria would become a republic."[13] So, although
the long-range Russian aim was to reconcile Serbia and Bulgaria, when A. A. Savinskii went to Sofia as Russian minister
early in 1914, his verbal instructions from Sazonov were "to
stand aloof from the Radoslavov government and to wait
for its downfall." If he "could manage to assist in its overthrow
without any risk of exposure, that would be still better; after that negotiations with the Bulgarians could be resumed
again."[14]

In his initial audience with Ferdinand in February, 1914,
Savinskii told him that more than words were required of
Bulgaria. "She must prove by her actions that she is deserving
of Russian support."[15] Sazonov encouraged this stern attitude
and advised Savinskii that even a change of the Bulgarian
cabinet would not mean the end of the policy of "extreme
caution" as long as King Ferdinand wished to improve his
relations with Russia "without compromising his relations
with Austria." Still, with a change in government, "it would be

[11] O'Beirne to Grey, December 11, 1913, in G. P. Gooch and Harold
Temperley, eds., *British Documents on the Origins of the War 1898-1914*
(London, 1926-38), X, 288.

[12] Crackenthorpe to Grey, January 27 to February 20, 1914, *ibid.*,
pp. 313, 337.

[13] Buchanan to Grey, February 1, 1914, *ibid.*, p. 337.

[14] A. A. Savinsky (Savinskii), *Recollections of a Russian Diplomat*
(London [1927]), p. 200

[15] Savinskii to Sazonov, February 19, 1914, in MOEI, Vol. I, Doc.
No. 291.

possible . . . to accelerate the final settlement of the Bulgarian loan in Paris."[16]

Immediately on arriving in Sofia, Savinskii looked for ways to promote Russophile thinking within influential court, political, business and professional circles. His first requests for funds to subsidize the local press were refused by Sazonov with the comment "We do not value public opinion created in such a way."[17] But when the request was repeated on February 18, 1914, in connection with the approaching Bulgarian elections,[18] Sazonov approved, and 10,000 rubles were transferred to Savinskii for this purpose.[19] In May, 1914, Sazonov refused Savinskii's request[20] for more money in view of the opposition of the Minister of Trade,[21] opposition which was overcome only after the beginning of war, when Savinskii renewed his subsidies to keep certain Bulgarian editors well disposed toward Russia.

Russian policy throughout this period was characterized by a patronizing tone toward Bulgaria arising from a belief that, as the liberator and protector of the Balkans, Russia's emperor enjoyed a position superior to that of minor Balkan kings, who should look to him as the arbiter of their differences, trust him without question and be eager to repay a long-standing debt of gratitude to Russia. For example, in an audience with King Ferdinand before the World War Savinskii said: "You must not forget that Russia has her own political tasks, which exceed all others in importance; that is what the Bulgarians have so often overlooked."[22] Again in

---

[16] Sazonov to Savinskii, March 2, 1914, *ibid.*, Doc. No. 358; also in *Entente Diplomacy and the World*, p. 441.

[17] Savinskii's report of March-April, 1916, in MOEI, Vol. VIII, Part 2, Supplement.

[18] Savinskii to the Chief of Near Eastern Department, Trubetskoi, February 18, 1914, *ibid.*, Vol. I, Doc. No. 27.

[19] Sazonov's letter to the Minister of Finance, February 27, 1914, *ibid.*, Doc. No. 342; and telegram to Savinskii, *ibid.*, p. 456, note 1.

[20] Savinskii to Sazonov, May 18, 1914, *ibid.*, Vol. III, Doc. No. 9.

[21] Sazonov to Savinskii, May 27, 1914, *ibid.*, III, 13, note 1.

[22] Savinsky, *Recollections*, p. 213. For a similar though slightly different version of the statement (made February 18, 1914), see Savinskii's letter to Sazonov, February 19, 1914, in MOEI, Vol. I, Doc. No. 291.

a telegram to Sazonov, Savinskii remarked: "The traditional character of our relations with Bulgaria, while giving us special rights, also implies some duties on our part."[23] Sermons by Savinskii in this vein were hardly likely to sway Ferdinand and his ministers, who realized that Russia's motives were not always altruistic and who weighed the issue on the scale of tangible advantage to Bulgaria.

As part of the policy of aloofness, Savinskii met and sympathized with politicians opposing Radoslavov, letting his distrust of Radoslavov be known, expecting that Russian pressure to deny Bulgaria foreign loans would bring him to his knees.

Meanwhile, Germany and Austria were slowly harmonizing their divergent views on Bulgaria. On March 15, 1914, Count Tisza urged a realignment of policies, placing great importance on Bulgaria and her reconciliation with Greece and Turkey to create a threat to Serbia.[24] Rumania, despite King Charles, was drawing closer to Russia though still formally tied to the Central Powers. This enhanced Bulgaria's value to the Central Powers. No alliance was offered her, however; rather, with the German government prodding and the Rumanian objecting, negotiations for a large loan progressed favorably in Berlin.[25]

Alarmed by the implications of such a loan and recognizing that Russian financial pressure on Bulgaria was actually driving her into the arms of Germany, Savinskii urged steps to counter the Berlin negotiations by denying British and French money to the German banking consortium. Sazonov requested such action in telegrams to his ambassadors in Paris and London.[26] In a quick about-face, Savinskii also urged that France be induced to lend Ferdinand personally about 100 million francs, simultaneously postponing the due date of the 75-

---

[23] Telegram of September 21, 1915, in Savinsky, *Recollections*, p. 290.
[24] See H. Marczali, "Papers of Count Tisza 1914-1918," *American Historical Review*, XXIX, January (1924), 303-10.
[25] Szögyény to Berchtold, March 1, 1914, in *Österreich- Ungarns Aussenpolitik*, Vol. VII, Doc. No. 9423; and Tarnowski to Berchtold, June 8, 1914, *ibid.*, Vol. VIII, Doc. No. 9837.
[26] Sazonov to Benckendorff, May 6, 1914, in *Entente Diplomacy and the World*, p. 451; and Izvol'skii to Sazonov, April 29, 1914, *ibid.*

million-franc repayment previously mentioned.[27] The French government accepted this proposal in mid-May, with the expectation that the advance would be conditioned upon a change in the Bulgarian cabinet.

By the end of May the French banks had not yet agreed to advance the money. Instead, the French government proposed offering Ferdinand a 600-million-franc loan which would not be contingent on Radoslavov's dismissal but would be advanced in installments in order to provide frequent levers for influencing Ferdinand's policy. Izvol'skii forwarded the draft proposal to St. Petersburg, but the offer was never made, as it was delayed until the Sarajevo crisis had disturbed the money market and halted such activity.[28] German bankers, headed by the firm Disconto-Gesellschaft, acting more quickly, advanced 100 million francs and obtained an option on the loan.[29] Its terms were hard and provided for two series of credits to Bulgaria, each series totaling 250 million francs and bearing interest at 5 percent. Repayment was guaranteed chiefly by the state's tobacco revenue. The first series was to repay the 75-million-franc French bank advance and 120 million francs in Disconto-Gesellschaft advances, the balance being available to the Bulgarian government. The second series was for the construction of a railroad to Porto Lagos on the Aegean Sea by German and Austro-Hungarian entrepreneurs (50 million francs), for purchases from Germany and Austria-Hungary (100 million francs), and for other purposes as Bulgaria desired. The agreement required ratification by Bulgaria by July 30, 1914, and was cancelable by the banks should war break out.[30] Savinskii tried to thwart ratification

---

[27] Savinskii to Sazonov, April 22, 26 and 27, 1914, in MOEI, Vol. II, Doc. Nos. 268, 301 and 307.

[28] See *Entente Diplomacy and the World*, pp. 451-56; and MOEI, Vol. II, Doc. No. 418, and Vol. IV, Doc., Nos. 19 and 33.

[29] Viner, p. 442.

[30] The text as published in *L'Echo de Bulgarie* is contained in Arthur Raffalovich, *Le marché financier* (Paris), XXIII (for the years 1913-1914; published in 1915), 723 ff. The guarantee based on the government tobacco monopoly was later successfully opposed, and replaced by one

by the Bulgarian National Assembly.[31] All the opposition parties fought the agreement, but during a stormy session Radoslavov pronounced it approved, without a roll call and amidst general tumult.[32]

By the late spring of 1914 Savinskii was chafing at the restraints of the Russian policy of aloofness in Bulgaria and was advocating that Ferdinand be asked point-blank to part with Radoslavov, to end Bulgaria's hostility to Serbia, to abandon his "personal regime" and to manifest his friendship to Russia by consecrating the Cathedral of St. Alexander Nevsky in Sofia.[33] He also warned of increasing Austrian activity in Bulgaria and recommended that Russia tighten its cultural and commercial bonds with Bulgaria by expanding its consular service and setting up Russian credit institutions there.[34] None of these recommendations were accepted.

Thus by the time of the Sarajevo crisis it was clear to the Russians that a pro-German leadership sat firmly at the helm in Bulgaria. Bulgaria had no formal alliances, but the Russian policy of aloofness had failed, leaving her a legacy of hard feeling and diminished prestige with Bulgaria's leaders.

RUSSIA WOOS BULGARIA

After the Sarajevo assassination Austria-Hungary delivered to Germany, on July 5, 1914, a memorandum (prepared before the Sarajevo event) which soon became the basis of their new

based on the exploitation of the Bulgarian state coal mines. Savinskii to Sazonov, July 21, 1914, in MOEI, Vol. IV, Doc. No. 310. See also *Evropeiskie derzhavy i Turtsiia vo vremia mirovoi voiny: Konstantinopl' i prolivy*, ed. Evgenii A. Adamov (Moscow, 1925-26), II, 236, note 1; hereafter abbreviated as *Konstantinopl' i prolivy*.

[31] Savinskii to Sazonov, June 4, 1914, in MOEI, Vol. III, Doc. No. 162.

[32] See G. I. Kaptchev, *La Débâcle nationale Bulgare, devant la Haute-Cour* (Paris, 1925), p. 24. Savinskii alleged that the loan was accepted by Radoslavov and his finance minister (and by implication Ferdinand) because the Germans "had taken care, while we hesitated, to interest them personally in the financial transaction." He gives no proof. See Savinsky, *Recollections*, p. 217.

[33] Savinskii to Sazonov, May 1, 1914, in MOEI, Vol. II, Doc. No. 336. Savinsky, *Recollections*, p. 221, dates this letter as April 15, 1914.

[34] Savinsky, *Recollections*, pp. 221 ff.

Balkan policy, a policy aimed at accepting Bulgaria's previous overtures and at building an alliance centered on Bulgaria and including Rumania, Greece and Turkey.[35] Although Berchtold proposed to go slowly out of deference for Rumania,[36] it was not long before the Austrian minister in Sofia, with German support,[37] placed the draft of a secret treaty before Ferdinand. The draft provided (a) that mutual assistance would be rendered by Austria-Hungary and Bulgaria if either party was without provocation attacked by two states one of which had a common frontier with Austria-Hungary, (b) that Bulgaria would remain friendly with Rumania, and (c) that Austria-Hungary noted Bulgaria's claim to Macedonia, Ferdinand delayed comment throughout July.[38] Meanwhile, however, the German legation reported Radoslavov's assurance that, now that the loan had been granted, Bulgaria sought to adhere to the Triple Alliance.[39] To pave the way Radoslavov had already authorized the Bulgarian minister in Bucharest to declare that, if Rumania left the Triple Alliance, Bulgaria would free herself of her obligation not to attack Rumania.[40] As the general European war broke out, however, Bulgaria backed off. First she made a counterproposal to Germany to draw out more specific backing for her claim of Macedonia.[41] When Berlin replied favorably, asking in turn what military obligations Bulgaria would undertake,[42] Ferdinand instead proclaimed Bulgaria's neutrality. He had sought the diplo-

---

[35] Text in Kautsky, ed., pp. 70-77; covering letter of Francis Joseph to William II, *ibid.*, p. 68.

[36] Tschirschky to Foreign Office, July 8, 1914, *ibid.*, p. 82.

[37] Zimmerman to Michahelles, July 8, 1914, *ibid.*, p. 80.

[38] Tarnowski to Foreign Office, July 19, 23 and 31, 1914, in *Österreich-Ungarns Aussenpolitik*, Vol. VIII, Doc. Nos. 10389, 10555 and 11188.

[39] Michahelles to Foreign Office, July 25, 1914. A marginal comment of William II was: "Hurry it up," and on Michahelles' report that "Ferdinand was overjoyed," he minuted: "I believe it." Kautsky, ed., p. 190.

[40] Radoslavov to Radev, July 30, 1914, in *Diplomaticheski dokumenti po namiesata na Bulgariia v evropeiskata voina* (Sofia, 1920-21), Vol. I, Doc. No. 239 (hereafter cited as *Diplomaticheski dokumenti*).

[41] Michahelles to Foreign Office, August 2, 1914, in Kautsky, ed., p. 500.

[42] Bethmann-Hollweg to Michahelles, August 2 and 3, 1914, *ibid.*, pp. 512 and 527.

matic support of the Triple Alliance, and he was willing to occupy Macedonia in conjunction with a localized Serbo-Austrian war. But, pointing to the uncertain positions of Greece and Rumania, he now told the Central Powers that Bulgaria could not pick a war on three fronts and hence must remain neutral.[43] It may be assumed that Ferdinand's astute mind recognized the advantage in marking time and observing the tide of battle.[44] Thus war began with Bulgaria neutral, following a cautious, watchful policy and receptive to bidding from both sides for her services.

On August 2, 1914, Turkey signed a secret treaty of alliance with Germany,[45] and thereafter the Central Powers redoubled efforts to form an alliance among Turkey, Bulgaria and Rumania. In Turkey the German alliance was kept very secret, and only the impetuous Enver Pasha appears to have worked for its immediate application. The other ministers hung back, stressing Turkey's unpreparedness for war and the need for an understanding with Bulgaria. To obtain such an understanding Talaat Pasha and Halil Pasha went to Sofia in August, 1914. Rumors were rife that Turkey and Bulgaria had signed a treaty, but apparently only a draft was initiated, pending assurances from Rumania. The Bulgarian documents indicate that both Bulgaria and Turkey sought to stay neutral as long as possible to observe the course of the war and that Talaat and Radoslavov agreed on a joint maneuver for the purpose—Turkey, when pressed by Germany, would excuse her own inactivity by the absence of a Bulgarian guarantee, and Bulgaria would withhold the guarantee, pointing to Rumania's ambiguous position.[46]

[43] See Toshev (Bulgarian minister at Constantinople) to Radoslavov, September 7, 1914, in *Diplomaticheski dokumenti*, Vol. I, Doc. No. 410.

[44] In this connection Radoslavov annotated a telegram of August 12, 1914, from Vienna which reported Austrian insistence that Bulgaria attack Serbia: "A decisive [Austrian] action against Serbia will arouse our public in favor of war." *Ibid.*, Doc. No. 338.

[45] Text in Kautsky, ed., p. 519. It became known to Bulgaria on August 6, 1914; see Toshev to Radoslavov, in *Diplomaticheski dokumenti*, Vol. I, Doc. No. 294. For details of the negotiations see Howard, pp. 89-91.

[46] Toshev to Radoslavov, August 12 and 15, 1914, in *Diplomaticheski*

Assuming that Bulgaria was not committed to the Central Powers, and worried about Serbia's exposed position, Russia at the outbreak of war set about to "let bygones be bygones," to drop its anti-Radoslavov policy[47] and to woo Bulgaria as an active ally. Certain Bulgarian officials continued to profess full sympathy with the Central Powers, and many observers felt it was hopeless to try to win Bulgaria to the Allied cause because her territorial aspirations could be satisfied only at the expense of one of the allies—Serbia.

However, Russia was unprepared for the alternative policy of organizing a coup d'état in Bulgaria or landing a Russian army on the Bulgarian coast to rally pro-Russian elements and forestall an attack on Serbia. Nevertheless in August, 1914, a group of Russian officials who disliked Ferdinand and believed him to be firmly in the German camp advocated such a landing at Varna, to dictate to or depose King Ferdinand.[48] Russian naval weakness made the plan impractical. A third course, to try to hold Bulgaria neutral by threats, had already been discredited by the failure of the policy of aloofness.

Savinskii did take up with Radoslavov a possible landing of Russian troops at Varna and the use of Burgas as a Russian naval anchorage in the event of a Russo-Turkish war.[49] Radoslavov temporized, finally telling Savinskii that Bulgaria would not resist a fait accompli[50] but at the same time as-

dokumenti, Vol. I, Doc. Nos. 342 and 353; and Radev to Radoslavov, August 22, 1914, *ibid.*, Doc. No. 371.

[47] See the telegram of August 14, 1914, from the Bulgarian Chargé d'Affaires in St. Petersburg to Radoslavov, referring to an interview with Trubetskoi, who asserted that Russia was not interested in personalities but was ready to forget the past if the sincerity of the present Bulgarian government was demonstrated. *Ibid.*, Vol. I, Doc. No. 351. Girs (Giers) also urged such a policy; see Girs to Sazonov, August 26, 1914, in MOEI, Vol. VI, Part 1, Doc. No. 153, note.

[48] A. Nekludoff, *Diplomatic Reminiscences before and during the War* (London, 1920), p. 302.

[49] Sazonov to Savinskii, September 21, 1914, in MOEI, VI, Part 1, 288, note 2; Savinskii to Sazonov, September 22, 1914, *ibid.*, Doc. No. 295; and Sazonov to Savinskii, November 4, 1914, in *Konstantinopl' i prolivy*, II, 289.

[50] Savinskii to Sazonov, April 2, 1915, quoting Radoslavov, in MOEI,

suring the Austrians that Bulgaria would fight in such an eventuality.[51]

At this time many Russian diplomats overestimated Bulgaria's sympathy for her Russian "brothers" and believed that, although Ferdinand might be able to hold Bulgaria neutral, he could not take her into war against Russia. They cited the many Bulgarians, including General Radko Dimitriev, Bulgarian minister to Russia, who had volunteered for the Russian army and the contributions and admiring letters pouring into the Russian legation at Sofia.[52] They neglected Ferdinand's iron grip on the country despite its further manifestation in the August, 1914, decrees proclaiming a state of siege which forbade public meetings and provided for control of the press and proroguing of the National Assembly.[53]

The new Russian policy was signalized by the note of August 3, which warned Bulgaria against hostile acts toward Serbia and made a vague offer of territorial concessions from Serbia in return for Bulgaria's friendship.[54] Simultaneously Sazonov instructed the Russian chargé in Belgrade, Shtrandtman, to obtain from the Serbian Prime Minister Pašić authority for Russia to open negotiations on Serbia's behalf for Bulgarian assistance to Serbia in return for (a) immediate cession of eastern Macedonia to the Vardar and (b) on victory, cession of Macedonia to the boundary specified in the secret annex to the Serbo-Bulgarian Treaty of February 29, 1912 (including cession of the disputed town of Struga).[55] Shtrandtman reported

VII, Part 2, 117, note. The Emperor minuted on this telegram: "It would be well to examine this." See also Savinskii to Sazonov, April 9, 1915, *ibid.*, Doc. 503; and Savinskii to Sazonov, July 15, 1915, in *Konstantinopl' i prolivy*, II, 310.

[51] Tarnowski to Burian, March 16, 1915 (as deciphered by the Russian Ministry of Foreign Affairs), in MOEI, VII, Part 1, Doc. No. 383.

[52] Up to February 27, 1915, these contributions totaled 173, 298 francs. *The Near East*, March 19, 1915, p. 541. See also Savinskii to Sazonov, September 22, 1914, in MOEI, Vol. VI, Part 1, Doc. No. 295.

[53] Radoslavov to Bulgarian envoys abroad, August 10, 1914, in *Diplomaticheski dokumenti*, Vol. I, Doc. No. 325.

[54] MOEI, Vol. V, Doc. No. 484.

[55] Sazonov to Shtrandtman, August 5, 1914, *ibid.*, Vol. VI, Part 1, Doc. No. 2.

Pašić's objections to such cessions and Serbia's reliance on Rumania and Greece to deter a Bulgarian attack on Serbia's rear. Although the Prime Minister did consent to Russia's proposal to offer concessions, he maintained that "it is best not to define the exact scope of them now."[56] To identic notes of the three Entente governments to Serbia on August 30, 1914, which formally raised the issue of concessions to Bulgaria, Serbia replied that, if Greece and Rumania also did so, she might cede territory after the war, providing that she obtained a seaport and the Serbo-Croat lands to which she aspired. It was noted that the lands then held were more highly regarded than any Serbia might later receive, and willingness to cede anything at all was qualified with the remark that all cessions required approval by the National Assembly, which would be adverse to the relinquishment of lands so dearly paid for in Serbian blood.[57] Serbian inflexibility, together with British, French and, to a lesser extent, Russian reluctance to resort to compulsion, forced a long and unsuccessful search for a formula more palatable to the Serbs.

In a talk with Radoslavov on August 9, 1914, Savinskii offered Bulgaria limited gains in Macedonia in return for her neutrality alone.[58] Coupled with the British Foreign Minister's advice to Bulgaria to stay neutral,[59] this offer further encouraged Radoslavov in the cautious, watchful policy he had adopted. On August 12, 1914, the Bulgarian government officially declared to Russia its intention to preserve "loyal neutrality."[60] Early in September Sazonov suggested to Britain and France that the Entente promise concessions by Serbia to Bulgaria and guarantee King Ferdinand his crown in return for Bulgaria's active participation on the side of the Entente.[61] Serbia's stubborn refusal of specific concessions and Britain's

---

[56] Shtrandtman to Sazonov, August 6, 1914, *ibid.*, Doc. No. 19.
[57] Shtrandtman to Sazonov, September 1, 1914, *ibid.*, Doc. No. 205.
[58] Savinskii to Sazonov, August 9, 1914, *ibid.*, Doc. No. 46.
[59] See Benckendorff to Sazonov, August 14, 1914, *ibid.*, Doc. No. 96.
[60] Savinskii to Sazonov, August 12, 1914, *ibid.*, Doc. No. 81.
[61] Sazonov to Benckendorff, September 2 and 4, 1914, *ibid.*, Doc. Nos. 206 and 217.

objections, both to a promise of Serbian territory and the guarantee of Ferdinand's crown,[62] caused this suggestion to be dropped.

The fleeting moment in August when Serbia felt endangered and ready to make concessions vanished with the repulse of the first Austrian invasion of Serbia later in the same month.[63] Thereafter, in order to forestall Allied promises to Bulgaria of Macedonian territory, the Serbs threatened a separate peace with Austria and war against Bulgaria.[64] Their simultaneous complaints of a very real ammunition shortage[65] betrayed the bluff.

Although the Allies tried to keep Serbia's refusal of concessions secret,[66] reports leaked out to the Bulgarians and raised doubts that the Entente could make good any promises to them. On one such report Ferdinand minuted, "This justifies my old prediction."[67]

A further obstacle to the reconstruction of the Balkan Bloc by the Entente was the attitude of Rumania, from whom concessions in the Dobruja were required. Rumanian Prime Minister Bratianu was playing a waiting game. To the Entente he declared that Bulgaria's threat to Rumania's rear prevented an attack by Rumania on Austria-Hungary,[68] and to prevent a reconciliation with Bulgaria he maintained that any concessions to her were impossible.[69] Bratianu even encouraged Bulgarian aggression against Serbia, by declaring in great

[62] Benckendorff to Sazonov, September 3, 1914, *ibid.*, p. 209, note 3; and September 4, 1914, *ibid.*, p. 199, note 2.

[63] Shtrandtman to Sazonov, August 27, 1914, *ibid.*, Doc. No. 171.

[64] For example, see Shtrandtman's report of November 9, 1914, *ibid.*, Doc. No. 487.

[65] For example, see Shtrandtman's report of November 7, 1914, *ibid.*, Doc. No. 481.

[66] Chaprashikov (Niš) to Radoslavov, September 4, 1914, in *Diplomaticheski dokumenti*, Vol. I, Doc. No. 402.

[67] Radev to Radoslavov, September 3, 1914, *ibid.*, Doc. No. 398. The Germans naturally fostered rumors of Serbian intransigence.

[68] Izvol'skii to Sazonov, September 20, 1914, in MOEI, Vol. VI, Part 1, Doc. No. 285.

[69] Radev to Radoslavov, September 25, 1914, in *Diplomaticheski dokumenti*, Vol. I, Doc. No. 438.

secrecy to the Bulgarian minister at Bucharest, on August 10, 1914, that Rumania would stay neutral in the event of a Bulgarian attack on Serbia, providing Bulgaria renounced her claims to Rumania's Dobruja territory. But he did not accept Radoslavov's counterproposal that Rumania make a written declaration of friendly neutrality which Bulgaria could publish the day she mobilized. Bratianu preferred to stay on the fence until it became easier to pick the winning side.[70]

Greece, too, early in the war, showed unwillingness to make concessions to Bulgaria. When Venizelos was in power, Britain balked at compelling Greece to concede territory for fear of weakening him. When Venizelos was out of power, a pro-German faction ruled which would have resisted such pressure.[71] Britain's strong backing of Greece was not at all pleasing to Sazonov.[72]

Meanwhile Russia found need to warn Bulgaria against encouragement of armed bands (*Komitadzhi*) in Macedonia. Bulgaria disclaimed responsibility. Shtrandtman, in Belgrade, wrote Sazonov in October that he thought small bands financed by Austria had initially performed acts of terrorism against the Serbs and then repressive retaliatory measures provoked further unrest; at the same time he connected the disturbances with a master plan of Bulgaria for hegemony in the Balkans.[73] When Austro-Hungarian gunboats prevented Russian supply vessels from reaching Serbia, Russia demanded that Bulgaria

[70] Radev memorandum personally presented in Sofia, August 14, 1914, *ibid.*, Doc. No. 347; and Radev to Radoslavov, August 21, 1914, *ibid.*, Doc. No. 364.

[71] Benckendorff to Sazonov, September 9, 1914 (reporting a conversation of Venizelos with the British Minister and others), in MOEI, Vol. VI, Part 1, Doc. No. 236; and Sazonov to Benckendorff, September 10, 1914, *ibid.*, Doc. No. 241.

[72] Sazonov to Benckendorff, September 6, 1914, *ibid.*, Doc. No. 226.

[73] Sazonov to Savinskii, August 9, 1914, *ibid.*, Doc. No. 41; Shtrandtman to Sazonov, October 13, 1914, *ibid.*, Doc. No. 387; Madzharov to Radoslavov, October 29, 1914, in *Diplomaticheski dokumenti*, Vol. I, Doc. No. 487; and Radoslavov to Chaprashikov, September 24, 1914, *ibid.*, Doc. No. 436.

take steps to keep the Danube open.[74] Bulgaria demurred,[75] but afterward larger Russian convoys safely reached Serbia. Except for the passage of German sailors and supplies to Turkey before Turkey became a belligerent and a few minor episodes—one of which evoked French complaints concerning transshipments to Turkey—Bulgaria was apparently circumspect in preserving neutrality during the early months of the war.[76]

Late in October Savinskii saw Pašić in Niš to press for concessions to Bulgaria. Pašić indicated that the line of the Vardar River was the maximum concession Serbia would ever make.[77]

In their views on the Bulgarian problem Sazonov and Grey, the British foreign minister, differed in that Sir Edward was interested in the solution chiefly as a factor affecting Greece's entry in the war—the Greeks before moving had to be sure of Bulgaria's neutrality[78]—whereas Sazonov stressed efforts to get Bulgaria's participation and advocated that the Entente guarantee her Macedonia according to the Serbo-Bulgarian treaty of March 13, 1912.[79]

Grey and French Foreign Minister Delcassé thought Bulgaria might fight Turkey, if not with Serbia against Austria.[80] Accordingly, with Sazonov's concurrence,[81] Bax-Ironside, the

---

[74] For text of the Russian note of September 23, 1914, see *Diplomaticheski dokumenti*, Vol. I, Doc. No. 434.

[75] Bulgarian note of October 1, 1914, *ibid.*, Doc. No. 446.

[76] For the text of the French note of December 4, 1914, see *ibid.*, Doc. No. 557; and for the text of the Bulgarian reply of January 6, 1915, *ibid.*, Doc. No. 604. The Chief of the German General Staff wrote on the subject of the supply of Turkey, "Everything that could be provided was sent by means of the very limited communication through Rumania, by the most varied other ways, by the air and under the water. It was not enough to cover Turkey's needs." Erich von Falkenhayn, *General Headquarters, 1914-1916, and Its Critical Decisions* (London [1919]), p. 77.

[77] Savinskii to Sazonov, October 29, 1914, in MOEI, Vol. VI, Part 1, Doc. No. 423.

[78] British *aide-mémoire* of November 3, 1914, *ibid.*, Part 2, Doc. No. 454.

[79] Russian *aide-mémoire* of November 5, 1914, *ibid.*, Doc. No. 466.

[80] Benckendorff to Sazonov, November 10, 1914, *ibid.*, Doc. No. 493; and Izvol'skii to Sazonov, November 7, 1914, *ibid.*, Doc. No. 478.

[81] Sazonov to Benckendorff, November 9, 1914, *ibid.*, Doc. No. 483; and Sazonov to Savinskii, November 10, 1914, *ibid.*, Doc. No. 492.

British minister in Sofia, told Radoslavov that for Bulgaria's help against Turkey, the Entente would guarantee her Eastern Thrace to the Enos-Midia line, Macedonia east of the Vardar and south of the line of the 1912 Serbo-Bulgarian treaty, and financial help.[82] King Ferdinand's government was not moved.

In early November, despite Serbia's ammunition shortage and Austrian pressure, Pašić rebuffed Shtrandtman's suggestion that only concessions to Bulgaria as the price of her help could relieve Serbia; the army and the country, he said, preferred to be trampled down rather than yield to Bulgaria.[83] Meanwhile Radoslavov had convinced Savinskii that Austria had offered Bulgaria all of Macedonia and part of old Serbia in the event of Austrian victory.[84] Actually the Central Powers had offered Bulgaria "that which she could take by force of arms" from their enemies.[85] But by mid-November Savinskii was urging that Bulgaria be persuaded to attack Austria by a guarantee of all of Macedonia to the 1912 treaty line, with the negotiations to be kept secret from Serbia.[86] Shtrandtman, of course, protested from Belgrade that this would alienate Serbia and shatter Russia's position in the Balkans.[87]

The worsening situation of the Serbs did bring Grey and Delcassé closer to Sazonov's point of view that the Entente should guarantee concessions to Bulgaria, if necessary without waiting for Serbian consent. Simultaneously word was received of Radoslavov's declaration of neutrality toward Rumania and Serbia.[88] The Entente accordingly presented identic notes to Bulgaria on November 24, 1914. The notes acknowledged Bulgaria's neutrality and promised to take it into ac-

[82] Text of verbal note in *Diplomaticheski dokumenti*, I, 327.
[83] Shtrandtman to Sazonov, November 7 and 9, 1914, in MOEI, Vol. VI, Part 2, Doc. Nos. 481 and 487.
[84] Savinskii to Sazonov, November 2, 1914, *ibid.*, Doc. No. 452.
[85] Radoslavov to Toshev (Vienna), February 15, 1915, in *Diplomaticheski dokumenti*, Vol. I, Doc. No. 678.
[86] Savinskii to Sazonov, November 13, 1914, in MOEI, VI, Part 2, 87, note 2; and November 17, 1914, *ibid.*, p. 92, note 1.
[87] Shtrandtman to Sazonov, November 15, 1914, *ibid.*, Doc. No. 522.
[88] British *aide-mémoires* to Russian Ministry of Foreign Affairs, November 18, 1914, *ibid.*, Doc. Nos. 531-32.

count at the end of the war and to procure for Bulgaria "important territorial gains." They indicated readiness to increase the gains should Bulgaria fight Turkey or Austria-Hungary.[89] Plainly those counsels most concerned with Serbia had been heeded, in preference to the recommendations of Savinskii and others who protested at the vagueness of the offer and who would have promised Serbian territories without further consultation with Niš.[90] A hint as to the opinion of Nicholas II appears in his cryptic marginal comment "Enough promises to Bulgaria" (dated November 7, 1914) on one of Shtrandtman's telegrams warning of Bulgarian claims.[91] Bulgaria replied to the Allied notes by reaffirming her neutrality.[92]

Russian diplomats were obviously handicapped by having to act in accord with their allies and particularly by the absence of a supreme Allied command. The time consumed in inter-Allied negotiations sometimes vitiated the Allied effort. There was, no doubt, friction between the British and Russian ministers in Sofia. But there were also basic differences within the British and Russian foreign offices and legations. For example, Sazonov, Savinskii, Lloyd George, the Buxton brothers and O'Beirne[93] all believed that Bulgaria could be won by suitable concessions. Grey, Shtrandtman and Bax-Ironside were usually respectful of Serbian disinclination to cede territory to Bulgaria. Sir Arthur Nicolson and Baron Schilling, his counterpart in the Russian Foreign Ministry, were both skeptical of attracting Bulgaria by concessions. Within each country, first one faction, then another seized the initiative. Far more important than Russo-British rivalry as a cause of Allied failure was the absence of unified Allied strategy.

[89] Savinskii to Sazonov, November 20 and 24, 1914, ibid., Doc. Nos. 540 and 556.
[90] Savinskii to Sazonov, November 22, 1914, ibid., p. 106, note 3.
[91] Ibid., p. 7, note 1.
[92] Radoslavov's reply of December 9, 1914 (summarized), ibid., p. 121, note 5.
[93] The two Buxton brothers were influential members of Parliament with a keen interest in Bulgaria. O'Beirne was British minister to Bulgaria from July to October, 1915, following a tour as counselor in Petrograd.

Serbia constantly pressed her need for a common frontier with Greece as a limit on concessions she could make Bulgaria.[94] To circumvent this obstacle, Sazonov suggested to Grey and Delcassé that Albania be partitioned between Greece and Serbia to provide a common Greek-Serbian border west of Macedonia.[95] Grey objected on the grounds that the move might suggest the possibility of a great expansion of Bulgaria and disturb Bulgaria's neighbors. Instead he suggested further steps to make sure of Bulgaria's neutrality.[96]

In early December fear of an impending Austrian onslaught induced Pašić to seek the assistance of Greece, with which he thought Serbia might hold out. The Greeks indicated a willingness to help providing the Entente would guarantee Greece against Bulgarian attack.[97] Grey preferred to keep Bulgaria neutral and to avoid promises of large concessions to Bulgaria in Macedonia, of a kind to which the Greeks vociferously objected.[98] Sazonov did not place much hope in Greek help and preferred to press Serbia for concessions to Bulgaria in return for Serbian expansion at the expense of Austria-Hungary. The Greeks withdrew their offer of help when Bratianu refused their request that he tell Bulgaria that Rumania would attack her if she attacked Greece or Serbia (while Greece was helping Serbia).[99]

The published Bulgarian documents of the period indicate that Radoslavov expected to stay neutral until the war reached a decisive stage. In confidential talks with Entente diplo-

[94] For example, see Shtrandtman to Sazonov, October 13, 1914, in MOEI, Vol. VI, Part 1, Doc. No. 387.
[95] Sazonov to Izvol'skii and Benckendorff, November 27, 1914, *ibid.*, Part 2, Doc. No. 561.
[96] Sazonov to Benckendorff, November 29, 1914, *ibid.*, Doc. No. 368. Grey also opposed such a division because it conflicted with Italian aspirations; see British *aide-mémoire* of December 3, 1914, *ibid.*, Doc. No. 590.
[97] Demidov (Athens) to Sazonov, December 1, 1914, *ibid.*, Doc. Nos. 581 and 582.
[98] British *aide-mémoire* of December 3, 1914, *ibid.*, Doc. No. 590.
[99] Sazonov to Benckendorff and Izvol'skii, December 6, 1914, *ibid.*, Doc. No. 608; and Poklevskii to Sazonov, December 6, 1914, *ibid.*, Doc. No. 611.

mats he professed sympathy for their cause, maintained that Bulgarian neutrality benefited them and denied that a Bulgarian threat prevented Rumania from attacking Austria-Hungary.[100] Simultaneously he was friendly with the Central Powers, excusing Bulgaria's inaction by her shortage of munitions and exposed position and claiming credit for restraining Rumania. On the assumption that they would want to weaken Serbia in any case, he hoped to get promises of rewards for neutrality, at Serbian expense. In short, he sought to assure Bulgaria of gains without fighting, no matter which side won. Thus the vague offers of Russia and her allies in November, 1914, stood little chance of acceptance, and it seems fair to assume that even the larger bait of all Macedonia which Savinskii and others of like views were disposed to dangle before Bulgaria would not have been sufficiently enticing.

Moreover, the Entente's offer of November 24, 1914, was even more vague and less favorable than the Bulgarians had anticipated. During direct talks with Pašić, which he had asked for during the dark days of November, 1914, the Bulgarian negotiator reported a conciliatory spirit on the part of the Serb leader, [101] as well as evidence that the government-inspired press was preparing the country for concessions to Bulgaria[102] and that the Serbian National Assembly in secret session had not objected to Pašić's statement that concessions would be necessary.[103] Madzharov had recently reported from Petrograd that Sazonov was ready to guarantee Bulgaria the 1912 Treaty frontier.[104] And the British minister at Athens

[100] See Savinskii to Savonov, August 9 and September 22, 1914, *ibid.*, Part 1, Doc. Nos. 46 and 295; November 6 and 13, 1914, *ibid.*, Part 2, Doc. Nos. 474 and 508; Demidov to Sazonov, December 1, 1914, *ibid.*, Doc. No. 581; Radev to Radoslavov, October 13, 1914, in *Diplomaticheski dokumenti*, Vol. I, Doc. No. 474; and Radoslavov to Hadzhi Mishev, February 15, 1915, *ibid.*, Doc. No. 676.

[101] Chaprashikov to Radoslavov, November 7, 1914, in *Diplomaticheski dokumenti*, Vol. I. Doc. No. 516.

[102] Chaprashikov to Radoslavov, November 8, 1914, *ibid.*, Doc. No. 522.

[103] Chaprashikov to Radoslavov, November 18, 1914, *ibid.*, Doc. No. 533.

[104] Madzharov to Radoslavov, November 5, 1914, *ibid.*, Doc. No. 514. Miliukov was reported by a Bulgarian agent to have revealed that Tru-

had spoken to the Bulgarian minister there about promises
of not only the Enos-Midia line in Thrace but also the port of
Rodosto (Tekirdag) on the Marmara.[105] The Bulgarians may
therefore have regarded the Entente offer as merely an opening
move to fix bargaining positions.

In early December Savinskii held conversations with Radoslavov and the Bulgarian Minister of War, General Fichev,
in which Savinskii indicated that Bulgaria might receive
the uncontested zone of Macedonia if she came to Russia's
side.[106] Sazonov followed up these conversations in the hope
that Radoslavov would name the price of Bulgarian participation, which Russia could then press Serbia to pay.[107] Radoslavov refused to quote any such price to Savinskii or,
through the Bulgarian minister at Niš, to Prince Trubetskoi,
newly appointed Russian minister to Serbia, whose arrival
in the Balkans caused a great deal of excitement. Trubetskoi
had previously been the head of the Near Eastern Department
of the Russian Foreign Ministry, and his mission was regarded
by Bulgaria as highly significant. When he passed through
Bucharest, Radev, the Bulgarian minister there, saw him and
reported that Trubetskoi was empowered to effect the reconciliation of Bulgaria and Serbia on the basis of the Treaty
of 1912 if Bulgaria would undertake to employ a 200,000-man
army against Austria-Hungary.[108] Radoslavov's instructions

betskoi thought significant concessions would be made to Bulgaria.
Bulgarian Chargé d'Affaires at Petrograd to Radoslavov, September 17,
1914, in MOEI, Vol. VI, Part 1, Doc. No. 272. This telegram was deciphered by the Russians.
  [105] Pasarov (Athens) to Radoslavov, October 31, 1914, in *Diplomaticheski dokumenti*, Vol. I, Doc. No. 494.
  [106] Savinskii to Sazonov, December 3 and 6, 1914, in MOEI, VI, Part 2,
187, notes 2 and 3. The "uncontested zone" of Macedonia refers to that
part of Macedonia which, according to the Treaty of Alliance between
Bulgaria and Serbia of March 13, 1912, would fall to Bulgaria if Macedonia
was later partitioned between Bulgaria and Serbia. According to the
same treaty, the disposition of another area, the "contested zone," on
which Serbia and Bulgaria could not agree, was left to the arbitration
of the Tsar of Russia.
  [107] Sazonov to Savinskii, December 8, 1914, *ibid.*, Doc. No. 619.
  [108] Radev to Radoslavov, December 5, 1914, in *Diplomaticheski dokumenti*, Vol. I, Doc. No. 565.

to Chaprashikov in Serbia regarding the latter's future conversations with Trubetskoi were intentionally vague—Bulgaria
"held to the principles of the Tsar-Liberator, San Stefano
and the Treaty of 1912." He refused to permit Chaprashikov
to say whether Bulgaria would fight if these principles were
recognized or to name any price.[109] Trubetskoi told Chaprashikov that Bulgarian neutrality was enough for the present but that action against Turkey would be required later in
exchange for concessions in Macedonia which the Triple
Entente would force Serbia to yield. He added a special message to Ferdinand that he could expect Russian support of
his authority, thus in effect delivering Sazonov's proposed
guarantee of the previous September which Grey had then
blocked.[110] This meeting between Trubetskoi and the Bulgarian
envoy occurred just as the Serbs recaptured Belgrade and
decisively threw back the second Austrian offensive against
them. Gone now was their conciliatory attitude of the past
few perilous weeks. The change in the Serbian attitude was
exemplified by the Serbian Crown Prince's proclamation of
December 23 promising political and civil rights after the war
to "brothers whom we liberated from the Turks."[111] This
indicated that Serbia had little intention of ceding Macedonia
to Bulgaria. The mission of Prince Trubetskoi was a failure.

In an effort to obtain Greek support of Serbia, during the
time of the second Austrian offensive against Serbia the Triple
Entente had guaranteed Greece against Bulgarian attack. On
December 9, 1914, the British, French and Russian ministers
in Sofia delivered identic notes informing Bulgaria of this
guarantee and promising her "just territorial acquisitions in
Macedonia" in return for "friendly neutrality" alone.[112] Again

---

[109] See Radoslavov's comments on the Radev telegram cited in the
preceding note; also Chaprashikov to Radoslavov, December 8, 1914,
with Radoslavov's comments, *ibid.*, Doc. No. 575.
[110] Chaprashikov to Radoslavov, December 14, 1914, *ibid.*, Doc. No. 596.
[111] Text *ibid.*, Doc. No. 600.
[112] Text of Russian note in MOEI, Vol. VI, Part 2, Doc. No. 627.

the effort was without particular effect, and during the following winter months the Entente made no further offers to
Bulgaria.

In November Russia decided to support Serbian claims to
Bosnia, Hercegovina and an outlet on the Adriatic.[113] Sazonov proposed that the three powers specifically promise
these territories to Serbia in order to induce her to make concessions to Bulgaria. But Britain and France wished to postpone such a promise, as Serbian and Italian aspirations were
in conflict and both Grey and Delcassé were particularly interested in securing Italian participation on the side of the
Entente.[114] On January 28, 1915, Sazonov, Buchanan and
Paléologue drafted a note to Bulgaria which was significant
although it never passed the draft stage. It promised Bulgaria
concessions in Macedonia conditional upon the acquisition by
Serbia of territory at the expense of Austria-Hungary.[115] Except for the matter of Kavalla, this draft was essentially the
same in content as the notes finally presented May 29, 1915,
which will be discussed later. Blame for the delay of four
months must rest upon the British and French. Both Grey
and Delcassé offered counterproposals so vaguely worded
that Sazonov objected.[116] Grey favored asking Bulgaria her
price and, desiring "not to disillusion Serbia," restrained Russia
from stronger pressure on her.[117] Delcassé twice proposed
delay, to await, first, the outcome of the Dardanelles bom-
bardments[118] and, later, Italy's imminent declaration of war,

[113] *Ibid.*, p. 80, note 2.
[114] See Sazonov to Izvol'skii and Benckendorff, January 12, 1915, *ibid.*,
Doc. No. 760; Benckendorff to Sazonov, February 4, 1915, *ibid.*, Vol.
VII, Part 1, Doc. No. 129; and Izvol'skii to Sazonov, March 16, 1915,
ibid., Doc. No. 23.
[115] Sazonov to Benckendorff and Izvol'skii, January 28, 1915, *ibid.*,
Vol. VII, Doc. No. 94.
[116] For example, see Sazonov to Izvol'skii, February 3, 1915, *ibid.*,
Doc. No. 125; and Benckendorff to Sazonov, February 4, 1915, *ibid.*,
Doc. No. 129.
[117] See Benckendorff to Sazonov, February 15, 1915, *ibid.*, Doc. No. 199;
and British *aide-mémoire* to Russian Foreign Ministry, March 20, 1915,
ibid., Doc. No. 399.
[118] Izvol'skii to Sazonov, February 16, 1915, *ibid.*, Doc. No. 205.

which was expected to have a spurring effect on Bulgaria.[119] Grey and Delcassé obviously accorded a higher priority to the entry of Italy than to any Balkan question. Sazonov's disagreement with this view was partly justified in the light of the slight contribution of Italian arms to final victory.

Unfortunately the Allied offer to Bulgaria drafted in January was delayed until after the Russian defeats in Galicia and the repulse by the Turks of the initial Allied attack at Gallipoli. In the interim, with the Dardanelles threatened by an Allied fleet and Przemyśl (Peremyshl) won by the Russians, Ferdinand's willingness to draw closer to the Entente had reached a high point.[120] Even then, however, he was concerned about possible Russian control of the Straits, and Russia on her part was apprehensive of a Bulgarian capture of the Straits without Russian help. Unable to mount an attack on the Straits herself, Russia slackened pressure on Bulgaria, and in early March, 1915, Savinskii reported he was avoiding meetings with Radoslavov.[121] Russian leaders repeatedly asserted the need of Russian blood being spilt in the capture of the Straits[122] and their preference that Balkan nations play a secondary role in a Straits campaign.

In the early spring of 1915, in connection with a contemplated Russian attack on the Bosporus, the Russian high command impressed on Sazonov the need to get the use of the Bulgarian port Burgas as a preliminary. Sazonov obtained from the ministry's legal counsel an opinion that, since Bulgaria had signed but not ratified the Hague Convention of 1907, Russia

---

[119] Izvol'skii to Sazonov, April 19, 1915, *ibid.*, Vol. VII, Part 2, Doc.No. 559. Sazonov expressed his agreement; *ibid.*, p. 246, note 1.

[120] See, for example, Radoslavov to Toshev, March 15, 1915 (deciphered by Russian Ministry of Foreign Affairs), *ibid.*, Doc. No. 769; Tarnowski to Burian, March 24, 1915 (deciphered as preceding), *ibid.*, Doc. No. 421; Sonnino to Carlotti, March 2, 1915 (deciphered as preceding), in *Konstantinopl' i prolivy*, II, 257; and Savinskii to Sazonov, March 9, 1915, in MOEI, Vol. VII, Part 1, Doc. No. 335.

[121] Savinskii to Sazonov, March 9, 1915, in MOEI, Vol. VII, Part 1, Doc. No. 335.

[122] As an example, see General Leont'ev's comments, *ibid.*, VI, Part 2, 18, note 1; and Savinskii to Sazonov, June 4, 1915, *ibid.*, Vol. VIII, Part 1, Doc. No. 63.

was not bound by its articles, which limited use of a neutral's ports by a belligerent's navy.[123] At the Emperor's request Sazonov raised the question with the Allies as to an occupation of Burgas "even without Bulgaria's agreement."[124] The British replied that "to occupy Burgas without Bulgaria's consent would . . . be a most serious political error that might even prove disastrous,"[125] a view to which the British held consistently thereafter[126] and which Sazonov respected despite occasional nudges from the Russian navy. The plan to assault the Bosporus was finally postponed because of Russian naval weakness.[127]

Overconfident of her military position, Russia was unwilling to modify her own war aims in the Straits and to induce Ferdinand to march on Constantinople, al hough opening of the Straits would have strengthened Russia immeasurably.

The recalcitrant attitude of the Serbs toward concessions continued throughout the winter and spring. Rumors of the promises the Entente powers were making to Italy on the Adriatic coast soon leaked out and stiffened Serbian resistance to Entente demands.[128] Greece, likewise, had not agreed to the cession of Kavalla and protested against the rumored Allied offer of that port to Bulgaria.[129]

[123] See the documents in *Konstantinopl' i prolivy*, II, 289-95.
[124] Letter from Chief of Staff of Army Headquarters to Sazonov, March 19, 1915, in MOEI, Vol. VII, Part 1, Doc. No. 397.
[125] *Aide-mémoire* presented in Petrograd on March 23, 1915, *ibid.*, Doc. No. 412.
[126] Benckendorff to Sazonov, April 14, 1915, in *Konstantinopl' i prolivy*, II, 306.
[127] See *ibid.*, pp. 236-310.
[128] See Trubetskoi to Sazonov, December 27, 1914, and January 21 and 29, 1915, in MOEI, Vol. VI, Part 2, Doc. No. 698, and Vol. VII, Part 1, Doc. Nos. 59 and 103; and Shtrandtman to Sazonov, May 29, 1915, *ibid.*, Vol. VIII, Part 1, Doc. No. 32. In March Pašić asked the Allies not to begin negotiations with Bulgaria regarding Serbian compensations as "it might move the Serbian army to despair." Izvol'skii to Sazonov, March 22, 1915, *ibid.*, Vol. VII, Part 1, Doc. No. 409. Sazonov now endeavored to restrict promises to Italy which conflicted with Serbian aspirations, but gave in to British and French pressure; see the article in this volume by Michael Boro Petrovich, "The Italo- Yugoslav Boundary Question, 1914-1915."
[129] See British *aide-mémoire* to Russian Foreign Ministry. May 12, 1915, in

On May 7, 1915, the participation of Italy having been arranged, assurances of Entente support for Serbian claim.s against Austria-Hungary based on the principle of nationality were given Pašić,[130] and on May 29, 1915, identic Allied notes were handed Bulgaria, offering in return for a Bulgarian attack on Turkey: (a) the immediate cession of Eastern Thrace to the Enos-Midia line; and (b) the postwar cession of Macedonia to the line Kriva Palanka (Egri-Palanka), Sopot on-the-Vardar, and Okhrida, provided that Serbia acquired Bosnia, Hercegovina and an outlet on the Adriatic Sea, and that Bulgaria abstained from any occupation of Macedonia until after the end of the war. The Allies also pledged all their influence toward the cession of Kavalla to Bulgaria by Greece (in return for which territorial compensation in Asia Minor was to be offered Greece). They expressed willingness to influence negotiations between Bulgaria and Rumania for the purpose of solving the Dobruja question and promised the financial help which Bulgaria might need.[131]

A few days before the Allied démarche in Sofia, Sazonov sent instructions to Shtrandtman, with which Britain and France concurred, to present an *aide-mémoire* to Pašić affirming the Entente's determination to seek Bulgarian participation in order to shorten the war. Shtrandtman was to tell Pašić confidentially and orally that the Entente was "taking into its own hands the matter of Serbo-Bulgarian relations" and to inform him of the sacrifices which would be required of Serbia. When Pašić made the familiar retort, "Every Serb will prefer to be trampled under with Serbia, rather than make a concession to the Bulgarians," and Shtrandtman warned of Pašić's possible resignation, Sazonov instructed the Russian envoy to avoid further discussion of the matter.[132]

MOEI, Vol. VII, Part 2, Doc. No. 738; and the Greek *aide-mémoire*, to Russian Foreign Ministry, May 31, 1915, *ibid.*, Vol. VIII, Part 1, Doc. No. 42.

[130] Trubetskoi to Sazonov, May 7, 1915, *ibid.*, Vol. VII, Part 2, Doc. No. 705.

[131] For the text of the Russian note see *ibid.*, Vol. VIII, Part 1, Doc. Nos. 1 and 17.

[132] Sazonov to Shtrandtman, May 26, 1915, *ibid.*, Doc. No. 12; Shtrandt-

After repulsing the Austrian army in December, the Serbian
army had remained inactive except for an expedition into
northern Albania to reinforce Serbian claims to that territory.
Russian appeals for a Serbian offensive were especially urgent
at the end of May, 1915, but the Serbs preferred to husband
their slim resources for defensive fighting.[133]

On June 10, 1915, Pašić formally told the Entente that
Serbia was unable to accept the suggested conditions of Bulgaria's entry in the war and moreover was unable to give
the Entente authority to promise her territory.[134]

Serbo-Bulgarian relations were further embittered by the
Komitadzhi activities which again flared up in Macedonia during the spring of 1915. The Russians intercepted telegrams
from Tarnowski in Sofia to Vienna dated in January and
February which revealed that the Austrians and Germans
were financing these armed bands and inciting them to attack
the Serbs. They were also pressing Radoslavov to support
a *Komitadzhi* attack on the Niš-Salonika railroad. Radoslavov
had assured Tarnowski of support but was in fact delaying
action on various pretexts.[135] When in April the Serbs reported an attack on a frontier post,[136] the Russian Tsar ordered
"sharp representations to be made to Bulgaria."[137] The Bulgarians disclaimed responsibility.[138] Grey and Delcassé dis-
suaded Sazonov from pressing the matter further.[139]

During the winter of 1914-15 it was widely believed in
Russian official circles that Bulgarian leaders, perhaps Ferdinand himself, were in the pay of the Central Powers. Sug-

man to Sazonov, May 29 and 30, 1915, *ibid.*, Doc. Nos. 32 and 39; and
Sazonov to Shtrandtman, June 1, 1915, *ibid.*, p. 57, note 2.
   [133] An appeal of Grand Duke Nikolai was sent to Prince Alexander on
May 30, 1915; *ibid.*, Doc. No. 41.
   [134] Shtrandtman to Sazonov, June 10, 1915, *ibid.*, Doc. No. 95.
   [135] Tarnowski to Burian, January 23, February 17 and 20, 1915, *ibid.*,
Vol. VII, Part 1, 91, note 1, and Doc. Nos. 213 and 229.
   [136] Note of the Serbian government to the Russian Ministry of Foreign
Affairs, April 3, 1915, *ibid.*, Part 2, Doc. No. 466.
   [137] Russian Chief of Staff to Sazonov, April 3, 1915, *ibid.*, Doc. No. 472.
   [138] *The Near East*, April 9 and 23, 1915.
   [139] British *aide-mémoire* to the Russian Ministry of Foreign Affairs,
April 8, 1915, in MOEI, Vol. VII, Part 2, Doc. No. 498.

gestions reached the Ministry of Foreign Affairs from the President of the Duma, from the Army High Command and from the embassy in Paris that Russia try the same weapon. Sazonov rejected these early suggestions, in part because he felt that Bulgaria's leaders would not feel embarrassed about accepting money from both sides while continuing their ambiguous policy.[140] Sazonov changed his mind in January, 1915, and agreed[141] to support an Izvol'skii-sponsored plan to bribe Bulgarian politicians for the purpose of bringing Bulgaria into the war on Russia's side. According to this plan a French bank would negotiate in Sofia for the financing of a Bulgarian railroad line to Porto Lagos (on which the German bankers had taken no action although the Disconto-Gesellschaft loan of July, 1914, provided for it). The money would be put up only after Bulgaria's entry in the war on the side of the Entente, at which time the founding shares in the projected railroad company previously assigned by the bank to prominent Bulgarian politicians would become redeemable at a fixed price.[142] On January 15 Izvol'skii reported that Delcassé was ready to cooperate and had promised to confer with the British about the project.[143] Later in the month the Russian Minister of Finance, Bark, then on a mission to London and Paris, expressed his agreement with the proposal.[144] To handle the details from the Russian side, Bark later suggested the president of the Siberian Bank, Grube, "experienced in the accomplishment of delicate assignments from his previous experience in Persia."[145] By late February, however, Delcassé

[140] Letter of Director of Chancery of Russian Ministry of Foreign Affairs to Director of Diplomatic Chancery of Military Headquarters (*Stavka*). December 17, 1914, *ibid.*, Vol. VI, Part 2, Doc. No. 660.

[141] Sazonov to Izvol'skii, January 9, 1915, in *Konstantinopl' i prolivy*, II, 249.

[142] Izvol'skii to Sazonov, January 7, 1915, in MOEI, Vol. VI, Part 2, Doc. No. 733.

[143] Izvol'skii to Sazonov, January 15, 1915, in *Konstantinopl' i prolivy*, II, 251.

[144] See MOEI, Vol. VII, Part 1, Doc. No. 155.

[145] Bark to Krivoshein, February 14, 1915, in *Konstantinopl' i prolivy*, II, 252. Bark's report on his London and Paris financial mission men-

was convinced that Radoslavov and Tonchev, his minister of finance, were too closely tied to the Central Powers to be approached. He told Izvol'skii that the French would postpone action until after the cabinet change in Bulgaria which he expected to follow the Allied Dardanelles operations.[146] No change took place. Meanwhile pressure built up in Petrograd for immediate action.[147] Finally Russia took the initiative and sent Grube to Bulgaria to work out another bribery plan. His report of July 1, 1915, endorsed the views of the Russian and French ministers there that bribery would not be decisive at that moment,[148] a stand on which they all soon reversed themselves.

Sazonov went ahead and obtained French and British adherence to a plan Grube had outlined for secretly buying up Bulgarian grain, using as intermediaries Bulgarian politicians who promised to push for joining the Entente.[149] Grube drew up the plan in consultation with the Allied legations in Sofia and with Gennadiev, the former Bulgarian foreign minister, who had been selected as a major intermediary. It called for oral agreements with intermediaries (to include, among others, Radoslavov's brother-in-law, a deputy of the National Assembly and a vice-president of a large bank) who would purchase grain from Bulgarian peasants for cash and would receive commissions varying in amount according to their political influence. Des Closières, a French banker, was to direct operations. Bulgaria had not been able to export grain the year before, and it was estimated that the grain carried over from 1914, combined with the 1915 harvest surplus, would make some 900,000 tons available, at a cost of about

---

tions discussion there of the advantage of a Lagos rail connection as an outlet for Russian commerce—a long-range view; see B. A. Romanov, ed., "Finansovye soveshchaniia soiuznikov vo vremia voiny," *Krasnyi Arkhiv* (Moscow), V (1924), 58.

[146] Izvol'skii to Sazonov, February 24, 1915, in *Konstantinopl' i prolivy*, II, 256.

[147] MOEI, Vol. VIII, Part 1, Doc. No. 68, gives the recommendations of Army Headquarters.

[148] *Ibid.*, Doc. No. 224.

250 million francs, plus another 12 million to be paid in commissions. All three Entente powers were to share in the financing, with France and Britain, who needed grain, as the ultimate purchasers.[150] Des Closières, who agreed to manage the deal for a 500,000-franc commission, began the purchases on August 25, 1915.[151]

The political purpose of the plan was not achieved. German agents were also active in buying grain, and the Bulgarian government decided for war before the Des Closières group had bought anywhere near the anticipated quantities.[152] Gennadiev, head of a group of seventeen deputies providing Radoslavov with his majority in the legislature, did bring his group to speak out against measures which finally led to war with Serbia, but their stand had little effect as the National Assembly did not meet before Bulgaria's entry into the war.

In the spring of 1915 practically all the news of the eastern front published in Sofia came from Austrian and German sources.[153] To remedy this situation, in June Savinskii organized the correspondents of Russian newspapers in Sofia into a news bureau which prepared leading articles, letters and background stories for the local press. By July he was also directly subsidizing five Sofia newspapers, paying these subsidies and supporting the news bureau from a sum of 40,000 francs provided by Grube "out of private funds" with Minister of Finance Bark's approval.[154] In the same month Savinskii reported that both the Austrians and Germans were

---

[149] Sazonov to Savinskii, July 16, 1915, *ibid.*, Doc. No. 326

[150] For a protocol on the plan of operation, see annex to Savinskii-Sazonov telegram of August 11, 1915, *ibid*, Vol. VIII, Part 2, Doc. No. 481.

[151] Sazonov to Savinskii, August 21, 1915, *ibid.*, Doc. No. 542; and Savinskii to Sazonov, August 25, 1915, *ibid.*, Doc. No. 577.

[152] Savinskii's report of March-April, 1916, published as a supplement to MOEI, Vol. VIII, Part 2, mentions total payments of 50,000,000 francs for grain.

[153] Savinskii to Sazonov, May 12, 1915, in MOEI, Vol. VII, Part 2, Doc. No. 744.

[154] Savinskii to Sazonov, September 14, 1915, *ibid.*, vol. VIII, Part 2, Doc. No. 711.

supporting large papers, and, in view of the newsprint shortage
threatening the existence of the organs of six Bulgarian political parties, he recommended that the Russians supply free
newsprint to these papers. He submitted a budget to Petrograd asking for 10,000 francs monthly for his news bureau,
10,000 francs monthly for continuation of the direct subsidies
to five newspapers and 26,666 francs monthly for newsprint.
Apparently Petrograd postponed action on this request and
no newsprint was actually provided.[155]

Even after Russia abandoned her anti-Radoslavov policy
at the outbreak of war, Savinskii kept in close touch with
opposition party leaders and leaked information to them of
Entente offers to Bulgaria despite the fact that he thought
them a weak-willed lot, incapable of vigorous action to change
the country's policy.[156] He thus gave Radoslavov reason to
feel that he was still bent on unseating him. Yet when Bulgaria's adherence to the Central Powers grew imminent, there
was no Bulgarian group to which Russia could turn for a coup
d'état. Conversations were held in Petrograd in March 1915
with Mikhail Monev, leader of a Bulgarian Macedonian organization, but these were limited to an exchange of views
on what Russia could promise Bulgaria in Macedonia. The
extent of Savinskii's talks with Macedonian leaders in Sofia
seem to have been the same. Through their consul at Dede-
gach (Alexandroupolis) the Russians did establish close relations with *Komitadzhi* in Eastern Thrace, apparently primarily to learn of Turkish military strength in Thrace and
only secondarily to utilize the movement—never very well
developed, it seems—as the nucleus of a political organization
aiming for Bulgaria's entry into the war on Russia's side.[157]

[155] Savinskii to Sazonov, July 6, 1915, with comment of Ministry
official, *ibid.*, Part 1, Doc. No. 250.
[156] Savinskii to Sazonov, March 2, 1915, *ibid.*, Vol. VII, Part 1, Doc.
No. 286.
[157] Telegram from Russian Ministry of Foreign Affairs to Vice-Consul
at Dedeagach, June 30, 1915, *ibid.*, Vol. VIII, Part 1, Doc. No. 209;
summaries of other correspondence between the preceding, *ibid.*, p. 249,
note 4; and Savinskii to Sazonov, July 6, 1915, *ibid.*, Doc. No. 249.

Savinskii also received authentic and often important news from the "outs" and disgruntled "ins" of Bulgarian politics, who tended to flock to representatives of the big powers for help. Unfortunately, he seems to have interpreted these close relations with Bulgarian politicians as proof of their devotion to Russia and as evidence of his own charm and ability, rather than as a manifestation of habits of some forty years standing. This led him to underestimate the danger that Bulgaria might fight Russia.

Meanwhile Radoslavov had again been bargaining with the Central Powers. Because of the outbreak of war Bulgaria had not received money under the agreement with Disconto-Gesellschaft of the previous July except for the initial advance of 120,000,000 francs. Savinskii urged Radoslavov to seek help from the Entente rather than Berlin,[158] but in February, 1915, a further agreement was reached with the German banking house under which another 150,000,000 francs would be advanced.[159] Bulgaria denied any political conditions, and her envoy in Vienna was insistent on this point in private conversations with his German colleague.[160] However, in a report from Sofia to Vienna, which the Russians intercepted, Tarnowski stated that his German colleague had been instructed by the German Foreign Ministry to remind Sofia that the April installment of the loan was intended to help defray the costs of Bulgarian mobilization.[161] The Chief of the German General Staff wrote in his memoires that in May, 1915, Germany dropped plans for an offensive against Serbia because Bulgaria refused to join in at that moment.[162] Indeed, with Ferdinand's approval, after receipt of the loan Radoslavov, arguing that the Entente had promised "just com-

---

[158] Savinskii to Sazonov, January 25, 1915, *ibid.*, Vol. VII, Part 1, Doc. No. 77.

[159] Savinskii to Sazonov, February 5, 1915, *ibid.*, Doc. No. 138.

[160] Toshev to Radoslavov, March 10, 1915, in *Diplomaticheski dokumenti*, Vol. I, Doc. No. 735.

[161] Telegram of Tarnowski to Burian (deciphered by the Russians), March 27, 1915, in MOEI, Vol. VII, Part 2, Doc. No. 435.

[162] Falkenhayn, p. 93.

pensation in Macedonia" and the Enos-Midia line in return for neutrality, on June 5, 1915, extracted a promise from Vienna that in return for her benevolent neutrality Bulgaria would receive the "contested" and "uncontested" zones of Macedonia plus the land she had lost to Rumania and Greece by the Treaty of Bucharest, should either of them fight the Central Powers.[163]

In addition, the Allies were now stalemated at Gallipoli, and by April-May the tide of battle on the eastern front had turned against Russia, confirming the reports of the Bulgarian military attaché in Petrograd that the Russian army was weak (when these reports became known to the Russians, they forced his recall).[164] Thus it is not surprising that, after delaying until mid-June, Radoslavov replied to the Allied note of May 29, 1915, by asking for more definite pledges.[165]

Sazonov proposed that various versions of a slightly more favorable offer be made to Bulgaria and that a time limit for acceptance be attached.[166] With Italy in the war an additional voice had been added to Allied deliberations, but the chief resistance to Sazonov's proposal again came from the British, who raised the danger of provoking a Serbo-Greek attack on Bulgaria.[167]

Before Bulgaria entered the war, two further proposals were made to her by the Entente, one on August 3,[168] and the other

[163] Radoslavov to Toshev, February 15, 1915, in *Diplomaticheski dokumenti*, Vol. I, Doc. No. 678; Toshev to Radoslavov, May 10, 1915, *ibid.*, Doc. No. 829; text of Austrian note of June 5, 1915, *ibid.*, Doc. No. 894.

[164] See Tarnowski to Burian, January 19, 1915 (deciphered by the Russians), in MOEI, Vol. VII, Part 1, Doc. No. 38.

[165] Savinskii to Sazonov, June 15, 1915, *ibid.*, Vol. VIII, Part 1, Doc. No. 117.

[166] Russian *aide-mémoire* of June 19 and 21, 1915, to Buchanan and Paléologue, *ibid.*, Doc. Nos. 136 and 149.

[167] The British *aide-mémoire* of June 25, 1915, exaggerated this danger, speaking of such an attack as the "probable result" of Sazonov's proposal. *Ibid.*, Doc. No. 180.

[168] The first proposal followed an exchange of telegrams between George V and Nicholas II, the texts of which are in *Konstantinopl' i prolivy*, II, 285-86. The importance of Bulgaria to the success of the Dardanelles expedition was recognized. A further factor bringing the British and Russian opinions into harmony was the replacement of Bax-Ironsides by

on September 13. Neither promised her as much in Macedonia for fighting as Austria-Hungary had for benevolent neutrality. The August 3 proposal offered Bulgaria for war on Turkey the "uncontested zone" of Macedonia, "Kavalla and hinterland," plus Eastern Thrace to the Enos-Midia line, and would have made the aggrandizement of Serbia at the expense of the Habsburg Empire and the gains of Greece in Asia Minor at the expense of the Ottoman Empire subordinate to the required concessions to Bulgaria.[169] No Bulgarian reply was received.

Allied feelings toward Serbia were ruffled during this time by Serbia's refusal to assist the hard pressed Russians on the eastern front through a diversion against Austria as well as by Serbia's sortie into Albania,[170] which irritated Italy.[171] In response to Allied pressure, on September 1 Serbia finally agreed to concede about half the "uncontested zone" in return for compensations elsewhere,[172] but there are indications that Pašić considered these terms so onerous that he explored the alternative of a separate peace.

The last Allied effort in Sofia, on September 13, 1915, included a flat guarantee of the "uncontested zone" of Macedonia for war on Turkey.[173] The Bulgarian government did not budge. The offer was not based on a change of Serb attitude but was a final attempt to deter Bulgaria from her course toward war against the Entente. Disastrous Russian reverses with the loss of Lwów and Warsaw had reduced Russian influence in Serbia, and a few days before the last offer to Bulgaria Grey had refused Sazonov's suggestion that the British withhold further credits to Serbia to make her more tractable.[174]

O'Beirne (formerly counselor of embassy at Petrograd) as British minister to Bulgaria.

[169] Text in *Diplomaticheski dokumenti*, I, 684-86.

[170] British *aide-mémoire* of June 16, 1915 (with Sazonov's approval indicated), in MOEI, Vol. VIII, Part 1, Doc. No. 120.

[171] Shtrandtman to Sazonov, June 20, 1915, *ibid.*, Doc. No. 145.

[172] Text of note *ibid.*, Vol. VIII, Part 2, Doc. No. 618.

[173] Text in Savinskii to Sazonov, September 14, 1915, *ibid.*, Doc. No. 708; and in *Diplomaticheski dokumenti*, I, 691-92.

[174] British *aide-mémoire* to Russian Ministry of Foreign Affairs, September 11, 1915, in MOEI, Vol. VIII, Part 2, Doc. No. 689.

BULGARIA ENTERS THE WAR

Although victorious on the eastern front, in the spring of
1915 the Central Powers were still threatened by the Allied
Gallipoli campaign. The German generals realized that the
relief of Turkey was possible only by opening the direct supply
route through Serbia and Bulgaria and that an easy victory
over Serbia required a Bulgarian attack on Serbia's rear. Accordingly, in July Germany sent Prince von Hohenlohe-Langen-
burg to convince Ferdinand of the certainty of German victory
and to indicate the rewards that could be Bulgaria's at Serbia's
expense.

Ferdinand had secluded himself from foreign diplomats after
war broke out, though attempting to stay on good terms with
all of them. Savinskii did not talk with him from the outbreak
of war until shortly before the Entente finally broke relations
with Bulgaria. Only a special envoy bearing a personal message from Nicholas II could have gained an audience. Russia
never sought this path.[175] France sent Ferdinand's cousin,
the Duc de Guise, in early 1915, and the British sent General
Sir Arthur Paget as George V's envoy in March, 1915. But
neither brought any definite offers.

When Germany made its bid in July, 1915, Prince von
Hohenlohe brought a specific proposal. To judge from oblique
references in later Austrian and German diplomatic reports,
von Hohenlohe fired Ferdinand's imagination with suggestions
as to his future role in the Balkans after Serbia and the Kara-
georgevich dynasty had disappeared.[176] Savinskii's arguments,
framed in Pan-Slav terms and delivered through Radoslavov,
were a poor match. Hohenlohe was successful, and Ferdinand
secretly sent a trusted staff officer, Colonel Ganchev, to Ger-

---

[175] Sazonov ruled out any intercourse between Nicholas II and Ferdinand on the grounds that Ferdinand was untrustworthy; see *ibid.*,
VI, Part 1, 74, note 3.

[176] Falkenhayn, p. 159; and R. W. Seton-Watson, "Unprinted Documents: Austro-German Plans for the Future of Serbia (1915)," *Slavonic
Review*, VIII, No. 21 (March 1929), 705-24.

man Headquarters at Pless to discuss a military convention.[177]

At this time the rail link between Dedeagach, Bulgaria's port on the Aegean Sea, and her own railroad net passed through a strip of Turkish-held territory in the lower Maritsa valley. Radoslavov, pleading pro-Entente and anti-Turk sentiment in Bulgaria, urged that Turkey cede Eastern Thrace as far as Enos-Midia to prevent a pro-Entente cabinet change.[178] Although both Austria-Hungary and Germany recognized this as an extreme demand, they pressed Turkey to concede at least the border strip through which the railroad ran. Turkey hesitated but finally ceded the narrow strip when Bulgaria actually mobilized for war.[179]

The negotiations with the Central Powers led to a secret treaty and two secret conventions signed on September 6, 1915. The treaty was aimed at Serbia with provisions to commit Bulgaria against Greece and Rumania should either attack Germany.[180] One of the secret conventions promised Bulgaria (a) the "contested" and "uncontested" zones of Macedonia, (b) that part of Serbia east of the line of the Morava River from its confluence with the Danube to the confluence of its Serbian and Bulgarian branches, then along the watershed between these rivers, passing near Kačanik to the crest of the Šar Mountains, then following the line of the Treaty of San Stefano, and (c) territory in the Dobruja and Thrace at the expense of Rumania and Greece should either side with the Entente. This convention also provided for a loan to Bulgaria of 200,000 francs in four monthly installments, the

[177] Falkenhayn, p. 159. See also *The Near East*, August 13, 1915; and H. D. Napier, *A Military Attaché in the Balkans* (London, 1924), pp. 248-64. Radoslavov minuted on a telegram from Rizov (Berlin) dated July 7, 1915, "Inform that the cabinet council approved the decision to send a high officer for negotiation." Thus the decision was taken in early July, undoubtedly on Ferdinand's order, by a council of cabinet members. *Diplomaticheski dokumenti*, Vol. I, Doc. No. 726.

[178] Radoslavov to Kolushev, May 29, 1915, in *Diplomaticheski dokumenti*, Vol. I, Doc. No. 880; and Radoslavov to Toshev, May 15, 1915, *ibid.*, Doc. No. 843.

[179] *Ibid.*, I, 701-51.

[180] The text is given *ibid.*, p. 687; and in English translation in R. H. Lutz, *The Fall of the German Empire* (Stanford, 1932), pp. 750-51.

first when Bulgaria mobilized, and promised further aid should the war last more than four months.[181] Military operations were arranged in more detail in the secret military convention signed at Pless, which provided for (a) an attack on Serbia by the armies of Austria-Hungary and Germany employing six divisions within thirty days, and by the Bulgarian army employing four divisions within thirty-five days, (b) the placing of the three armies under the command of Field Marshal von Mackensen, (c) the dispatch of a German mixed infantry brigade to secure the port of Varna, (d) German pressure on Turkey to persuade her to undertake the defense of Dedeagach if necessary, (e) German financial and material assistance to Bulgaria, (f) the concentration of the Bulgarian army against Serbia and the occupation by it of Macedonia, (g) the transit of military supplies across Bulgaria to Turkey and (h) mutual defense against any enemy attacking any one of the signatories.[182]

The timing of Bulgaria's entry clearly indicates that her leaders moved when they did because of their confidence in German arms[183] and their eagerness to help crush Serbia and thereby seize Macedonia.

Despite Bratianu's avowed Entente sympathies and Greece's alliance with Serbia, Radoslavov was able to get assurances from Rumania of her neutrality should Bulgaria attack Serbia, and Greece adopted an ambiguous position that led him to believe she would not help Serbia.[184]

---

[181] Text in *Diplomaticheski dokumenti*, I, 689; and in English translation in Lutz, pp. 750-51.

[182] Text in *Diplomaticheski dokumenti*, I, 684-86; and in English translation in Lutz, pp. 744-46.

[183] Radoslavov is quoted as saying at the moment of the signing of the treaty with Germany on September 6, 1915: "It is done. Let the blessing of God, the Lord of chance and destiny, rest upon it. God and the Germans—we have confidence in both." R. von Mach, *Aus bewegter Balkanzeit*, quoted in G. P. Gooch, *Recent Revelations of European Diplomacy* (4th ed.; London, 1940), pp. 225-26.

[184] See Radev to Radoslavov, September 3, 13, 26 and 29, 1915, in *Diplomaticheski dokumenti*, Vol. I, Doc. Nos. 1057, 1099, 1110 and 1127; Radoslavov to Pasarov (Athens), September 16, 1915, *ibid.*, Doc. No. 1077; Pasarov to Radoslavov, September 25 and October 7, 1915, *ibid.*, Doc. Nos. 1112 and 1152.

On September 21 the Bulgarian army was mobilized, and a state of armed neutrality declared. Anti-war feeling was very high, however. All opposition party leaders joined in a manifesto protesting the Radoslavov policy and, in a collective audience with Ferdinand, warned against war. The particularly outspoken Agrarian leader Stambuliiski was jailed, and the National Assembly postponed for two months.[185]

The Bulgarian mobilization, the troop concentration against Serbia, the relaxation of controls against passage of contraband to Turkey and the increasing number of German officers with the Bulgarian army provoked the Russians to vigorous protest. Finally on October 4 they gave Bulgaria an ultimatum citing these developments and threatening to break diplomatic relations if within twenty-four hours the Bulgarian government did not "openly break with the enemies of Slavdom and Russia and . . . remove from her army the officers of powers that are at war with the Entente."[186] Bulgaria's reply denied the validity of the charges and expressed "brokenhearted regret" that efforts to arrive at a close alliance with Russia had failed.[187]

Ferdinand played his chameleon role to the end. He staged a friendly farewell with each of the departing Allied ministers, showing a desire to hedge against an unforeseen disaster to German arms. "I cannot forget that French blood flows in my veins," he told the French Minister.[188] He visited Savinskii, who was then convalescing at the Russian legation, and tried to ingratiate himself as a precaution against a possible victorious Russian return to Sofia.[189]

On October 6 the German-Austrian offensive began against Serbia, and five days later Bulgaria fell on Serbia's rear. Serbia was crushed, and by the end of 1915 the entire coun-

---

[185] *Dnevnitsi (stenog.) na XVII Obiknoveno Narodno Sobranie* (Sofia, 1928), p. 1.

[186] For text see *Diplomaticheski dokumenti*, I, 697.

[187] For text see *ibid.*, p. 698.

[188] H. R. Madol, *Ferdinand von Bulgarien* (Berlin, 1931), p. 212. Ferdinand was a descendant of Louis Philippe of France.

[189] Savinsky, *Recollections*, pp. 301 ff.

try was held by the Central Powers. Turkey was secure, and
Russia effectively isolated.

Russian diplomacy failed to win Bulgaria. But it was the
Central Powers' impressive military victories and their ability
to satisfy Bulgarian aspirations in Macedonia at the expense
of their enemy Serbia which were the dominant factors in
losing Bulgaria for the Entente. Russia might have played
her cards more shrewdly had she not been overconfident of
her military prowess at critical moments and had she made
more effective efforts to convince Ferdinand of ultimate Allied victory or to organize his overthrow. Misjudging the
real locus of power and driving forces in Bulgarian politics
and suffering from the absence of unified direction of Allied
or even Russian war policy, Russian diplomacy stumbled
upon the persi tent problems of Macedonia, Serbo-Bulgarian
relations and the lingering animosity of the Balkan wars.
The Central Powers expoited their advantage in these respects
to win an early though fleeting victory on the Balkan field.

ALFRED J. RIEBER

Russian Diplomacy
and Rumania

On the eve of the First World War Rumania occupied an
important strategic position in southeastern Europe. Russia
was working actively to strengthen its influence in Bucharest
primarily because Rumania could help open a line of advance
to Constantinople if the long-awaited opportunity to seize the
Straits materialized. At a special imperial conference on
February 8, 1914, General Zh. B. Zhilinskii, then Chief of the
General Staff, pointed out that in the event of a general European war Rumanian neutrality would free an entire army
corps from service along the Danube for use in landing operations in the Straits.[1] Alternatively, Russian diplomats considered the advantages of moving on the Straits along the
traditional overland route through Rumanian territory. During
the First World War, Deputy Foreign Minister A. A. Neratov
sketched out a plan whereby Russia would take advantage
of an Allied victory over the Central Powers to seize the Straits.
In order to avoid the risk of exposing the Russian forces to
attack by the Turkish navy, powerfully reinforced in August,
1914 by the Goeben and the Breslau, he proposed sending an
army across Rumania toward Constantinople.[2] Thus, whatever

---

[1] Friedrich Stieve, *Isvolsky and the World War* (London, 1926), pp.
233, 236.

[2] Memorandum of Neratov, December 27, 1914, in *Mezhdunarodnye
otnosheniia v epokhu imperializma*, Series III (Moscow, 1931-38), VI,
Part 2, 270. The abbreviation MOEI used hereafter refers to this title,
Series III.

road Russia might take to the Straits, Rumania's cooperation
in the venture could make the difference between victory
and defeat.

Geographically Rumania was destined to play a key role
in the Austro-Russian rivalry in the Balkans. In any war
between the powers, a friendly Rumania would protect over
three hundred miles of Russia's southwestern frontier and
open the only direct route for Russia to reach Serbia with
military aid, though the absence of a rail connection between
the three countries would slow down the transport of supplies.

In wartime, Berlin and Vienna would bid high for access
to Rumania's natural resources, especially oil and grain. Even
in 1913, 14 percent of Rumania's cereal exports went to Austria-
Hungary.[3] When the war broke out, the French learned that
Austria-Hungary needed over a million tons of grain, "much
of which is in Rumania."[4] It would be to Russia's advantage,
above all in case of a long war, to prevent these resources
from falling into the hands of the Central Powers.

Russian military leaders estimated that Rumania could
field an army of 500,000, presumably well trained and well led.
In 1916 General Brusilov had high hopes for a significant
Rumanian contribution to the military operations in Galicia,
but he was quickly disillusioned. "The mediocre condition of
the Rumanian army was to become well known," he later
wrote, but at the time "we did not know anything about it,
and all this was a surprise to us."[5]

For the Central Powers, Rumania's political influence was
as important as her economic and strategic value. The loyalty
of the Rumanian recruits in the Austro-Hungarian army could
be guaranteed only by friendly relations between Vienna and
Bucharest. If Rumania become a benevolent neutral or an
ally of the Central Powers, Russia would find it very difficult

[3] Royal Institute of International Affairs, *The Balkan States* (London,
1936), p. 134.
[4] Sazonov to Poklevskii, August 4, 1914, in MOEI, V, 401.
[5] "L'Offensive de 1916, II," *Revue des Deux Mondes*, June 15, 1929,
p. 917.

to exert any political influence in the Balkans during the war. The obstacle of Rumania between the other states and the Russian army would oblige Bulgaria and Greece to hesitate before committing themselves to the Entente. Consequently, as the crisis of the summer of 1914 deepened, both Russia and the Central Powers strove to win Rumania over to their side.

In negotiating with Rumania, the Russians were handicapped by several long-standing disadvantages. They had not fully recovered the loss of prestige and popularity which they had suffered in Rumania as a result of the Congress of Berlin in 1878. The Rumanians still resented the Russian annexation of the three southern districts of Bessarabia. The territorial gains in the Dobruja hardly seemed to them adequate compensation for their contribution to the storming of Plevna. As late as 1912, on the one-hundredth anniversary of the Russian annexation of Bessarabia, there were patriotic demonstrations in Bucharest against the Russians, and the Rumanian press attacked the Russian spoliation of this "Rumanian province."[6] During the war the Central Powers were quick to encourage this Rumanian claim against Russian territory.

The alliance between Austria-Hungary and Rumania and the strongly pro-German sympathies of King Charles (Carol) I were major obstacles to the achievement of Russia's aims. A scion of the younger branch of the Hohenzollerns, the King had been instrumental in the conclusion of a secret treaty of defensive alliance with the Monarchy on October 30, 1883. The agreement, which was later bolstered by Germany's adherence, provided that, if Rumanian or Austro-Hungarian territories bordering on Rumania should be attacked without provocation, the two contracting parties would render mutual assistance. Renewed at three-year intervals, the treaty was extended for the last time on February 5, 1913.[7] Since there

---

[6] A. Nekludoff (Nekliudov), *Diplomatic Reminiscences before and during the World War, 1911-1917* (2d ed.; London, 1920), p. 49.

[7] A. F. Pribram, *The Secret Treaties of Austria-Hungary, 1879-1914,* (Cambridge, England, 1922), I, 260, 262, 264.

was some doubt about the legality of the agreement under the
Rumanian Constitution of 1866, the king rather than the
treaty proved to be the real challenge to Russian policy. Article 93 of the constitution provided that the king should
have the power to conclude "conventions of commerce [and]
navigation and others of the same nature" but that they would
be valid only after parliamentary ratification. There was no
mention of military or political alliances in this paragraph,
and the king had no powers other than those specified in the
constitution.[8] It was true that Foreign Minister Dimitrie
Sturdza had countersigned the treaty, but the parliament had
not been informed of it. Though over the years the secret
became common knowledge among Rumanian political leaders,
the alliance was never formally ratified. Two astute observers,
the Austrian ambassador in Bucharest, Count Otto Czernin,
and the French ambassador at St. Petersburg, Maurice Paléologue, were convinced that the treaty would be ineffective
in the event of war. On the other hand, they agreed, as long
as King Charles was alive, Rumania would not join the Entente.[9]

Once the war broke out, the Russians no longer had a free
hand in dealing with Rumania. They had to consider the
interests of their allies in the give-and-take of diplomatic
bargaining. Serbia stubbornly opposed Rumanian territorial
demands in the Banat of Temesvar. England and France
had to be consulted on the progress of the talks and sometimes
exerted unwelcome pressure on the Russians to compromise.
Rumania negotiated alone and consequently her position was
stronger.

Long before the war the Russian Foreign Office had worked
patiently to overcome some of these handicaps. M. N. Girs
(Giers) and N. N. Shebeko, the Russian ministers in Bucharest
from 1902 to 1914, took an active interest in improving rela-

[8] R. W. Seton-Watson, *A History of the Roumanians* (Cambridge,
England, 1934), p. 365.
[9] Otto Czernin, *In the World War* (New York, 1920), pp. 4, 90; Maurice
Paléologue, *La Russie des Tsars pendant la Grande Guerre* (Paris), I,
(1921), 171.

tions with Rumania.[10] During the Balkan wars Sazonov moved boldly to strengthen ties with Bucharest by supporting Rumanian claims to Silistria. In July, 1913, he went so far as to assure Rumania that Russia would not hinder an attack on Bulgaria.[11] Sazonov summed up his views on Rumania in his memorandum to the Tsar of December 8, 1913. He argued that the Straits problem could be solved to Russia's satisfaction only through European complications. Convinced there was a strong possibility of winning Rumanian support in the event of a general war, Sazonov insisted that Russian diplomacy should strive to create "favorable conditions for as close a rapprochement with Rumania as possible."[12]

On the eve of the war the general feeling among European diplomats was that Russia had gone far toward the achievement of its aims in Rumania. Writing to Sazonov in August, 1913, A. P. Izvol'skii remarked, "I have always regarded as your political masterpiece, and I do still, your weaning of Rumania from Austria. It was always my dream, but I could never see how to bring it about."[13] Normally an alarmist, S. Poklevskii, the new Russian ambassador to Bucharest, responded enthusiastically to the reception he received from government circles upon his arrival in Rumania in January, 1914. There were clear indications to him that "a great and decisive change is taking place in [Rumanian] public opinion in favor of Russia."[14]

The growth of anti-Austrian feeling was so pronounced that the German General Staff had "ceased to place any serious reliance . . . on Rumanian adherence if war broke out."[15] Count Czernin concluded that Austria-Hungary could regain its lost prestige only by giving Rumania satisfaction in Tran-

[10] Serge Sazonov, *Fateful Years, 1909-1916* (London, 1928), p. 103.
[11] E. C. Helmreich, *The Diplomacy of the Balkan Wars, 1912-1913* (Cambridge, Massachusetts, 1938), pp. 300-303, 376.
[12] Stieve, p. 189.
[13] *Ibid.*, p. 166.
[14] Poklevskii to Sazonov, January 22, 1914, in MOEI, I, 89.
[15] General Erich von Falkenhayn, *General Headquarters, 1914-1916, and Its Critical Decisions* (London [1919]), p. 203.

sylvania.[16] However, by opposing a moderate solution, Francis
Joseph and the powerful Hungarian statesman Count Tisza
played into the hands of Russia, which was free to promise
Transylvania to Rumania as a reward for military assistance.

The predominant position of French culture in Rumanian
society had helped to advance Russian interests. The Liberal
Party, which came into power on January 16, 1914, was led
by an ardent admirer of France, Ionel Bratianu; and several
leading Rumanian statesmen, including Take-Ionescu, former
Minister of the Interior, and N. Filippescu, Conservative Party
leader, were strong supporters of France.

On the eve of the war Sazonov persuaded the Tsar to make
a goodwill visit to Bucharest, which proved to be a triumph
for the Russians. After the departure of the imperial family
Sazonov remained in order to talk privately with Bratianu.
He came away convinced that Bratianu was prepared to negotiate for the improvement of Russo-Rumanian relations,
but he did not know how far the Rumanian premier was willing
to go.[17]

By June, 1914, Rumania was in an anomalous position.
A secret treaty and the will of the King bound Rumania to
the Triple Alliance, but public sentiment and the majority
political party favored the Entente. Austrian influence, dominant in 1883, had declined. Russian influence, weak in 1878,
had grown. Though there was room for caution in estimating
Rumania's probable posture in the event of war, the Entente
position in Bucharest was clearly strong and likely to become
even stronger in the event of Austrian aggression in the Balkans.

The initial reaction of the Rumanian people to the news
of the Sarejevo tragedy was, according to Count Czernin,
an expression of sincere sympathy with the House of Habsburg.[18] The Austrian ultimatum to Serbia helped to change
this attitude, and Sazonov moved quickly in its wake to try

---

[16] Czernin, p. 90.
[17] Sazonov, *Fateful Years*, p. 114.
[18] Czernin, p. 97.

to associate Rumania with Russian policy at Vienna and Belgrade.[19] He urged Poklevskii to find out what Rumania's position would be in the event of a general European war. Bratianu admitted that the harsh terms of the ultimatum had produced a "bad impression" on the Rumanian government and even on the King. But he refused to make any commitment without knowing first "exactly and specifically" what Russia intended to do. In any case all the Rumanian leaders insisted they would "not allow the Balkan equilibrium which was established by the Treaty of Bucharest to be destroyed." On the other hand, Bratianu concluded, Rumania was unable in the face of Bulgarian hostility to help Serbia and could only advise acceptance of all of Austria's demands.[20] Not satisfied by this answer, Sazonov insisted on knowing what Rumania would do if war became "inevitable" and if Bulgaria were to take this opportunity to attack Serbia.[21] Bratianu's vague replies were followed by the first disquieting reports from Berlin that Rumania intended to join the Central Powers against Russia, and Sazonov, who was deeply distressed by the news, redoubled his efforts in Bucharest.[22]

Under pressure Bratianu finally conceded that "in any case Russia need not fear any hostile action on the part of Rumania." Poklevskii took courage from these words. "In previous conversations Bratianu was less specific, and consequently it is quickly clear that Rumania favors remaining neutral at the present time."[23] Now at the height of the crisis Sazonov

[19] Daily Report of the Foreign Ministry, July 24, 1914, in MOEI, V, 46; and Diamandi to Bratianu, July 24, 1914, quoted in Constantine Diamandi, "Ma Mission en Russie (1914-1918), I: Le drame d'une conscience royale," *Revue des Deux Mondes*, February 15, 1929, p. 799.

[20] Poklevskii to Sazonov, July 25, 27, 1914, in MOEI, V, 84, 164; and Diamandi, "Ma mission," p. 801.

[21] Sazonov to Poklevskii, July 26, 1914, in MOEI, V, 116.

[22] Poklevskii to Sazonov, July 27, 1914, and Sazonov to Poklevskii, July 28, 1914, *ibid.*, pp. 165, 179.

[23] Poklevskii to Sazonov, July 28, 1914 ,*ibid.*, p. 197. Though Russia did not know it, Count Czernin had reported to Vienna three days earlier that on the basis of his conversations with the King and Bratianu it was clear that Rumania would not enter either a localized or general European war but would remain neutral until the outcome of the struggle became

might still have reasonably assumed that his prewar analysis of Rumanian policy was correct. Rumania and Italy, he had written in 1913, "suffer from megalomania, and they are not strong enough to realize their plans openly, they have to content themselves with an opportunist policy, constantly watching to see on which side the power lies and going over to that side."[24] But in a moment of uncertainty Sazonov reversed his opinion, with fatal results for his Rumanian policy.

On July 29 Sazonov began to negotiate for Rumanian intervention against Austria before it was clear who in Eastern Europe held the preponderance of power. He told Bratianu that, if Serbia were attacked, Russia would declare war on Austria-Hungary, with the sole aim of saving the tiny kingdom. He urged Rumania to give a "categorical answer" on its position and added that Russia would "not exclude the possibility of profits for Rumania if she joins us in the war against Austria-Hungary." Poklevskii was also informed that, if he considered it appropriate, he could assure Bratianu that Russia was "ready to support the annexation of Transylvania by Rumania in return for a declaration of war against Austria-Hungary."[25]

A day later the Russian Foreign Office was thrown into confusion by an increased flow of contradictory information on Rumania's intentions. In a state of near panic, Sazonov ordered Poklevskii to send the embassy's secret archives to Odessa. He had "positive information" that there was a chance Rumania would attack Russia. On the other hand, he spoke of "some indications" that "there is still a chance of ensuring nonintervention or perhaps even of getting Rumania to come

clear. Czernin to Berchtold, July 25, 1914, in *Osterreich- Ungarns Aussen-politik von der bosnischen Krise 1908 bis zum Kriegsausbruch 1914: Diplomatische Aktenstücke des Osterreichisch- Ungarischen Ministeriums des Aussern* (Vienna, 1930), VIII, 628. For a complete account of the negotiations between the Central Powers and Rumania on the eve of the war, see F. I. Notovich, *Diplomaticheskaia bor'ba v gody pervoi mirovoi voiny*, Vol. I (Moscow, 1947), chap. 3.
[24] Stieve, p. 190.
[25] Sazonov to Poklevskii, July 29, 30, 1914, in MOEI, V, 207, 253-54.

over openly to our side by promising concessions. In the latter case we would be willing to promise our support for the acquisition of Transylvania by Rumania."[26] The phrasing of this last message was dangerously imprecise.

Following his instructions, Poklevskii told Bratianu that it was possible for Russia to strengthen Rumania's position if Bucharest assumed a friendly attitude in the present crisis. Bratianu was quick to take advantage of the situation by asking whether Russia would regard the preservation of Rumanian neutrality as evidence of a friendly attitude. Poklevskii, "guided by the general spirit of the July 31 telegram, replied in the affirmative."[27] By so doing he gave away, unofficially, but no less positively, the principal Russian bargaining point and received nothing in return. Bratianu was now aware of the great price that Russia would pay for Rumanian neutrality, let alone her intervention.

There is no evidence to support the contention that the Russian offer of Transylvania enabled Bratianu "to defeat the pro-Germans in a critical Rumanian Crown Council on August 3, and to assure Rumanian neutrality for the time being."[28] On the contrary, according to the only eyewitness account of the Crown Council, Bratianu did not mention the Russian offer at all.[29] There was no reason why he should have done so. Rumanian public opinion was clearly anti-Austrian. Already on July 30 Poklevskii knew that the Liberal cabinet had voted to take a temporizing position in the event of a general European war. Furthermore, he was convinced that the Rumanian army "lives in the hope of acting together with us against Austria-Hungary."[30] Even Marghiloman, who

[26] Sazonov to Poklevskii, July 31, 1914, ibid., p. 290. For reports on Rumanian hostility toward Russia, see Savinskii to Sazonov, July 29, 1914, ibid., p. 236, and Sverbeev to Sazonov, July 30, 1914, ibid.

[27] Poklevskii to Sazonov, August 2, 1914, ibid., p. 372.

[28] C. Jay Smith, Jr., The Russian Struggle for Power, 1914-1917 (New York, 1956), p. 24.

[29] Alexandru Marghiloman, Note politice 1894-1924 (Bucharest, 1927), pp. 230-35.

[30] Poklevskii to Sazonov, July 30, 31, 1914, in MOEI, V, 276, 305.

had pro-German sympathies, noted in his diary on July 20
that "at Sinaia [the residence of the king] everyone was opposed
to action and, above all, against action on the side of Austria."[31]

It should, then, have come as no surprise to Sazonov that the
Crown Council agreed almost unanimously that there was
no just cause for Rumania to fulfill its treaty with Austria.
Instead, Rumania would "put the frontier defenses in order"
and prepare public opinion for eventual war. Though there
was no declaration of neutrality, Russia was reassured that
Rumania would not attack her.[32] Thus by refusing to meet
its obligations to either the Triple Alliance or the Treaty of
Bucharest, Rumania sought to increase the price of its intervention by playing off one alliance against the other.

NEGOTIATIONS: THE FIRST PHASE, NEUTRALITY

Encouraged by the results of the Crown Council, Sazonov
worked feverishly in the first month of war to win Rumania
over to the side of the Entente. From the beginning his efforts
were hampered by Poklevskii's rash promise of August 2.
Even before the first battles on the eastern front Sazonov
renewed his appeals to Bucharest, this time promising that,
if Rumania agreed to attack the Monarchy immediately,
Russia would not end the war "until those lands (*pays*) of the
Austro-Hungarian Monarchy inhabited by a Rumanian population were reunited to the Rumanian crown."[33] Though
Rumania was mainly unwilling to sign a bilateral treaty with
Russia on the basis of such a vague offer, Bratianu preferred
to give as his excuse for inaction the fear of a Bulgarian attack
from the south.[34] Poklevskii urged that Russia satisfy Bratianu's request for an Allied guarantee of Bulgarian neutrality,
but he did not agree with Bratianu that this could best be

[31] Marghiloman, p. 229.
[32] Poklevskii to Sazonov, August 3, 1914, in MOEI, V, 390.
[33] Sazonov to Benckendorff and Izvol'skii, August 7, 1914, *ibid.*, VI,
Part 1, 20.
[34] Diamandi, "Ma mission," p. 807.

done by compensating Bulgaria at the expense of Serbia and Greece.[35]

Sazonov asked for French and British endorsement of his offer as well as a promise "to go to war with any power which attacked Rumania" while she was fighting on the Russian side. London and Paris agreed, but the British held out against guaranteeing the territories promised to Rumania.[36] Now Rumania took advantage of growing French and British suspicion of Russian plans in the Balkans in order to disrupt the common diplomatic front which Sazonov was trying to build. As Sazonov became bolder, his allies advised caution. London and especially Paris warned him that "it would be dangerous to put too much pressure on Rumania" and that Rumanian neutrality must be regarded as "a most happy event."[37] Soon afterward the French rallied to Sir Edward Grey's proposal for a neutral Balkan bloc of Bulgaria, Greece and Rumania.[38]

At the same time Bratianu explained he could not accept the Russian offer but promised to bear it in mind "if [the Russians] do not demand an immediate answer and will keep the question open." Quite correctly Poklevskii concluded that Bratianu wanted the same territorial compensation for neutrality as Sazonov had just offered for military assistance. But the Russian ambassador himself fell victim to Bratianu's maneuver and urged Sazonov to refrain from demanding an immediate answer for fear this would rouse the King to lead Rumania into the enemy camp.[39] From this moment Poklevskii joined the Allied diplomats in accepting at face value Bratianu's explanations of the favorable influence Rumanian neutrality

[35] Poklevskii to Sazonov, August 7, 1914, in MOEI, VI, Part 1, 27.

[36] Buchanan to Sazonov, August 9, 1914; Sazonov to Benckendorff and Izvol'skii, August 9, 1914; Benckendorff to Sazonov, August 9, 1914; Sazonov to Benckendorff, August 10, 1914; and Izvol'skii to Sazonov, August 11, 1914, ibid., pp. 33-35, 38, 47, 57.

[37] Izvol'skii to Sazonov, August 11, 1914, and Doumergue to Paléologue, August 12, 1914, ibid., pp. 57, 71.

[38] Buchanan to Sazonov, August 22, 1914, ibid., pp. 138-39; Raymond Poincaré, Au service de la France (Paris), V (1928), 96, 101.

[39] Poklevskii to Sazonov, August 12, 1914, in MOEI, VI, Part 1, 76.

would have on Italy, Bulgaria and the outcome of the war in the east.[40] Apparently on his own initiative he suggested to Bratianu that in exchange for a written promise of neutrality until the end of the war, Rumania might, in the event of an Allied victory, receive those provinces of Austria-Hungary where there was a majority of Rumanians. In the meantime Rumania's territorial integrity would be guaranteed. After thinking the proposal over for a few hours, Bratianu agreed on the condition that no one in Bucharest—not even the King or the Allied ambassadors—should know about it. Po-klevskii now pressed Sazonov vigorously to accept this formula.[41] His forceful arguments were based on the weak assumption that a formal, written guarantee of Rumanian neutrality was worth much more to Russia than the Crown Council decision —so much, in fact, that the better part of three Austro-Hun-garian provinces was not too high a price to pay.

Receiving no reply from Sazonov, Poklevskii devised an ingenious proposal which might satisfy Sazonov's desire for Rumanian action and at the same time reassure Rumania that Russia looked with favor upon the realization of her national aspirations. It would be opportune, he suggested to Sazonov, to invite the Rumanian government to occupy with its army that part of the Bukovina peopled by Rumanians and then under the control of Russian forces. Even if Bu-charest rejected the proposal, Poklevskii reasoned, the offer would "dispel the dangerous notion that Russia wishes to annex the Rumanian provinces of Austria."[42] Seeing an op-portunity to bring Rumania into the conflict, Sazonov broadened the original plan. On September 16 he encouraged Rumania to "occupy, without delay, the southern Bukovina and Tran-sylvania." The occupation line would be settled by military

---

[40] Poklevskii to Sazonov, August 28, September 1, 1914, *ibid.*, pp. 174, 195-96.

[41] Poklevskii to Sazonov, September 2, 9, 1914, *ibid.*, pp. 203-4, 228-29.

[42] Poklevskii to Sazonov, September 14, 1914, in *Tsarskaia Rossiia v mirovoi voine* (Leningrad, 1925), p. 160. (hereafter cited as TRMV); Sazonov to Kudashev, September 14, 1914, in MOEI, VI, Part 1, 252.

leaders on the spot and would, in any case, "be based solely on military considerations, without prejudice to the future delimitation of the frontier, which will be determined by the two governments on an ethnic basis."[43]

This was little more than Sazonov had offered Bratianu as a reward for Rumanian neutrality. Uncertain of an Allied victory, Bratianu was wary of accepting a Russian proposal to occupy enemy territory. Instead he favored Russian concessions in Bessarabia. In early September he launched a vigorous and skillful campaign to obtain the southern districts of that disputed province.[44] A large Rumanian delegation in Rome led by Take-Ionescu and Filippescu assured the Russian ambassador that, if Russia restored the southern districts of Bessarabia to Rumania, Bucharest would declare war immediately on Austria-Hungary and send all five of its army corps into Transylvania. They said Bratianu had authorized this proposal and was prepared to persuade the King that the interests of the nation were at stake.[45] According to the Rumanian ambassador to Russia, Bratianu actually intended "to keep the right to choose the time and means of intervention after having obtained the necessary guarantees." At this very moment he sent his close collaborator, Constantine Diamandi, back to St. Petersburg "with the aim of obtaining in exchange for [Rumanian] neutrality the same conditions which Russia wished to grant solely for immediate military cooperation."[46] However, Bratianu's calculations were upset by the enthusiasm with which the Rumanian public received the news of the Russian advance into Galicia and the Bukovina. Soon afterward Grand Duke Nikolai Nikolaevich publicly appealed to the national groups in the Austro-Hungarian Monarchy to throw off the Habsburg yoke and realize their national aspirations.

[43] Sazonov to Poklevskii, September 16, 1914, in MOEI, VI, Part 1, 257.
[44] See, especially, Notovich, I, 261, and Poincaré, V, 210.
[45] Krupenskii to Sazonov, September 16, 1914, in MOEI, VI, Part 1, 259.
[46] Diamandi, "Ma mission," pp. 809-10.

This was a critical moment for Russian policy. Great pressure was building up in Bucharest for Rumanian intervention. On September 20 King Charles noted in his diary: "In Bucharest, great agitation, manifestations, also the professors." Three days later he wrote: "Situation very serious, all against Bratianu," and by the end of the week, "All the political figures wish to march into Transylvania."[47] Bratianu admitted that, "if public opinion continued to put strong pressure on him by means of manifestations, then he and the Liberal Party would resign."[48] The Russian military group in Bucharest urged Poklevskii to make public the Russian invitation of September 16. They later insisted that "only a word" from them announcing that Russia supported Rumanian national aspirations would have aroused public opinion and rushed Rumania into war. But Poklevskii thought that it would be "incorrect, contrary to diplomatic tradition, to conduct negotiations in the streets." Consequently, the military group concluded, Russia lost a unique opportunity to pull Rumania into the conflict.[49]

Indeed, Poklevskii did not allow the excitement of the moment to overcome his natural caution. "I continue to consider it desirable," he cabled Sazonov, "to make specific promises in advance to Rumania in exchange for its neutrality in order to hold public opinion here, if military operations should take a temporarily favorable turn for our opponents."[50] His attitude evidently convinced Bratianu that he could reject the Russian offer to occupy Austro-Hungarian territory and still obtain Transylvania, for the Premier suggested that Rumania

[47] *Ibid.*, p. 818.

[48] Poklevskii to Sazonov, September 19, 1914, in V. P. Semennikov, ed., *Monarkhiia pered krusheniem, 1914-1917: Bumagi Nikolaia II i drugie dokumenty* (Moscow, 1927), p. 212. The Russian ambassador also noted that the only difference among Rumanian political leaders, regardless of party, was one of deciding when was the best moment to attack Austria. "Neither the press nor the public even mentions the idea of possible joint action of Austria and Rumania."

[49] *Ibid.*, pp. 210-14.

[50] Poklevskii to Sazonov, September 20, 1914, *ibid.*, p. 212.

would remain neutral for the duration if Russia promised Transylvania.[51]

Sazonov's determination began to waver. True, France and England now wanted Rumania to enter the war, but the Russians feared that they would be expected to pay part of the cost. The Allies appeared to be lending a sympathetic ear to Rumania's pleas for southern Bessarabia as a reward for intervention. The first hint of this stiffened the Tsar's attitude: "Now the active participation of Rumania seems to us less necessary than it was at the beginning of the war."[52] As his suspicions increased the Tsar declared, "I am against concessions to Rumania of even so much as an inch of Russian soil."[53] This viewpoint together with Bratianu's refusal ended for the moment any possibility of negotiating for Rumanian intervention.

What of Bratianu's offer to negotiate for neutrality? Sazonov considered Bucharest's demands "excessive." Yet he conceded that, in his opinion, it was "possible to give Rumania, in exchange for a written promise of neutrality, a promise of the three powers to recognize its rights to annex Transylvania as long as the Allies were not required to use military force to occupy this region."[54] Poklevskii's pessimism had finally infected his superior. Sazonov had virtually surrendered to Bratianu's position before Poklevskii reported that Austria-Hungary was offering Rumania enormous territorial compensation to join the Central Powers. In the face of strong French opposition, negotiations were quickly completed for Rumanian neutrality.[55]

The neutrality agreement signed in Petrograd on October 2 provided that Russia would oppose any threats to Rumanian

[51] Poklevskii to Sazonov, September 21, 1914, in MOEI, VI, Part 1, 283.

[52] Marginal note of Nicholas II dated September 13, on telegram of Demidov to Sazonov, September 11, 1914, *ibid.*, p. 259, note 1.

[53] Marginal note of Nicholas II dated September 19, on telegram of Krupenskii to Sazonov, September 16, 1914, *ibid.*, p. 260.

[54] Sazonov to Poklevskii, September 22, 1914, in TRMV, pp. 163-64.

[55] Poklevskii to Sazonov, September 22, 1914, Poklevskii to Sazonov, September 26, 1914, and Grey to Buchanan, September 27, 1914, in MOEI, VI, Part 1, 15, 290, 333.

territorial integrity, recognize the right of Rumania to annex
those provinces of Austria-Hungary which had a majority of
Rumanians, delimit the Bukovina frontier with Rumania on
the principle of ethnic majority, and permit Rumania to occupy
these areas when she desired. In return Rumania would pledge
benevolent neutrality toward Russia up to the moment of
actual occupation and delimitation. At the last minute Sazonov tried to tack on an appendix which specifically defined
benevolent neutrality. In this way he hoped to block the
transit of German officers and equipment across Rumania to
Turkey and open the way for Russian militay supplies to
reach Serbia. But the Rumanians refused to be pinned down
on this issue. However, they agreed that Russia was obliged
to employ only diplomatic means to protect Rumanian territorial integrity.[56]

This treaty brought to a close the first phase of Russo-Rumanian relations during the war. In signing it, Sazonov committed a grave error. With skill and some luck he might have
brought Rumania into the war in August or September, 1914.
A hasty promise of Transylvania to Bratianu in return for
neutrality cut down his bargaining power, and the Tsar's
intransigence on the Bessarabian question further weakened
his hand. All was lost when Poklevskii was unwilling to exploit
Bratianu's shaky position in Bucharest. By publicizing the
Russian offer of Transylvania and Bukovina, he might well
have stampeded Rumania into war. Still Sazonov did not
have to acknowledge his defeat by signing the neutrality
agreement. There was little doubt that Rumania would have
remained neutral without being offered Transylvania. The
terms of the treaty justified Bratianu's dilatory tactics and

[56] Sazonov to Diamandi, October 1, 1914; Appendix, Daily Report of
Ministry, October 3, 1914; Poklevskii to Sazonov, October 6, 1914; Daily
Report of Ministry, October 14, 1914; Poklevskii to Sazonov, October 17,
1914, *ibid.*, pp. 341-43, 358-61, 376, 401, 406. There is some confusion
in secondary sources on the exact date of the agreement. On October 1
Diamandi was unexpectedly confronted with the appendix and refused to
sign the agreement. Baron Schilling finally persuaded him to sign the
principal part without the appendix on the afternoon of October 2.

allowed him to choose the most favorable moment for his country to enter the war. The pro-Allied interventionists had the ground cut out from under them.[57] Thus when King Charles died, on October 12, 1914, Rumania made no move to join the Allies. She no longer had good reason to do so.

Sazonov later tried to vindicate his action by stating that he had wanted to bring about a breach between Rumania and the Central Powers in order to prevent Rumania from attacking Russia.[58] As we have seen, such reasoning was not justified. Allied diplomats in Bucharest and Petrograd had shared—and expressed—Poklevskii's view that "it goes without saying that Rumania can only enter the war on our side."[59]

Sazonov also maintained that he had wanted to end grain and oil shipments from Rumania to the Central Powers and the transfer of munitions to Turkey.[60] Yet by not incorporating these aims in the October 2 treaty, he lost the opportunity to force Rumanian compliance with his wishes. "It is impossible," Sazonov later told Diamandi, "to understand benevolent neutrality as you understand it."[61] Though Bratianu tried to minimize the importance of the transit trade, the Russians continued to receive reports that Rumanian grain, oil, naphtha, and benzne were being shipped to Germany and that German shipments to Turkey of munitions and dismantled submarines were passing through Rumania.[62] In spite of Sazonov's protests, Rumanian shipments to Germany continued uninterruptedly until Rumania entered the war in 1916.[63]

[57] Semennikov, ed., p. 215; Diamandi, "Ma mission en Russie, II: La guerre vue du versant oriental," *Revue des Deux Mondes*, November 30, 1930. According to Diamandi, "Bratianu would answer to critics who wanted to intervene by going to his strong box, pulling out a sheet of paper and pointing to the line in the treaty which stated that Rumania was free to choose the moment" of entering the war (pp. 423-24).

[58] Sazonov, *Fateful Years*, p. 265.

[59] Poklevskii to Sazonov, September 19, 1914, in Semennikov, ed., p. 212.

[60] Sazonov, *Fateful Years*, p. 265.

[61] Report on the Conversation of S. D. Sazonov and C. Diamandi, October 21, 1914, in MOEI, VI, Part 1, 418.

[62] Sazonov to Poklevskii, October 21, 1914, *ibid.*, p. 414; and Sazonov to Poklevskii, April 25, 1915, *ibid.*, VII, Part 2, 251.

[63] As late as March, 1916 Rumania concluded an economic agreement

As one Russian diplomat put it, this was strict neutrality with a vengeance.[64]

Finally, Sazonov declared that he had preferred Rumania's neutrality—her active participation in the conflict would have been inconvenient and positively risky, "since it imposed upon us duties which would be bound to disorganize our military plans."[65] It appears that Sazonov hoped to neutralize the Balkan area until the Russian army could win a decisive victory over Austria-Hungary. Then Balkan allies would rally to the tsarist standard as grateful pensioners. They would be indebted to Russia and not she to them. In this way Russia could extend her political influence over the approach to the Straits. The flaw in Sazonov's reasoning here lies in his mistaken estimate of Russia's military strength. During the negotiations of the treaty of neutrality Sazonov received information that the Russian General Staff passionately desired the immediate entrance of Rumania into the war.[66] Events proved them to have been correct. As an ally in the fall of 1914, Rumania would have joined Serbia to Russia, extended the Austrian line of battle and encouraged the Russian troops, who were already flushed with their first great victories in Galicia. The situation at that time was vastly more advantageous than in August, 1916, when Rumania entered the war. Then Serbia was gone, Bulgaria and Turkey were enemies, and Russia was exhausted by two terrible war years.

Poklevskii must share the blame for the Russian blunder. He supported negotiations for Rumanian neutrality in the belief that territorial concessions would secure public opinion in the event of Russian military defeat. That this analysis

with Austria-Hungary and Germany for the exchange of nonmilitary supplies, including wheat. "Dnevnik Ministerstva Inostrannykh Del za 1915-1916 gg.," April 6, 1916, in *Krasnyi Arkhiv*, XXXII (1929), 31.

[64] Eugene de Schelking, *Recollections of a Russian Diplomat: The Suicide of Monarchies* (*William II and Nicholas II*) (New York, 1918), pp. 201-2.

[65] Sazonov, *Fateful Years*, p. 266.

[66] Kuḍashev to Sazonov, September 28, 1914, in "Stavka i Ministerstvo Inostrannykh del," *Krasnyi Arkhiv*, XXVI (1928), 10.

was shortsighted is clear from the fact that the promises of concessions would be of no use if the means of fulfillment were no longer present.

The magnitude of the Russian error became evident a month later when a new Austrian attack threatened to destroy Serbia. Sazonov appealed to Rumania to intervene quickly, before Serbia succumbed and Austria-Hungary was able to reinforce Transylvania.[67] When the Bulgarian premier, Radoslavov, announced, under Allied pressure, that his country intended to remain neutral, Sazonov believed that a major obstacle to Rumanian intervention had been removed.[68] In the eyes of Bratianu, however, such was not the case. In fact, Rumania now insisted that Bulgaria join her in attacking Austria-Hungary.[69] This diplomatic reverse made Sazonov and the other Allied leaders realize that it would be more expedient to sponser the creation of a pro-Allied bloc based on a general territorial settlement among Serbia, Bulgaria, Rumania and Greece than to negotiate separately with the last three suspicious and jealous neutrals. The Entente leaders differed as to the details of this plan.

Besides her immediate military needs, Russia was developing plans at this very moment to settle the future of the Straits. Rumania was to play a key role in these operations, and Russian domination of the Balkans was vital to their ultimate success. Therefore, Sazonov had several good reasons to create a pro-Allied Balkan bloc controlled by Russia. Though France and Britain were favorably disposed toward Russian aims in the Straits, Sazonov believed that Russia could be assured the Straits only by obtaining them herself.[70] Consequently, he insisted that the active intervention of the Balkan bloc would

[67] Sazonov to Poklevskii, November 10, 1914, in MOEI, VI, Part 2, 52; Sazonov to Poklevskii, November 15, 1914, in TRMV, p. 170.

[68] Sazonov to Izvol'skii and Benckendorff, November 18, 1914, in TRMV, p. 171.

[69] Poklevskii to Sazonov, November 14, 1914, in MOEI, VI, Part 2, 81-82.

[70] Evropeiskie derzhavy i Turtsiia vo vremia mirovoi voiny: Konstantinopl' i prolivy (Po sekretnym dokumentam byvshego Ministerstva inostrannykh del) (Moscow, 1925-26), II, 133.

be opportune only "when Russian forces had effected a landing on the Balkan peninsula."[71]

In the complex negotiations following this resolve, Russia tried first to work out a Serbo-Greek-Rumanian alliance wh¡ch would neutralize Bulgaria.[72] Sazonov hoped to persuade Rumania to cede Lower Dobruja to Bulgaria in order to satisfy Sofia and also to convince Serbia that concessions to Bulgaria were necessary. But Bratianu insisted that Serbia and Greece first make territorial sacrifices to Bulgaria. He would not cede Lower Dobruja unless Bulgaria entered the war or Russia compensated Rumania with Bessarabia.[73]

In the long run, Neratov, the Russian Deputy Foreign Minister, pointed out, Russia would have to make some concessions in Bessarabia in order to win Rumanian support for the Straits project.[74] Evidently no one else in the Foreign Ministry agreed with him at this time. As a result, Russia and then Rumania refused to make the concessions needed to create the Balkan bloc.[75]

Unable to dictate to Rumania and unwilling to bargain with her, Russia lost the diplomatic initiative in the Balkans. The failure was due partly to Sazonov's promise of too much too early in the game for too little in return. Secure in the knowledge that Transylvania would be hers, Rumania was not anxious to enter the war at a time when there was so little chance of a quick victory. For Sazonov Bessarabia was too high a price to pay for Rumanian intervention. But did he fully understand that there was no way, short of sacrificing Russian territory, to rally the divided Balkan powers to the

---

[71] Sazonov to Poklevskii, December 16, 1914, in TRMV, p. 175.

[72] Sazonov to Izvol'skii and Benckendorff, December 2, 1914, in MOEI, VI, Part 2, 148.

[73] Kudashev to Sazonov, November 20, 1914; Poklevskii to Sazonov, December 2, 6, 1914; Krupenskii to Sazonov, December 22, 1914; Trubetskoi to Sazonov, January 11, 1915; ibid., p.p 110, 153, 179, 249, 358; and Poklevskii to Sazonov, January 14, 1915, ibid., VII, Part 1, 6.

[74] Memorandum of Deputy Foreign Minister A. Neratov, December 27, 1914, ibid., VI, Part 2, 272.

[75] Poklevskii to Sazonov, January 14, 1915, ibid., VII, Part 1, 6-7.

Entente? Because of his inability to see the great stakes involved, Sazonov had let slip an opportunity to lead a Balkan military coalition to victory over Austria-Hungary and Turkey.

Negotiations: The Second Phase, Stalemate

In the spring of 1915 dramatic events in Eastern Europe altered the course of Russo-Rumanian relations. In March the Russians were assured control of Galicia by capturing the great Austrian fortress of Przemyśl. A month later Allied forces began the invasion of Gallipoli. On April 26 the Treaty of London was signed, and, as previously agreed, Italy informed Rumania of her intention to enter the war.[76] Cautiously Bratianu began to explore the possibility of negotiating with the Allies in London.[77] But Sazonov blocked this maneuver and insisted that negotiations ought to begin in Petrograd.[78]

On April 22 Diamandi left Bucharest for Petrograd with the Rumanian proposals for intervention. Since Sazonov was aware of the precise nature of the demands, he was immediately on guard and urged Britain and France to support Russia in resisting what he called Rumania's excessive claims.[79] On May 3 Diamandi formally presented his report to the Russian Foreign Minister. In return for intervention, Rumania demanded cession of Transylvania, the entire Bukovina to the Prut River, including Czernowitz, the entire Banat to the gates of Belgrade and several Hungarian counties up to a line from Szeged to the confluence of the Tisza and Szamos (Somes) rivers. The proposals were presented as a block to be accepted or rejected.[80] Sazonov declared flatly that he could not accept such demands for they would mean abandoning a large Russian (Ukrainian) population and a strategic frontier

[76] Poincaré, V, 346.
[77] Buchanan to Sazonov, April 19, 1915, in MOEI, VII, Part 2, 189.
[78] Sazonov to Izvol'skii and Benckendorff, April 22, 1915, *ibid.*, p. 227.
[79] Poklevskii to Sazonov, April 22, 1915; Buchanan to Sazonov, April 29, 1915; Poklevskii to Sazonov, April 29, 1915; Neratov to Izvol'skii, April 30, 1915, *ibid.*, pp. 235, 291, 295, 297.
[80] Diamandi to Sazonov, May 3, 1915, *ibid.*, p. 333.

in the Bukovina. Sazonov also pointed out that cession of the
Banat would move the Rumanian border to the right bank
of the Danube facing Belgrade and would threaten the security
of the Serbian capital.[81] He might well have added that the
Banat was rich in iron and coal deposits. The Torontal district
was especially important because of the network of canals
which provided transportation for the natural resources of
the Banat and Transylvania. At the town of Resiczabanya in
the Banat was the southernmost of the great European steel
works which manufactured heavy guns and rolling stock.[82]

The Stavka was in complete agreement with Sazonov's opposition to the Rumanian demands. In fact, special staff
studies had recommended that Russia annex all of the Bukovina
for strategic, economic and religious reasons. If concessions
to Rumania in the southern Bukovina were necessary, then
the Stavka insisted that Russia should retain Czernowitz and
the crest of the Transylvanian Alps at any cost.[83] Contrary
to his earlier belief, Grand Duke Nikolai Nikolaevich now
declared that Rumania's intervention was a matter of "secondary importance." He pointed out that Russia's future
frontier in the Carpathian zone, in the Bukovina and in the
Hungarian plain must be drawn "in accordance with strategic
considerations."[84] Opposed to Rumania's territorial claims,
he concluded that firmness and the pressure of events would
ultimately decide Rumania's course of action.

General Polivanov was so skeptical of Rumania's military
power that he insisted the Russians should have a well-equipped
army of 300,000 men to help the Rumanians protect their
southern flank against a Bulgarian invasion. Yet at this

---

[81] Daily Report of the Ministry, May 3, 1915, and Sazonov to Poklevskii,
May 5, 1915, *ibid.*, pp. 336, 349-50.

[82] *Banat* (London, 1920), p. 69 (Handbook Prepared under the Direction
of the Historical Section of the Foreign Office, No. 6).

[83] Kudashev to Sazonov, February 16, 1915, with report of Danilov and
Samoilo, February 14, 1915, kn MOEI, VII, Part 1, 277, 282; Schilling
to Danilov, April 28, 1915, and Danilov to Schilling (n.d.), *ibid.*, Part 2
pp. 282, 513-15.

[84] Nikolai Nikolaevich to Neratov, May 3, 1915, *ibid.*, p. 337.

time, he admitted, any such operation would be highly impracticable.[85]

This firm position of Sazonov and the General Staff was shaken by a sudden turn in the fortunes of war. On May 3 German and Austrian forces under General Mackensen pierced the Russian lines at Gorlice and Tarnow and destroyed the Russian Third Army. This disaster forced the Russian armies in Galicia to fall back rapidly to avoid being enveloped. The military defeat cost Russia her strong position in negotiating with the Balkan neutrals. Sazonov was now vulnerable to increased pressure from his allies to balance the defeat in the field with a victory at the conference table.

The Russian General Staff began to reconsider its position in terms of winning the war rather than planning the peace and agreed grudgingly to concessions in the Bukovina and Banat. Sazonov based the Russian counterproposals of May 14 on their recommendations. He recognized Rumanian claims to that part of Transylvania on the Hungarian plain and suggested the Suchava (Suceava) River as the boundary in the Bukovina, leaving Czernowitz in Russian hands. Rumania would receive almost half the Banat, but Temesvar and the province of Torontal would be awarded to Serbia.[86] Before receiving these instructions, Poklevskii knew their general tenor. He warned that such demands would make Rumanian intervention impossible and "might even cause anti-Russian sentiment." He suggested that Russia concede Czernowitz and reserve to Serbia only one-third of Torontal (the Panchevo district) as a defensive "glacis" for her capital.[87] Sazonov was unmoved, and Bratianu immediately rejected the Russian counterproposals.[88]

After the failure of this first exchange, the French and British became more insistent. Sir Edward Grey did not

[85] Nekludoff, p. 387.
[86] Sazonov to Poklevskii, May 14, 1915, in MOEI, VII, Part 2, 446.
[87] Poklevskii to Sazonov, May 13, 1915, ibid., p. 442.
[88] Poklevskii to Sazonov, May 18, 1915, ibid., p. 475.

consider Sazonov's proposal satisfactory.[89] Paléologue tried to convince Sazonov that bargaining with Rumania would be useless. The Russian Foreign Minister replied that he was not opposed to negotiation but that Bratianu's attitude was too arrogant and dictatorial. He maintained that Russia was still a great power and that a momentary check to her armies did not make her forget the past nor her historic mission. The French ambassador argued that, in view of the military situation, the only questions that concerned him at the moment were whether Rumanian intervention was useful and whether it would be too costly to abandon a little more territory to Bratianu.[90]

Reluctantly Sazonov accepted Delcassé's proposal that the Seret River be the frontier in the Bukovina and that the Banat, including only the northeast section of Torontal, be ceded to Rumania. He demanded that, in return for his concession to Bratianu, Rumania enter the war by May 26, 1915.[91] Bratianu refused to renounce his claims for a "natural frontier" on the Prut. Sazonov was equally determined not to surrender a strong Russian strategic position in the Bukovina, but he was skillful enough to couch his protest in terms of ethnic considerations.[92]

Pressure on Sazonov to yield now increased from all quarters. Rumanian public opinion was ranged firmly on Bratianu's side. Even the opposition leaders wanted Czernowitz, which they considered "the spiritual and cultural center of Rumanian Bukovina."[93] The Allied ambassadors in Bucharest bombarded their governments with demands that Russia make greater concessions. Sazonov even accused Poklevskii of aligning himself with his colleagues and thereby "playing into the hands of

[89] Benckendorff to Sazonov, May 19, 1915, *ibid.*, p. 482.
[90] Paléologue, I, 359.
[91] Paléologue to Sazonov, May 18, 1915; Sazonov to Benckendorff and Izvol'skii, May 20, 1915, in MOEI, VII, Part 2, 470-71, 487-88. In the first draft of the telegram to London and Paris the Russians conceded the entire district of Torontal to Rumania.
[92] Sazonov to Diamandi, June 3, 1915, *ibid.*, VIII, Part 1, 76.
[93] Poklevskii to Sazonov, May 27, 1915, *ibid.*, p. 25.

our enemies."[94] Grey, who had heretofore been blaming the Rumanians for the impasse, appealed to Sazonov to concede the Prut line and most of the Banat, on the assumption that Rumania would then restore the Lower Dobruja to Bulgaria. The military situation was "not reassuring," he argued, and because of "the outlook in Galicia [there was] the possibility of your having to abandon Lwów."[95] Delcassé, who had supported the Russian counterproposals, was finding it difficult to resist parliamentary pressure on him to obtain still greater concessions from Sazonov.[96]

In reply to Sazonov's inquiries, the Stavka had to admit that, "from the purely military point of view," Rumanian intervention was "highly desirable," but insisted that further concessions be made only if Rumania promised to intervene immediately.[97] This opinion was decisive in convincing the Tsar and Sazonov to offer Czernowitz to the Rumanians.[93] However, Bratianu refused to accept anything short of his complete demands. If an agreement was reached, he added, Rumania would declare war on Austria-Hungary "two months, at the most, from the day the political convention between Rumania and the Powers is signed." He offered some hope that this period could be shortened to five weeks from the day the proposals were made if the Allies gave in at once.[99] While Poklevskii found it "extremely difficult to recommend one mode of action over another at the present moment," he suggested that, "if the Allies admit the possibility of accepting all the Rumanian demands, then we ought to do so at once [and], in exchange for this, force Rumania to enter the war five weeks from the day the proposal is made and immediately begin negotiations on a military convention."

[94] Sazonov to Poklevskii, May 29, 1915; Blondel to Delcassé, May 29, 1915, ibid., p. 46.
[95] Buchanan to Sazonov, June 3, 1915, ibid., pp. 78-79.
[96] Izvol'skii to Sazonov, June 6, 1915, ibid., p. 105.
[97] Nikolai Nikolaevich to Sazonov, June 7, 1915, ibid., p. 111.
[98] Daily Report of the Ministry, June 8, 1915, and Sazonov to Poklevskii, June 9, 1915, ibid., pp. 113, 114.
[99] Poklevskii to Sazonov, June 18, 1915, ibid., p. 166.

In any case some territory in southwest Torontal should be awarded to Serbia to cover Belgrade.[100]

The Chief of Staff, General Ianushkevich, concurred: "Now the most important consideration is not to lose a moment in bringing Rumania firmly into the Russian camp because it is certain that she will go over to the enemy camp if we abandon Galicia, which is possible." He therefore advised acceptance of all the political terms, but, relying on Poklevskii's two telegrams of June 18, insisted that Rumania enter the war five weeks from the day the offer was made to Bratianu. Ianushkevich wanted to begin discussions of a military convention immediately and further stressed that there were also certain purely military considerations which should influence the terms of the political agreement. First, Rumania should close her frontier completely to the transit of military shipments to Turkey as soon as the agreement was signed. Secondly, it was necessary to reserve a zone in the Banat for the defense of the Serbian capital; this area should be kept small, about sixty square miles, but should not be demilitarized. Finally, it was necessary to specify what aid Russia could furnish to Rumania; horses, provisions and cattle should be promised, but not, Ianushkevich concluded, munitions, artillery and rifles, "of which we ourselves have need."[101]

Before Sazonov had an opportunity to draft new proposals, Bratianu tried to stretch the proposed time limit of Rumanian intervention to "five weeks from the day the agreement was signed." While refusing to accept this further delay, Sazonov agreed to extend the Rumanian frontier to the Prut. His fear of betraying Serbia forced him to advocate a postwar conference at which the great powers could mediate the dispute between Serbia and Rumania on the future status of the Torontal district.[102] Bratianu still insisted on receiving the entire Banat, on extending the time limit to five weeks from

[100] Poklevskii to Sazonov, June 18, 1915, *ibid.*, p. 165.
[101] Ianushkevich to Sazonov, June 20, 1915, *ibid.*, pp. 185-86.
[102] Sazonov to Poklevskii, June 21, 1915, *ibid.*, p. 188.

the signing of the political agreement and, in addition, on France and Italy filling substantial Rumanian munitions orders before Rumania could declare war.[103] Because of the rapid deterioration of the Russian military position, Poklevskii concluded that "our negotiations with Bratianu on an early intervention by Rumania no longer seem to me to be realistic."[104] In this case his correct judgment went unheeded.

Then, in desperation, Asquith and Delcassé, meeting at Calais, agreed to accept Rumania's demands in the Banat but proposed to placate Serbia by offering her Croatia "as the only acceptable prize." Thus, as the French historian Pingaud remarks, Rumania played a curious but important part in founding the Yugoslav state.[105]

The French pressed Sazonov to accept these proposals. Doubtful of success on the western front, they saw themselves saved by a great flank attack from Italy and Rumania. Izvol'skii reminded his chief that "in case of the final failure of the negotiations with Rumania and the possible adverse turn of events [on the western front], French public opinion will certainly blame us for that turn."[106]

Consequently, the final details of an agreement with Rumania were worked out among the three Allies. On July 10 Sazonov informed Bratianu that the Allies were ready to satisfy all his demands in the Banat and the Bukovina if Rumania would (a) enter the war no later than five weeks from the day the political agreement was signed, (b) prevent "at once" the transit of military supplies to Turkey, (c) cede Balchik and Dobrich to Bulgaria, (d) create a demilitarized zone opposite Belgrade, (e) give compensation to any Serbs who wished to leave the Banat and guarantee the minority rights of those

[103] Poklevskii to Sazonov, June 23, 25, 1915, ibid., pp. 206, 227.
[104] Poklevskii to Sazonov, July 4, 1915, ibid., p. 292.
[105] Albert Pingaud, "L'Entente et la Roumanie en 1915, 3 mai-22 août 1915," Revue des Deux Mondes, May 1, 1930, p. 155. This version of the Calais meeting was based on the author's research in the French archives.
[106] Izvol'skii to Sazonov, June 29, 1915, in MOEI, VIII, Part 1, 244.

who chose to remain. The Allies promised also to satisfy
Rumania's need for munitions.[107]

At this crucial moment Sazonov committed another blunder.
Still distrustful of Bratianu, he instructed Poklevskii to find
out, before submitting the proposals of July 10, whether the
Rumanian premier was still willing to enter the war in five weeks
if all his demands were met. In vain the French and British
pointed out that this maneuver could only delay a final decision when time was of the utmost importance. The ill-
considered move cost the Allies two weeks, and when Bratianu
finally did reply, it was only to refuse to set a time limit at
all. The military situation had changed so radically since
June that he was willing to sign only a political agreement.
Conclusion of a military convention, he asserted, would depend
on the fortunes of war in Eastern Europe.[108]

It is easy to agree with the Marchese Carlotti that Bratianu
deserved a "kick in the right place." The French, however,
again appealed to Sazonov to yield to Bratianu. Delcassé
was in political trouble at home, and, in Izvol'skii's words,
a rupture of the negotiations "would produce a painful impression and might further undermine Delcassé's position."
The French were also deeply concerned about the shipments
of German munitions to Turkey. These supplies, which were
sustaining the Turkish defenders at Gallipoli, could be cut off by
a political agreement. With this in mind, Delcassé asked
Sazonov to consider the fact that "to wish to fix a time interval . . . is equivalent to renouncing the agreement."[109] The
French pressed Sazonov relentlessly and with their British
and Italian allies finally persuaded him to capitulate in the

---

[107] Sazonov to Poklevskii, July 10, 1915, *ibid.*, p. 356. In view of Delcassé's later reservations, Sazonov agreed not to insist on guarantees for
the Serbian minority. Izvol'skii to Sazonov, July 11, 1915, Sazonov to
Poklevskii, July 12, 1915, *ibid.*, pp. 369, 377.

[108] Sazonov to Buchanan, Paléologue and Carlotti, July 14, 1915, Izvol'skii to Sazonov, July 15, 1915, Sazonov to Izvol'skii, July 16, 1915,
Izvol'skii to Sazonov, July 16, 1915, Benckendorff to Sazonov, July 17,
1915, Izvol'skii to Sazonov, July 17, 1915, Poklevskii to Sazonov, July 23,
1915, *ibid.*, pp. 397, 406, 414, 416, 421, 422, 472-73.

[109] Izvol'skii to Sazonov, July 25, 1915, *ibid.*, p. 488.

interests of the Dardanelles campaign.[110] Though Sazonov agreed to all Bratianu's demands including no time commitment, he insisted that Rumania prevent any contraband of war from passing from the Central Powers to Turkey.[111]

At this crucial moment in the negotiations the Russian army surrendered Warsaw, an event which produced a "profound impression" in Rumania.[112] The Rumanian government declared its inability to sign even the political agreement.[113] The Allies now feared losing Rumania altogether and accepted Bratianu's request to inform Rumania verbally of their consent to her territorial claims, on the assumption that she would enter the conflict when the military situation improved.[114]

The summer negotiations ended in failure. Sazonov had tried to win Rumania to the Entente side, but he did no† want to concede everything to Bratianu without committing Rumania to a well-coordinated and well-planned intervention. Also, the Russian leaders were obsessed by a grand design for postwar Imperial Russia which required that Bessarabia remain Russian, that the frontiers be anchored firmly on strategic foundations and that Russia be assured of political domination of the Balkans. The political leaders were, in fact, more sensitive than some members of the Stavka to the strategic concessions which would influence the peace settlement. Sazonov was admirably farsighted, but he failed to understand the necessities of the moment. Russia was not in a position either in October, 1914, or May, 1915, to pursue the long-range policy. Military defeats, the pressure of the Western allies and the stubborn resistance of Bratianu forced Sazonov to compromise. He gave in grudgingly, and often too late. Vig-

---

[110] Benckendorff to Sazonov, July 25, 1915, and Sazonov to Izvol'skii, Benckendorff and Girs, July 29, 1915, *ibid.*, pp. 486, 518.

[111] Sazonov to Poklevskii, August 3, 1915, *ibid.*, p. 518, note 5.

[112] Pingaud, p. 159.

[113] Poklevskii to Sazonov, August 14, 1915, in MOEI, VIII, Part 2, 44, note 1.

[114] Poklevskii to Sazonov, August 21, 1915, *ibid.*, p. 118. The French even refused to accept Sazonov's suggestion that Rumania promise to block the transit of military supplies to Turkey for fear of "insulting the Rumanian government." Izvol'skii to Sazonov, August 13, 1915, *ibid.* p. 73.

orous action at the beginning of the war could have pushed
Rumania into the conflict. But it is doubtful whether more
timely concessions later would have persuaded Bratianu to intervene. The wily Rumanian statesman always had one eye on
the military situation. In the final analysis it was the position
of the Russian army that determined his action.

Sazonov's error of October 2, 1914, continued to plague him.
The Russians had to accept the provisions of the treaty of
neutrality as a basis for further diplomatic bargaining. This
meant in turn greater concessions to Rumania than the intervention was worth.

Bulgarian Intervention and Rumania

The entrance of Bulgaria into the war on the side of the
Central Powers in October, 1915, confirmed Bratianu's unwillingness to move and underlined the futility of further
negotiations between Russia and Rumania. The Bulgarian
mobilization and offensive against Serbia's rear brought no
response in Bucharest. Since the Allies realized that Serbia
would now be lost unless Rumania were persuaded to intervene, they renewed their desperate appeals to Bratianu.

The British proposed signing a military convention with
Greece, promised a British expeditionary force of 200,000
"seasoned" troops at Saloniki to attack Bulgaria and agreed
to dispatch to Russia within two months 500,000 rifles "to
develop strong and concerted action with Rumania in the
southern theater."[115] Faced by the prospect of fighting alone
for two months, Bratianu rejected the British offer. "If we
undertook to send 500,000 men," Buchanan told Sazonov,
"he would reconsider the question."[116]

The new Russian Chief of Staff, General M. V. Alekseev,
viewed the destruction of Serbia with grave concern. He was
willing to "make any concession to bring hesitant Rumania
over to our side." Five hundred thousand rifles would enable

---

[115] Buchanan to Sazonov, October 14, 1915, *ibid.*, pp. 486-87.
[116] Buchanan to Sazonov, October 17, 1915, *ibid.*, IX, 3.

the Russian army, he added, "to mount a serious offensive against Bulgaria as well as Austria on the southern front." Yet in the long run he saw little chance of preventing Germany from linking up with Turkey. Far better to give up the Straits, conclude a separate peace with Turkey and turn with full force against Germany than to risk disaster. Russia's first task was to destroy German militarism, he asserted, and "to pursue other aims is to chase after a mirage."[117] But the Tsar and the Russian Foreign Office saw one last chance to organize a march on the Straits. Nicholas II, commander in chief since August, authorized the concentration of five army corps (about 500,000 men) for an attack on Bulgaria on condition that the promised British rifles should be sent. At the same time Sazonov began negotiations, first, to get Bratianu's permission for the Russian army to cross Rumanian territory or, failing this, to bring Rumania into the conflict.[118] Startled by these energetic moves, Bratianu categorically refused to allow a Russian army transit rights and demanded a separate Allied army of 500,000 men at Saloniki in addition to the Russian troops massing in the north![119]

Throughout these negotiations the Stavka called for a tough-minded policy in Bucharest. Distrustful of Poklevskii, they urged the Tsar to send a qualified military man to speak to Bratianu "firmly and authoritatively." Even if Bratianu hesitated, they insisted, the Russian army could cross the Danube without difficulty because the "disorganization and unpreparedness of the Rumanian army" meant that Bucharest would "not be able to offer us much resistance."[120] Learning

[117] Alekseev to Sazonov, October 17, 1915, Kudashev to Sazonov, October 21, 1915, ibid., pp. 12, 41.

[118] Sazonov to Nicholas II, October 23, 1915, Sazonov to Buchanan and Paléologue, October 25, 1915, Poklevskii to Sazonov, October 26, 1915, Sazonov to Nicholas II, October 29, 1915, Sazonov to Poklevskii, October 31, 1915, ibid., pp. 54-55, 64, 73, 94, 112.

[119] Buchanan to Sazonov, November 2, 1915, Poklevskii to Sazonov, November 6, 1915, ibid., pp. 131, 180.

[120] Kudashev to Sazonov, November 2, 1915, in "Stavka i MID," Krasnyi Arkhiv, XXVIII (1928), 14-16, quoting from report of Staff Captain Bubnov, who had recently returned from Bucharest.

that Sazonov had ignored this proposal and receiving news of Bratianu's intransigence, General Alekseev recommended transfer of the Russian forces from Bessarabia to the Galician front. "We cannot seriously weaken our position on the western front because our fate will be decided there and not in the south."[121] To save Serbia, he urged a general Allied offensive from Galicia and Saloniki aimed at Budapest. Serbia could hold Bulgaria in check, and then Greece and Rumania would be dragged into the war. "Real strength and success will be more decisive," he declared, "than diplomatic negotiations and promises."[122]

Despite the apparent uselessness of continuing negotiations with Bratianu, Grey and Sazonov hoped to discuss unofficially with him the basis of a future military convention. While leaving Rumania complete liberty of action, such an agreement would have made possible a rapid and effective intervention when the proper moment came.[123] All these efforts were in vain. Bratianu could not be persuaded either to intervene or to prepare to do so.

Consequently, military disaster overwhelmed the Allies in the Balkans. Hopelessly outnumbered and outflanked, the Serbian army disintegrated, and the helpless Russian army of 250,000 which was massed in Bessarabia withdrew from the Rumanian frontier. As a result of these events, the isolated Allied forces in Saloniki and Gallipoli had no chance of breaking out of the beachhead perimeters. The Russians, backed by the French, had to bargain hard to persuade the British not to abandon the Saloniki venture.[124] But in January, 1916, the ill-fated Gallipoli campaign was brought to a close.

---

[121] Alekseev to Sazonov, November 6, 1915, in MOEI, IX, 183. See also Paléologue, *La Russie*, II, 98.

[122] Alekseev to Sazonov, November 22, 1915, in MOEI, IX, 325.

[123] Buchanan to Sazonov, November 10, 1915, Sazonov to Poklevskii, November 13, 1915, *ibid.*, pp. 198-99, 236.

[124] Gudim-Levkovich to Sazonov, November 22, 1915, Izvol'skii to Sazonov, December 2, 1915, Daily Report of Ministry, December 7, 1915, Alekseev to Sazonov, December 7, 1915, Alekseev to General Williams, December 11, 1915, *ibid.*, pp. 318, 420, 457, 478, 485, 519.

The Central Powers took advantage of the Allied withdrawal to put pressure on Rumania to join them.[125] Sazonov tried to secure Anglo-French military and diplomatic support against the Austro-German threats.[126] He also authorized Poklevskii to "inform Bratianu that, if need be, a Russian army [would] at once go to his aid."[127] Once again this raised the thorny problem of working out some kind of military cooperation between Rumania and Russia in advance of a possible German ultimatum.

Bratianu was very wary of accepting Sazonov's advice that the two staffs should draft a military convention. On the other hand, he insisted that a Russian army mass on the Danube to repulse a possible Bulgarian attack. He planned to use the bulk of the Rumanian army to fulfill the national ambition of liberating Transylvania.[128] The Stavka strongly condemned this political strategy, and General Alekseev presented an alternative plan. In view of the unwillingness of the Allies to strengthen their forces in Saloniki or to use their troops there for offensive operations, Alekseev noted, "the burden of defending Rumania will fall on us." Therefore, "from the purely military point of view, at the present moment the preservation of Rumanian neutrality would be more advantageous for us." This would hold true as long as Rumanian neutrality could be guaranteed against Austro-German pressure. If no guarantee was possible, then the Russian army could allot ten infantry divisions to defend the southern approaches to Bucharest against a Bulgarian thrust. The main Russian army would be concentrated in northern Moldavia to threaten the Austro-German right flank. Alekseev urged that all the Rumanian forces be used in the south where they would be supported by the allied forces at Saloniki, who would

---

[125] Paléologue to Sazonov, January 22, 1916, Poklevskii to Sazonov, January 23, 24, 1916, ibid., X, 47, 65, 71.
[126] Sazonov to Izvol'skii, Benckendorff, and Girs, January 24, 1916, Sazonov to Paléologue and Buchanan, January 27, 1916, ibid., pp. 68, 92-93, note 1.
[127] Sazonov to Izvol'skii and Benckendorff, January 26, 1916, ibid., p. 86.
[128] Poklevskii to Sazonov, January 28, 1916, ibid., p. 108.

pin down a large number of Bulgarian and German troops.[129]
Colonel Tatarinov was sent to Bucharest as the new military
attaché in order to conclude a military agreement along these
lines.[130] Within the next month negotiations failed to resolve
the basic differences in strategy.

To Alekseev's disgust, the French then intervened in the
dispute. Poincaré telegraphed the Tsar: "It is not surprising
that Rumania wants to advance primarily in the areas which
have been promised to her by the diplomatic agreements,
and it seems fitting that the Rumanian army, supported by
the Russian army, which is more solid and experienced, will
be inspired by fighting to liberate its own blood brothers."[131]
The Russian attitude stiffened. Sazonov protested that it
was not a mere divergence of views between the general staffs
which prevented an agreement. The very issue of cooperation
was still unsettled.[132] The Stavka won the Tsar over to its view.
"Our victory over the Germans," he agreed, "will decide the
Rumanian question."[133] In Bucharest, once again the Russian
military group accused Poklevskii of taking the French side
and thereby selling Russia short. The troublesome Rear Ad-
miral Veselkin tried to undermine the Russian ambassador's
position in Bucharest and had to be called to order by Sazonov.[134]
But this did not settle the dispute between the Russians and
the French. In fact Sazonov showed deep annoyance when
Paris unofficially suggested that negotiations might be speeded
up if the Italian military attaché in Bucharest were allowed
to participate. As for Italy, Sazonov snapped, "its influence
in Bucharest is utterly insignificant."[135]

[129] Alekseev to Sazonov, January 26, 1916, ibid., pp. 90-91.
[130] Daily Report of the Ministry, February 2, 1916, ibid., p. 134. Alekseev
doubted Poklevskii's ability to support the Russian position. Kudashev
to Sazonov, January 28, 1916, in "Stavka i MID," Krasnyi Arkhiv,
XXVIII, 28-29.
[131] Poincaré to Nicholas II, March 1, 1916, in MOEI, X, 305-6.
[132] Paléologue, La Russie, II, 205.
[133] Alekseev to Sazonov, March 5, 1916, in MOEI, X, 333.
[134] Poklevskii to Sazonov, February 25, 1916, Alekseev to Veselkin,
March 2, 1915, ibid., pp. 336, 371.
[135] Sazonov to Izvol'skii, March 22, 1916, ibid., p. 434.

As the danger of a German attack on Rumania receded, Bratianu lost interest in concluding any military agreement with Russia. In April he informed Colonel Tatarinov, who was about to leave for Russia, of a new Rumanian demand, that the Russian army actually take the offensive in the Dobruja and occupy Ruschuk. The exasperated Tatarinov reported that the French military agent, Captain Pichon, had even gone beyond this, arguing that the Rumanian government should demand Russian occupation of Sofia![136] Encouraged by France, Rumania wanted the Russian army to protect its left and right flanks while she staged a military promenade in Transylvania. Alekseev explained to Joffre in detail why he considered the Rumanian demands "excessive and unreasonable." According to Paléologue, Joffre then agreed with Alekseev that Rumanian intervention was not indispensable and that Bratianu must be informed that nothing but effective military cooperation as prescribed by the Allies would obtain the compensation he desired.[137] The Russian proposals and criticisms were well founded, and Rumanian unwillingness to see this had disastrous results.

RUMANIAN INTERVENTION

Rumanian intervention on the Allied side was determined by a Russian military victory. By mid-June, 1916, Russian forces under General Brusilov had advanced on a broad front in Galicia and recaptured Czernowitz. During the offensive Russian military leaders sought to gain Rumanian support. According to General Alekseev, this was the moment for Rumania to enter and, indeed, "the only moment when this intervention could interest Russia."[138] General Polivanov, who, though no longer Minister of War, was in close contact with

[136] Bazili to Sazonov, April 24, 1916, in "Stavka i MID," *Krasnyi Arkhiv,* XXVIII, 44-45.
[137] Paléologue, *La Russie,* II, 256-57.
[138] Murav'ev to Sazonov, July 7, 1916, in "Stavka i MID," *Krasnyi Arkhiv,* XXIX (1928), 1-2. See also Alekseev to Joffre, June 29, 1916, Alekseev to Sazonov, July 2, 1915, in Paléologue, *La Russie,* II, 301-2, 305.

Alekseev, explained that a Russian attack on Kraków depended
upon Rumania's attitude. If the Russian left flank could be
covered at once, operations could proceed immediately, but
any delay, he added, would necessitate more circumspect
maneuvers and thus rob the offensive of much of its decisive
potential.[139] Meanwhile the French, who were fighting for
survival at Verdun, also urged Rumania to join the Entente.[140]

However, Bratianu, still doubting that the decisive victory
was at hand and still avoiding a firm commitment to the
Allies, called for additional guarantees of supplies and military
assistance.[141] He was nonetheless ready to sign a military convention if his requests were met and Rumania was not bound
to enter the war at a specific date.[142]

The Russians refused categorically to give Bratianu a free
hand in choosing the date of Rumanian intervention. As
Baron Schilling pointed out to Paléologue in late June, "If
the Rumanians come in now or at least in the next few weeks,
their aid would be worth a good deal to us. But if their offensive were to begin only when we have already won a victory
over Austria-Hungary at great cost, then Rumanian intervention will be not only superfluous but undesirable."[143] Sazonov wired Poklevskii that the Russians could "sign only
an agreement which guaranteed Rumanian intervention in
the near future and on a specific date."[144] The French concurred and on July 18 associated themselves with a Russian
note demanding Rumanian intervention without delay. General
Alekseev fixed August 7 as the last possible day for Rumania
to declare war.[145]

Though the French and the Russians agreed that the Rumanian intervention should come quickly, they disagreed

---

[139] Conversation of July 5, 1916, in Paléologue, *La Russie*, II, 309.
[140] Poklevskii to Sazonov, June 29, 1916, in TRMV, p. 217.
[141] Poklevskii to Sazonov, July 4, 1916, in *ibid.*, p. 217-18.
[142] Poklevskii to Sazonov, July 5, 1916, *ibid.*, p. 218.
[143] Entry for June 25, 1916, in "Dnevnik MID," *Krasnyi Arkhiv*, XXXII,
60-61. See also June 30, 1916, *ibid.*, pp. 62-63.
[144] Sazonov to Bazili, July 7, 1916, in TRMV, p. 219.
[145] Paléologue, *La Russie*, II, 315.

on what its immediate direction and objective should be. General Alekseev wanted the bulk of the Rumanian army to launch an offensive over the Carpathians toward Budapest. This would shift the weight of the Brusilov offensive to the south and deal Austria a mortal blow. At the same time he urged the French to put Rumania's fear of Bulgaria to rest by striking north from Saloniki. "The entrance of Rumania into the war, which is necessary and advantageous, will thus become inevitable."[146] But the British and French were extremely reluctant to undertake any large-scale operation in this area.[147] Joffre, supported by Aristide Briand, wanted a strong Rumanian force to attack Bulgaria and join hands with the Allied forces at Saloniki.[148]

If French and Russian leaders looked to the Rumanian army to strengthen their immediate military position and perhaps advance their long-range national interests in Eastern Europe, they reckoned without the diplomatic skill of Ionel Bratianu. From the scanty documentation of the final sequence of events which led to the Rumanian intervention, it appears that the French and the Russians were forced to modify their views in the face of Bratianu's persistent demands for powerful military assistance from the Allies.

The immediate result of these negotiations was a compromise plan. On July 23 the Rumanian military attaché in Paris and representatives of the Entente signed the Chantilly convention, which provided for a Rumanian army of 150,000 men with Russian support to attack Bulgaria one week after the Allies had launched an offensive from Saloniki.[149] Thus the French agreed to attack from the south without assurances of massive Rumanian aid from the north, and the Russians

[146] Murav'ev to Sazonov, July 7, 1916, in "Stavka i MID," *Krasnyi Arkhiv*, XXIX, 2.

[147] For a thorough discussion of this problem based partially on unpublished archival material, see V. A. Emets, "Protivorechiia mezhdu Rossiei i Soiuznikami po voprosu o vstuplenii Rumynii v voinu, 1915-1916," *Istoricheskie Zapiski*, No. 56 (1956), pp. 73-75.

[148] George Suarez, *Briand, 1914-1916* (Paris), III (1939), 355.

[149] Paléologue, *La Russie*, II, 323. See also Bazili to Stürmer, July 28,

agreed to weaken their potential striking force in Galicia by diverting troops to the Dobruja.

However, Bratianu repudiated the Chantilly agreement because it committed Rumania to a two-front war, and unexpectedly declared that he would not attack the Bulgarians under any circumstances. The French again conceded, but the astonished General Alekseev now saw little reason to send Russian troops into the Dobruja if the mission was not to attack the Bulgarians immediately. At last, worn down by the lengthy negotiations, he too agreed that the Bulgarian operations could be left "to develop by themselves."[150]

Bratianu further asked for an extension of the final date from August 7 to August 14 and for an Allied attack from Saloniki against the Bulgarians ten, instead of seven, days before the Rumanian intervention, in order to free the Rumanian army for operations in Transylvania. Furthermore, as General Alekseev noted, though he would accept the new date, the Rumanian draft convention was textually vague on this point. The key sentence read, "Rumania pledges to attack Austria-Hungary after having mobilized all naval and land forces that she possesses, not later than August 14." Without the comma, August 14 would have referred to mobilization and not to intervention.[151] The French raised no objection to this detail, but it was only on August 10 that Alekseev was informed that Joffre also accepted the Rumanian demand for an Allied offensive ten days before the Rumanian intervention.[152]

Finally, Bratianu demanded that the Entente unconditionally guarantee to Rumania the entire Banat, the Tisza

1916, in TRMV, pp. 221-22. On July 21, B. V. Stürmer had replaced S. D. Sazonov as foreign minister. The change had no effect on these negotiations.

[150] Central State Archives, Folio 2003, Doc. 1, p. 210, as quoted in Emets, p. 73. See also Paléologue, La Russie, II, 324, 326-27, 329.

[151] Bazili to Stürmer, July 28, 1916, in TRMV, pp. 221-22.

[152] Central State Archives, Folio 2003, Doc. 1, p. 362, as quoted in Emets, p. 76.

frontier, Transylva ... nia and the Bukovina to the Prut. In
a last futile outburst ... of rage, Baron Schilling asserted: "The
Allies have already mad ... too many concessions to the Rumanians, [and] further step ... in this direction would not be
in keeping with the dignity of t ... e powers but would strengthen
Bratianu in the conviction that ... he could always haggle for
something else." Paléologue heat ... dly replied that the immediate entry of Rumania was wor ... h more than the concessions made by the Allies: "If the n ... gotiations with Rumania do not lead now to her interventio ... then there will
be deep disappointment in France, [and] sin ... ce the responsibility for the failure of the negotiations will b ... placed on
Russia, a wave of indignation, harmful to the inte ... rests of
the Franco-Russian alliance, will rise against her." Fr ... nce
was war weary, Paléologue concluded, and saw in Ruman ... a
"the last chance to tip the scales to our side because our recent,
heavy losses make us wonder how long France can hold out."
With equal vehemence, Schilling replied that "the concessions made by us to the Rumanians appear to be worth so
little to the French because all of them were made mainly
at Russia's expense." He pointed out the error of placing
such high hopes in Rumanian intervention, which would have
no direct bearing on the French front.[153] After Poincaré again
appealed directly to the Tsar to break the deadlock, the Russians capitulated to the last Rumanian demands.[154]

Bratianu emerged as the only victor of these disputes.
The negotiations had delayed Rumanian intervention by at
least three weeks. When solution of the last problem was
in sight, Boris Stürmer, who had assumed the duties of foreign
minister, submitted a draft political agreement in the form
of an ultimatum for Allied approval and presentation to Bratianu. The draft provided, first, for a guarantee of Rumanian
territorial integrity. Second, Rumania would attack Austria-

---

[153] Entry for July 27, 1916, in "Dnevnik MID," *Krasnyi Arkhiv*, XXXII,
68.
[154] Paléologue, *La Russie*, II, 333.

Hungary on a date fixed by the military convention and break diplomatic and economic relations with the enemies of the Allies. Third, the Allies would recognize the Rumanian right to annex the Bukovina to the Prut River; Transylvania and the Hungarian counties to the Tisza River, for the most part, but including Debrecen, and the entire Banat bounded by the Tisza and then the Danube. Restrictions were placed on the fortification of territory opposite Belgrade. Fourth, the Allies and Rumania were to give mutual assurances not to conclude a separate peace with Austria-Hungary until the territories named were occupied by either the Allies or Rumanians. Fifth, Rumania was to be guaranteed equal rights with the Allies.[155]

Bratianu was opposed to the no-separate-peace clause, and the French were able to convince the Russians that the clause was of no significance. In the final analysis, they asserted, the position of the great powers after the war would determine the territorial realignment of Europe.[156]

The military convention, too, was clearly a setback for the Russian plans. The Russians promised to maintain an energetic offensive on the Austrian front, especially in the Bukovina, to protect the port of Constantsa with their fleet and to prevent enemy sea or land attacks across the Danube mouths. To lend assistance, one Russian cavalry and two infantry divisions would be stationed in the Dobruja. The river and land forces here would be under Rumanian command. The Allies would send at least 300 tons of munitions a day to Rumania, and they would launch an offensive from Saloniki not later than August 20. Rumanian and Russian forces in Hungary would be under separate commands. In sum, coordination and cooperation between the Russian and Rumanian general staffs were held to a minimum. In return

---

[155] Stürmer to Izvol'skii, Benckendorff and Girs, August 8, 1916, in TRMV, pp. 224-25.
[156] Entry for August 12, 1916, in "Dnevnik MID," Krasnyi Arkhiv, XXXII, 69-70.

Rumania promised to enter the war not later than August 28, 1916.[157]

The agreement was signed on August 17, and twelve days later Rumania declared war on Austria-Hungary. It was much too late to be of significant aid to the stalled Russian offensive. Furthermore, Rumania's inept strategy led to a series of disastrous defeats which put her out of the war and forced the now crippled Russian army to take on the defense of an additional 600 kilometers of the eastern front.

Russian policy in Rumania was a failure because of imprudent diplomacy and military weakness. The Tsar, the Stavka and the Foreign Ministry could not agree on what course of action to take. Pokevskii's advice from Bucharest was invariably pessimistic. As a result, in a moment of uncertainty in 1914, Russia bid too high for Rumanian neutrality. Apparently Sazonov assumed that later Russian victories would force the Rumanians to intervene without further compensation. But after May 1915 the Russian defeats deprived Sazonov of the one strong bargaining point remaining to him. Time and again Bratianu took advantage of this shaky posture to break down Russian resistance to his demands. His task was made easier by the western Allies, who attached great importance to Rumanian intervention.

In 1915 and 1916, under heavy Allied pressure, the Russians made great concessions. Yet these sacrifices were of no avail until the Russian army was again victorious. Thus, Rumania entered the war on her own terms and at a moment deemed most favorable to her interests, not to Russia's. The result was a military catastrophe for both countries. The Russian diplomatic failure can be measured in terms of the added burden to a war-weary army that was the mainstay of the tsarist autocracy.

[157] Text of Russian-Rumanian Military Convention, August 17, 1961, in TRMV, pp. 226-30.

Bibliography

Abrash, Merritt. "Entente Policy towards Austria-Hungary, August 1914—March 1917." Unpublished Certificate Essay, Russian Institute, Columbia University, 1958.

Adamov, Evgenii A., ed. *See* Evropeiskie derzhavy i Turtsiia vo vremia mirovoi voiny: Konstantinopl' i prolivy.

Akademiia Nauk SSSR. *See* Istoriia Pol'shi.

Alexandra Fëdorovna (Tsaritsa). *See* Perepiska Nikolaia i Aleksandry Romanovykh; and Pis'ma imperatritsy Aleksandry Fëdorovny k imperatoru Nikolaiu II.

Allied Press Supplement (an occasional supplement to *Daily Review of the Foreign Press*, q.v.), September 1, November 8, 22, 29, December 6, 20, 1916.

Askenasy, Szymon. Uwagi [Observations]. Warsaw, 1924.

Asquith, Herbert Henry. Memories and Reflections, 1852-1927, by the Earl of Oxford and Asquith, K. G. 2 vols. Boston, 1928.

Balabanov, M. S. Tsarkaia Rossiia XX veka [Tsarist Russia of the Twentieth Century]. Moscow, 1927.

The Balkan States. *See* Royal Institute of International Affairs.

Banat. London, 1920 Handbook Prepared under the Direction of the Historical Section of the Foreign Office, No. 6.

Beneš, Eduard. "Les slaves et l'idée slave pendant et après la guerre," *Le Monde Slave* (Paris), No. 3 (March, 1926), pp. 321-81.

—— Souvenirs de guerre et de révolution. 2 vols. Paris, 1928-29.

Bertie, Francis. The Diary of Lord Bertie of Thame. 2 vols. London, 1924.

Berton, Peter. "The Secret Russo-Japanese Alliance of 1916." Doctoral dissertation, Columbia University, 1956.

Błociszewski, Józef. La restauration de la Pologne et la diplomatie européenne. Paris, 1927.

British Documents on the Origins of the War 1898-1914. *See* Gooch, G. P., and Harold Temperley, eds.

British War Office. See *Daily Review of the Foreign Press*.

British White Paper, Misc. No. 7, 1920, Cmd. 671.

Brusilov, A. A. "L'offensive de 1916, II," *Revue des Deux Mondes*, June 15, 1929, pp. 903-28.

—— A Soldier's Notebook. London, 1930.

Buchanan, George. My Mission to Russia and Other Diplomatic Memories. 2 vols. London, 1923.

Bulgaria. Ministerstvo na vunshnitie raboti. See Diplomaticheski dokumenti pro namiesata na Bulgariia v evropeiskata voina.

The Cambridge History of Poland, 1697-1935. Edited by W. F. Reddaway, J. H. Penson, O. Halecki and R. Dyboski. Cambridge, England, 1951.

Čapek, Karel, ed. See Masaryk, Tomaš. President Masaryk Tells His Story.

Chego zhdët Rossiia ot voiny [What Russia Expects of the War]. Petrograd, 1915.

Chéradame, André. Le plan pangermaniste démasqué. Paris, 1916.

Czernin, Otto. In the World War. New York, 1920.

Daily Review of the Foreign Press (published by the British War Office), August 4, 9, 11, 18, 26, 28, 30, September 16, 27, October 17, November 29, December 13, 20, 1916.

Danilov, Iurii. Russland im Weltkrieg. Jena, 1925.

Diamandi, Constantine. "Ma mission en Russie (1914-1918), I: Le drame d'une conscience royale," Revue des Deux Mondes, February 15, 1929, pp. 794-820.

—— "Ma mission en Russie, II: La guerre vue du versant oriental," Revue des Deux Mondes, November 30, 1930, pp. 421-32.

Diplomatic Documents Submitted to the Italian Parliament by the Minister for Foreign Affairs (Sonnino): Austria-Hungary. Session of May 20, 1915. (The Italian Green Book: Acts of Parliament, Legislature XXIV, Sessions 1913-15, Chamber of Deputies). London [1915].

Diplomaticheski dokumenti po namiesata na Bulgariia v evropeiskata voina [Diplomatic Documents on the Intervention of Bulgaria in the European War]. 2 vols. Sofia, 1920-21. Vol. I: 1913-1915. Vol. II (with the main title Diplomaticheski dokumenti po uchastieto na Bulgariia v evropeiskata voina [Diplomatic Documents on the Participation of Bulgaria in the European War]): 1915-1918 (do primirieto) [1915-1918 (Until the Armistice)]. A publication of the Ministry of Foreign Affairs.

Dmowski, Roman. Germaniia, Rossiia i pol'skii vopros [Germany, Russia and the Polish Question]. St. Petersburg, 1909.

—— Polityka polska i odbudowanie państwa [Polish Policy and the Restoration of the State]. 2d ed. Warsaw, 1926.

"Dnevnik Ministerstva Inos trannykh Del za 1915-1916 gg." [Journal of the Ministry for Foreign Affairs for 1915-1916 gg.], Krasnyi Arkhiv [Red Archive] (Moscow), Vols. XXXI and XXXII (1928-29).

Dnevnitsi (stenog.) na XVII Obiknoveno Narodno Sobranie [Record (Stenographic) of the Seventeenth Regular National Assembly]. Sofia, 1928.

Documents on the Outbreak of the World War. *See* K. Kautsky, ed.

The Eastern Question. London, 1920. British Foreign Office Peace Handbook, No. 15.

Emets, V. A. "Protivorechiia mezhdu Rossiei i Soiuznikami po voprosu o vstuplenii Rumynii v voinu" [Conflicts between Russia and the Allies over the Question of Rumania's Entrance into the War], *Istorichesie Zapiski* [Historical Notes] (Moscow), No. 56 (1956).

Entente Diplomacy and the World: Matrix of the History of Europe, 1909-14. Translated from the original texts in his possession by B. de Siebert. Edited, arranged and annotated by George Abel Schreiner. New York, 1921.

Evropeiskie derzhavy i Turtsiia vo vremia mirovoi voiny: Konstantinopl'i prolivy (Po sekretnym dokumentam b. Ministerstva Inostrannykh Del) [The European Powers and Turkey during the World War: Constantinople and the Straits (Based on Secret Documents of the Former Ministry for Foreign Affairs)]. Edited by Evgenii A. Adamov. 2 vols. Moscow, 1925-26. A publication of the People's Commissariat for Foreign Affairs.

Ezhegodnik gazety *Rech'*, 1915 [Annual of the Newspaper *Rech'*, 1915]. Petrograd, 1915.

Ezhegodnik gazety *Rech'*, 1916 [Annual of the Newspaper *Rech'*, 1916]. Petrograd, 1916.

Falkenhayn, Erich von. General Headquarters, 1914-1916, and Its Critical Decisions. London [1919].

Fay, Sidney B. The Origins of the World War. New York, 1930.

Fiłasiewicz, Stanisław, comp. La question polonaise pendant la guerre mondiale. Paris, 1920.

Fisher, Harold H. America and the New Poland. New York, 1928.
—— *See also* Genkin, Olga, and H. H. Fisher.

Florinsky, Michael T. Russia: A History and an Interpretation. 2 vols. New York, 1955.

Frankel, Henryk. Poland, the Struggle for Power, 1772-1939. London, 1946.

Frantz, Günther. Russland auf dem Wege zur Katastrophe. Berlin, 1926.

Genkin, Olga, and H. H. Fisher. The Bolsheviks and the World War. Stanford, 1940.

Gerson, Louis L. Woodrow Wilson and the Rebirth of Poland, 1914-1920. New Haven, 1953.

Golder, Frank A., ed. Documents of Russian History, 1914-1917. New York, 1927.

Gooch, G. P. Recent Revelations of European Diplomacy. 4th ed. London, 1940.

Gooch, G. P., and Harold Temperley, eds. British Documents on the Origins of the War 1898-1914. 11 vols. in 13. London, 1926-38. Vol. X.

Gosudarstvennaia Duma, IV sozyv, IV sessiia, zasedanie I: Stenograficheskie otchëty [State Duma, Fourth Convocation, Fourth Session, First Sitting: Stenographic Minutes]. Petrograd, 1915.

Gottlieb, Wolfram W. Studies in Secret Diplomacy during the First World War. London, 1957.

Grey, Edward Grey. Twenty-Five Years, 1892-1916, by Viscount Grey of Fallodon, K. G. 2 vols. New York, 1925.

Grzybowski, Kazimierz. "The Jakhontov Papers: Russo-Polish Relations (1914-1916)," Journal of Central European Affairs (University of Colorado, Boulder, Colorado), XVIII, No. 1 (April, 1958), 3-24.

Gurko, Vasilii. Memories and Impressions of War and Revolution in Russia. London, 1918.

Gurko, Vladimir. Figures and Features of the Past. Stanford, 1939.

Hanbury-Williams, John. The Emperor Nicholas II As I Knew Him. London, 1922.

Handelsman, Marcel. La Pologne: Sa vie économique et sociale pendant la guerre. Vol. I. Paris and New Haven, Connecticut, 1932. In the series Histoire économique et sociale de la guerre mondiale, Série polonaise; Publications de la Dotation Carnegie pour la paix internationale.

Hansard (London), March 2, 1915.

Helmreich, E. C. The Diplomacy of the Balkan Wars, 1912-1913. Cambridge, Massachusetts, 1938.

Hoelzle, Erwin. Der Osten im Ersten Weltkrieg. Leipzig, 1944.

Hoetzsch, Otto. Der Krieg und die grosse Politik. Leipzig, 1918.

Howard, H. N. The Partition of Turkey. Norman, Oklahoma, 1931.

Iakhontov, A. N., ed. "Tiazhëlye dni" [Difficult Days], in Arkhiv russkoi revoliutsii [Archive of the Russian Revolution]. Berlin. Vol. XVIII (1926).

——— See also Sovet Ministrov.

Ianushkevich, N. N. See "Perepiska V. A. Sukhomlinova s N. N. Ianushkevichem."

L'Intervento dell'Italia nei documenti segreti dell'Intessa. Rome, 1923.

Ioffe, Aleksandr Euseevich. Russkofrantsuzskie otnosheniia v

1917 g., fevral'-oktiabr' [Russo-French Relations in 1917, February-October]. Moscow, 1958.

Istoriia Pol'shi [History of Poland]. 3 vols. Moscow, 1954-55. A publication of the USSR Academy of Sciences.

Italy. Ministero degli affari esteri. *See* Diplomatic Documents Submitted to the Italian Parliament by the Minister for Foreign Affairs (Sonnino): Austria-Hungary.

Izvestiia Ministerstva Inostrannykh Del [News of the Ministry for Foreign Affairs] (St. Petersburg), No. 4. 1916.

"Kadety v dni galitsiiskogo razgroma" [The Cadets during the Days of the Rout in Galicia], *Krasnyi Arkhiv* [Red Archive] (Moscow), Vols. LIV-LV (1932) and LIX (1933).

Kaptchev, G. I. La Débâcle nationale Bulgare, devant la Haute-Cour. Paris, 1925.

Kareev, N. I. "Pol'skii vopros v istoricheskom osveshchenii" [The Polish Question in the Light of History], in Voprosy mirovoi voiny [Questions of the World War]. Edited by M. I. Tugan-Baranovskii, Petrograd, 1915.

Kautsky, K., ed. Documents on the Outbreak of the World War. New York, 1924.

Kliuchnikov, Iurii V., and Andrei Sabanin, eds. Mezhdunarodnaia politika noveishego vremeni v dogovorakh, notakh i deklaratsiiakh [International Politics of the Recent Period in Agreements, Notes and Declarations]. 3 vols. Moscow, 1925-29.

Komarnicki, Titus. Rebirth of the Polish Republic: A Study in the Diplomatic History of Europe, 1914-1920. London, 1957.

Komissiia pri TsIK SSSR po izdaniiu dokumentov epokhi imperializma. *See* Mezhdunarodnye otnosheniia v epokhu imperializma: Dokumenty iz arkhivov tsarskogo i vremennogo pravitel'stv, 1878-1917 gg.

Konstantinopl' i prolivy. *See* Evropeiskie derzhavy i Turtsiia vo vremia mirovoi voiny: Konstantinopl' i prolivy.

Korostovetz, V. The Rebirth of Poland. London, 1928.

Kozłowski, Leo, comp. Voina i Pol'sha [The War and Poland]. Moscow, 1914.

Kramář, Karel. "M. Kramář et la politique slave," *Le Monde Slave* (Paris), No. 11 (November, 1926), pp. 283-303.

Kryzhanovskii, Sergei Efimovich. Vospominaniia [Memoirs]. Berlin, 1938.

Kumaniecki, Kazimierz. Odbudowa państwowości polskiej [The Restoration of Polish Statehood]. Kraków, 1924.

Lapinskii, M. N., ed. *See* Russko-pol'skie otnosheniia v period mirovoi voiny.

Lebedev, Vladimir. "Chekhoslovatskaia politika tsarskogo pra-vitel'stva" [The Czechoslovak Policy of the Tsarist Government], *Volia Rossii* [Russia's Freedom] (Prague), No. 8-9 (May, 1924), pp. 209-26.

Lednicki, Alexander. "Voina i Pol'sha" [The War and Poland], *Russkaia Mysl'* [Russian Thought] (Moscow), No. 6 (1915).

Lemke, Mikhail K. 250 dnei v tsarskoi stavke [250 Days at the Tsarist Field Headquarters]. Petrograd, 1920.

Lempicki, Michał. Le grand problème international. Lausanne, 1915.

Lenin, Vladimir Il'ich. Sochineniia [Works]. 4th ed. Moscow, 1941-57. Vol. XXI (1948).

Lettres des Grands-ducs à Nicolas II. Paris, 1926.

Lippmann, Walter. The Cold War: A Study in U.S. Foreign Policy. New York, 1947.

Un livre noir: Diplomatie d'avant-guerre et de guerre d'après les documents des archives russes, Novembre 1910—Juillet 1914. With a preface by René Marchand. 3 vols. Paris [1922-34].

Lloyd George, David. Memoirs of the Peace Conference. 2 vols. New Haven, 1939.

—— War Memoirs. 6 vols. London, 1933-36.

Lutz, R. H. The Fall of the German Empire. Stanford, 1932.

MacMurray, J. V. A. Treaties and Agreements with and concerning China, 1894-1919. 2 vols. Washington, 1929.

Madol, H. R. Ferdinand von Bulgarien. Berlin, 1931.

Mamatey, Victor S. The United States and East Central Europe 1914-1918: A Study in Wilsonian Diplomacy and Propaganda. Princeton, 1957.

Marchand, René. *See* Un livre noir: Diplomatie d'avant-guerre et de guerre d'après les documents des archives russes.

Marczali, H. "Papers of Count Tisza 1914-1918," *American Historical Review*, Vol. XXIX (January, 1924).

Marghiloman, Alexandru. Note politice 1894-1924 [Political Notes]. Bucharest, 1927.

Martin, William. "La question polonaise et l'Europe au cours de la guerre," *Quarterly Review* (London), CCXXX (1918).

Masaryk, Tomaš. The Making of a State. Translated and edited by Henry Wickham Steed. New York, 1927.

—— President Masaryk Tells His Story. Edited by Karel Čapek. New York, 1935.

Mezhdunarodnaia politika noveishego vremeni v dogovorakh notakh i deklaratsiiakh. *See* Kliuchnikov, Iurii V., and Andrei Sabanin, eds.

Mezdunarodnye otnosheniia v epokhu imperializma: Dokumenty iz arkhivov tsarkogo i vremennogo pravitel'stv, 1878-1917 gg. [International Relations in the Period of Imperialism: Documents from the Archives of the Tsarist and Provisional Governments, 1878-1917]. Series III: 1914-1917. 10 vols. Moscow, 1931-38.

Michel, Paul-Henri. La Question de l'Adriatique (1914-1918): Recueil de Documents. Paris, 1938.

Miliukov, Pavel. "Dnevnik P. N. Miliukova" [P. N. Miliukov's Diary], Krasnyi Arkhiv [Red Archive] (Moscow), LIV-LV (1932), 3-48.

—— "Territorial'nyia priobreteniia Rossii" [Russia's Territorial Acquisitions], in Chego zhdët Rossiia ot voiny [What Russia Expects of the War]. Petrograd, 1915.

—— "Tseli voiny" [The War Aims], in Ezhegodnik gazety Rech', 1916 [Annual of the Newspaper Rech', 1916]. Petrograd, 1916. Pages 29-128.

—— Vospominaniia [Memoirs]. 2 vols. New York, 1955.

Napier, H. D. A Military Attaché in the Balkans. London, 1924.

The Near East (London), March 19, April 9 and 23, and August 13, 1915.

"Neizvestnye dokumenty iz tsarskogo arkhiva" [Unknown Documents from the Tsarist Archives], Volia Rossii [Russia's' Freedom] (Prague), No. 8-9 (May, 1924), pp. 227-40.

Nekludoff (Nekliudov), Anatolii V. Diplomatic Reminiscences before and during the World War, 1911-1917. Translated by Alexandra Paget. 2d ed. London, 1920.

The New York Times, March 9 and May 29, 1916.

Nicholas II. See Perepiska Nikolaia i Aleksandry Romanovykh.

Nikolai II i velikie kniaz'ia. See Semennikov, Vladimir Petrovich, ed.

Nol'de, Boris E. Dalëkoe i blizkoe: Istoricheskie ocherki [Far and Near: Historical Sketches]. Paris, 1930.

—— "Les desseins politiques de la Russie pendant la Grande Guerre," Le Monde Slave (Paris), No. 2 (1931), pp. 161-77.

Notovich, F. I. Diplomaticheskaia bor'ba v gody pervoi mirovoi voiny. Vol. I: Poteria soiuznikami Balkanskovo poluostrova. Moscow, 1947.

Novoe vremia [New Times] (Moscow), July 21, August 25, October 6 and November 15, 1916.

Odezwy i rozporzadzenia z czasów okupacji rosyjskief Lwowa 1914-1915 rr. [Proclamations and Decrees during the Russian Occupation of Lvov, 1914-1915]. Lvov, 1916.

Official Statements of War Aims and Peace Proposals, December 1916 to November 1918. Edited by James B. Scott. Washington, 1921.

Österreich-Ungarns Aussenpolitik von der bosnischen Krise 1908 bis zum Kriegsausbruch 1914: Diplomatische Aktenstücke des Österreichisch-Ungarischen Ministeriums des Äussern. Compiled by Ludwig Bittner, Alfred Francis Pribam, Heinrich Srbik and Hans Uebersberger; and edited by Ludwig Bittner and Hans Uebersberger. Vienna, 1930.

Padenie tsarskogo rezhima: Stenograficheskie otchëty doprosov i pokazanii, dannykh v 1917 g. v. Chrezvychainoi sledstvennoi komissii Vremennogo pravitel'stva [The Fall of the Tsarist Regime: Stenographic Records of the Interrogation and Testimony Given in 1917 in the Extraordinary Investigating Commission of the Provisional Government]. Edited by P. E. Shchegolev. 7 vols. Leningrad, 1924-27.

Paléologue, Maurice. An Ambassador's Memoirs. Translated by F. A. Holt. 5th ed. 3 vols. London, 1925. A translation of *La Russie des Tsars pendant la Grande Guerre.*

—— La Russie des Tsars pendant la Grande Guerre. 3 vols. Paris, 1921-22.

Papánek, Ján. La Tchécoslovaquie. Prague, 1923.

Papers Relating to the Foreign Relations of the United States. *See* U. S. Department of State.

Pares, Bernard. The Fall of the Russian Monarchy. New York, 1939.

Paulová, Milada. Jugoslavenski Odbor: Povijest jugoslavenske emigracije za svijetskog rata od 1914-1918 [Yugoslav Committee: History of the Yugoslav Emigrés during the World War of 1914-1918]. Zagreb [1925].

Perepiska Nikolaia i Aleksandry Romanovykh [Correspondence of Nicholas and Alexandra Romanov]. Moscow, 1923-27.

"Perepiska V. A. Sukhomlinova s N. N. Ianushkevichem" [Correspondence of V. A. Sukhomlinov and N. N. Ianushkevich], *Krasnyi Arkhiv* [Red Archive] (Moscow), Vol. I (1922).

Pingaud, Albert. "L'Entente et la Roumanie en 1915: 3 mai–22 août 1915," *Revue des Deux Mondes* (Paris), May 1, 1930, pp. 119-61.

—— Histoire diplomatique de la France pendant la grande guerre. Paris, n.d. Vols. I-II.

Pipes, Richard. The Formation of the Soviet Union. Cambridge, Massachusetts, 1954.

Pis'ma imperatritsy Aleksandry Fëdorovny k imperatoru Nikolaiu II [Letters of Empress Alexandra Fëdorovna to Emperor Nicholas II]. 2 vols. Berlin, 1922.

Poincaré, Raymond. Au service de la France. 10 vols. in 6.

Paris, 1926-[1933?]. Published in English under the title *The Memoirs of Raymond Poincaré.*

—— The Memoirs of Raymond Poincaré, translated and adapted by Sir George Arthur, with a preface by the Duke of Northumberland. 4 vols. London, 1926-30. A translation of *Au service de la France.*

Pokrovskii, M. N. *See* Tsarskaia Rossiia v mirovoi voine.

Pokrovskii, M. N., ed. Ocherki po istorii oktiabr'skoi revoliutsii [Studies in the History of the October Revolution]. Vol. I. Moscow, 1927.

Polen (Vienna), Vol. I, No. 18 (1915).

Polivanov, A. A. Memuary [Memoirs]. Vol. I. Moscow, 1924.

Popov, A. "Chekho-slovatskii vopros i tsarskaia diplomatiia" [The Czechoslovak Question and Tsarist Diplomacy], *Krasnyi Arkhiv* [Red Archive] (Moscow), XXXIII (1929), 3-33; XXXIV (1929), 3-38.

Pribram, A. F. The Secret Treaties of Austria-Hungary, 1879-1914. Cambridge, England, 1922.

Privat, Edmond. La Pologne sous la rafale. Paris, 1915.

"Progressivnyi blok v 1915-1917 gg." [The Progressive Bloc in 1915-1917], *Krasnyi Arkhiv* [Red Archive], L (1932).

Raffalovich, Arthur. "Bulgarie," in Le marché financier. Paris. XXIII (1915), 719-39.

Recke, Walther. Die polnische Frage als Problem der europaeischen Politik. Berlin, 1927.

Revue de Pologne (Paris), No. 1-2 (1915); Nos. 1-2, 3 (1916).

Ribot, Alexandre. Lettres à un ami. Paris, 1924.

Riha, Thomas. "Miliukov and the Progressive Bloc in 1915: A Study in Last-Chance Politics," *The Journal of Modern History*, XXXII, No. 1 (March, 1960), 16-24.

Romanov, B. A., ed. "Finansovye soveshchaniia soiuznikov vo vremia voiny" [Financial Conferences of the Allies during the War], *Krasnyi Arkhiv* [Red Archive] (Moscow), Vol. V (1924).

Rosen, Roman Romanovich. Forty Years of Diplomacy. 2 vols. London and New York, 1922.

Royal Institute of International Affairs. The Balkan States. London, 1936.

"La Russie tsariste et la question tchécoslovaque," *Le Monde Slave* (Paris), No. 1 (November, 1924), pp. 123-38; No. 2 (December, 1924), pp. 294-300.

Russko-pol'skie otnosheniia v period mirovoi voiny [Russo-Polish Relations during the World War Period]. Edited by M. N. Lapinskii. Moscow, 1926.

Sabanin, Andrei, ed. *See* Kliuchnikov, Iurii V., and Andrei Sabanin, eds.

Salandra, Antonio. L'Intervento (1915): Ricordi e pensieri. Milan, 1930.

—— Italy and the Great War: From Neutrality to Intervention. Translated by Zoe Kendrick Pyne, with a foreword by the Rt. Hon. Sir James Rennell Rodd. London [1932]. A translation of *La neutralità italiana (1914): Ricordi e pensieri* (Milan, 1928) and *L'Intervento (1915): Ricordi e pensieri.*

Savinsky [Savinskii], A. A. Recollections of a Russian Diplomat. London [1927].

Sazonov, Sergei D. Fateful Years, 1909-1916. London, 1928. A translation of his *Vospominaniia,* q.v.

—— Vospominaniia [Memoirs]. Paris, 1929. Published in English translation under the title *Fateful Years, 1909-1916,* q.v.

Sbornik sekretnykh dokumentov iz Arkhiva byvshago Ministerstva Inostrannykh Del [Collection of Secret Documents from the Archives of the Former Ministry of Foreign Affairs]. Petrograd, 1917-18. A publication of the People's Commissariat for Foreign Affairs.

Schelking, Eugene de [Evgenii Nikolaevich Shel'king]. Recollections of a Russian Diplomat: The Suicide of Monarchies (William II and Nicholas II). New York, 1918.

Schreiner, George Abel, ed. *See* Entente Diplomacy and the World: Matrix of the History of Europe, 1909-14.

Scott, James B., ed. *See* Official Statements of War Aims and Peace Proposals, December 1916 to November 1918.

Selver, Paul. Masaryk. London, 1940.

Semennikov, Vladimir Petrovich. Politika Romanovykh nakanune revoliutsii (ot Antanty k Germanii) [The Policy of the Romanovs on the Eve of the Revolution (from the Entente to Germany)]. Moscow, 1926.

Semennikov, Vladimir Petrovich, ed. Monarkhiia pered krusheniem, 1914-1917 : Bumagi Nikolaia II i drugie dokumenty [The Monarchy before Its Downfall, 1914-1917: Papers of Nicholas II and Other Documents]. Moscow, 1927.

—— Nikolai II i velikie kniaz'ia : Rodstvennye pis'ma k poslednemu tsariu [Nicholas II and the Grand Dukes: Family Letters to the Last Tsar]. Leningrad, 1925.

Seton-Watson, Robert William. A History of the Czechs and Slovaks. London, 1925.

—— A History of the Roumanians. Cambridge, England, 1934.

—— "Magyar Forgeries in England," *The New Europe* (London), January 18, 1917, pp. 16-23.

—— Masaryk in England. Cambridge, England, 1943.

—— "Unprinted Documents: Austro-German Plans for the Future of Serbia (1915)," *Slavonic Review* (London), VIII, No. 21 (March, 1929), 705-24.

—— "William II's Balkan Policy," *Slavonic Review* (London), VII, No. 19 (June, 1928), 1-29.

Seyda, Marjan. Polska na przełomie dziejów. 2 vols. Poznań, 1927-31.

Seymour, Charles. American Diplomacy during the World War. Baltimore, 1934.

Shavel'skii, Georgii. Vospominaniia [Memoirs]. 2 vols. New York, 1954.

Shchegolev, P. E., ed. *See* Padenie tsarskogo rezhima.

Shel'king, Evgenii Nikolaevich. *See* Schelking, Eugene de.

Siebert, B. de. *See* Entente Diplomacy and the World: Matrix of the History of Europe, 1909-14.

Smith, C. Jay, Jr. The Russian Struggle for Power, 1914-1917: A Study of Russian Foreign Policy during the First World War. New York, 1956.

Smogorzewski, Kazimierz. La Pologne et la guerre à travers les livres polonais. Paris, 1929.

Sonevytsky, Leonid C. Bukovina in the Diplomatic Negotiations of 1914," *The Annals of the Ukrainian Academy of Arts and Sciences in the U.S.* (New York), VII, No. 1-2 (23-24) (1959), 1586-1629.

Sosnowski, Jerzy Jan. Prawda dziejowa, 1914-1917 [Historical Truth, 1914-1917]. Warsaw, 1925.

Sovet Ministrov. "Osobye zhurnaly 1914-1916." Library of Congress microfilm, from the papers of A. N. Iakhontov.

"Stavka i Ministerstvo Inostrannykh Del" [Field Headquarters and the Ministry for Foreign Affairs], *Krasnyi Arkhiv* [Red Archive] (Moscow), Vols. XXVI-XXX (1928).

Steed, Henry Wickham, trans. and ed. *See* Masaryk, Tomaš. The Making of a State.

Stieve, Friedrich. Isvolsky and the World War (Based on the Documents Recently Published by the German Foreign Office). Translated by E. W. Dickes. London and New York, 1926.

—— Iswolski im Weltkrieg : Der diplomatische Schriftwechsel Iswolskis aus den Jahren 1914-1917. Berlin, 1925.

Suarez, Georges. Briand, 1914-1916. Vol. III. Paris, 1939.

Sukhomlinov, V. A. "Dnevnik" [Diary], *Dela i dni* [Works and Days] (Petrograd), Vol. I (1920).

—— *See* "Perepiska V. A. Sukhomlinova s N. N. Ianushkevichem."

Taube, Mikhail. La politique russe d'avant-guerre et la fin de l'empire des tsars, 1904-1917. Paris, 1928.

Taylor, A. J. P. The Struggle for Mastery in Europe, 1848-1918. Oxford, 1954.

—— "The War Aims of the Allies in the First World War," in Essays Presented to Sir Lewis Namier. Edited by Richard Pares and A. J. P. Taylor. New York, 1956.

Temperley, Harold, ed. See Gooch, G. P., and Harold Temperley, eds.

Le Temps (Paris). September 24, 1914; November 17, 24, 1916.

The Times (London). September 25, 1914.

Toscano, Mario. Il Patto di Londra. Bologna, 1934.

Trubetskoi, Grigorii. Russland als Grossmacht. Stuttgart, 1913.

Tsarskaia Rossiia v mirovoi voine [Tsarist Russia in the World War]. Vol. I, with an introduction by M. N. Pokrovskii. Leningrad, 1925.

U. S. Department of State. Papers Relating to the Foreign Relations of the United States: The Lansing Papers, 1914-1920. 2 vols. Washington, 1939-40.

—— Papers Relating to the Foreign Relations of the United States, 1916. Supplement: The World War. Washington, 1929.

—— Papers Relating to the Foreign Relations of the United States, 1917. Supplement I : The World War. Washington, 1931.

Viner, Jacob. "International Finance and Balance of Power Diplomacy," Southwestern Political and Social Science Quarterly (Austin, Texas), Vol. IX, No. 9 (March, 1929).

Vydrun, R. In Sovremennyi mir [The Modern World] (Petrograd), No. 9 (1915).

Wolfe, Bertram D. Three Who Made a Revolution. New York, 1948.

The World War. See U. S. Department of State. Papers Relating to the Foreign Relations of the United States, 1916; and Papers Relating to the Foreign Relations of the United States, 1917.

Zeman, Z. A. B. The Break-up of the Habsburg Empire, 1914-1918 : A Study in National and Social Revolution. London and New York 1961.

Zeman, Z. A. B., ed. Germany and the Revolution in Russia, 1915-1918: Documents from the Archives of the German Foreign Ministry. London, 1958.

Index